## Bearing Witness

Since the 1990s, modern slavery has been recognized as a global problem, with campaigners around the world providing assessments of its nature and extent, its drivers, and possible solutions for ending it. However, largely absent from the global antislavery movement's discourse and policy prescriptions are the voices of survivors of slavery themselves. Survivors' authentic voices are underemployed vital tools in the fight against human trafficking and modern slavery in all its forms. Through close readings of over 200 contemporary slave narratives, Andrea Nicholson repositions the history of the genre and exposes the conditions and consequences of slavery, and the challenges survivors face in liberation. Far from the trope of "capture, enslavement, escape," she argues that narratives are rich and vitally important sources that enable the antislavery community to gain important insights and build more effective interventions.

**Andrea Nicholson** is Associate Professor in the School of Politics and International Relations, and a member of the Rights Lab, University of Nottingham. Her research primarily concerns survivor testimony and the support frameworks in place for survivors of human trafficking and modern slavery. She has previously undertaken research and consultancy for a range of nongovernmental and governmental organizations, including the EU Fundamental Rights Agency and the UN Special Rapporteur on Contemporary Forms of Slavery.

# Slaveries since Emancipation

*General Editors*
Randall Miller, *St. Joseph's University*
Zoe Trodd, *University of Nottingham*

Slaveries since Emancipation publishes scholarship that links slavery's past to its present, consciously scanning history for lessons of relevance to contemporary abolitionism and that directly engages current issues of interest to activists by contextualizing them historically.

**Also in this series:**

Genevieve LeBaron, Jessica R. Pliley, and David W. Blight, eds., *Fighting Modern Slavery and Human Trafficking: History and Contemporary Policy*

Hannah-Rose Murray, *Advocates of Freedom: African American Transatlantic Abolitionism in the British Isles*

Catherine Armstrong, *American Slavery, American Imperialism: US Perceptions of Global Servitude, 1870–1914*

Elizabeth Swanson and James Brewer Stewart, eds., *Human Bondage and Abolition: New Histories of Past and Present Slaveries*

R. J. M. Blackett, *The Captive's Quest for Freedom: Fugitive Slaves, the 1850 Fugitive Slave Law, and the Politics of Slavery*

Anna Mae Duane, ed., *Child Slavery before and after Emancipation: An Argument for Child-Centered Slavery Studies*

# Bearing Witness

*Contemporary Slave Narratives and the Global Antislavery Movement*

**ANDREA NICHOLSON**
*University of Nottingham*

Shaftesbury Road, Cambridge CB2 8EA, United Kingdom

One Liberty Plaza, 20th Floor, New York, NY 10006, USA

477 Williamstown Road, Port Melbourne, VIC 3207, Australia

314–321, 3rd Floor, Plot 3, Splendor Forum, Jasola District Centre, New Delhi – 110025, India

103 Penang Road, #05–06/07, Visioncrest Commercial, Singapore 238467

Cambridge University Press is part of Cambridge University Press & Assessment, a department of the University of Cambridge.

We share the University's mission to contribute to society through the pursuit of education, learning and research at the highest international levels of excellence.

www.cambridge.org
Information on this title: www.cambridge.org/9781009018470

DOI: 10.1017/9781009039741

© Andrea Nicholson 2022

This publication is in copyright. Subject to statutory exception and to the provisions of relevant collective licensing agreements, no reproduction of any part may take place without the written permission of Cambridge University Press & Assessment.

First published 2022
First paperback edition 2025

*A catalogue record for this publication is available from the British Library*

Library of Congress Cataloging-in-Publication data
NAMES: Nicholson, Andrea, author.
TITLE: Bearing witness : contemporary slave narratives and the global antislavery movement / Andrea Nicholson, University of Nottingham.
DESCRIPTION: New York, NY : Cambridge University Press, 2022. | Includes bibliographical references and index.
IDENTIFIERS: LCCN 2022022861 | ISBN 9781316510803 (hardback) | ISBN 9781009039741 (ebook)
SUBJECTS: LCSH: Slave narratives. | Slavery – History.
CLASSIFICATION: LCC HT869 .N64 2022 | DDC 306.3/62–dc23/eng/20220714
LC record available at https://lccn.loc.gov/2022022861

ISBN 978-1-316-51080-3 Hardback
ISBN 978-1-009-01847-0 Paperback

Cambridge University Press & Assessment has no responsibility for the persistence or accuracy of URLs for external or third-party internet websites referred to in this publication and does not guarantee that any content on such websites is, or will remain, accurate or appropriate.

Man is the storytelling animal
Graham Swift, *Waterland*

# Contents

| | | |
|---|---|---|
| *List of Figures* | | *page* xi |
| *Preface* | | xiii |
| *Acknowledgments* | | xix |
| | Introduction | 1 |
| 1 | A Narrated Self: The Slave Narrative Genre | 19 |
| 2 | "I Was Free, I Still Wasn't Free": Defining Freedom | 48 |
| 3 | The Construction and Reconstruction of Survivor Identities | 71 |
| 4 | Bearing Witness: Trauma in Contemporary Slave Narratives | 95 |
| 5 | Assuming "Full" Freedom: Challenges in Recovery | 128 |
| 6 | Antislavery Strategies and the Survivor as Activist | 157 |
| | Conclusion | 174 |
| *Appendix: Table of Narratives Analyzed* | | 183 |
| *Bibliography* | | 199 |
| *Index* | | 225 |

# Figures

4.1 Drawing by Dwain on matters meaningful to him,
    including abstract representations of himself    *page* 111
4.2 Drawing by Pranus on an important moment for him,
    visualizing the incident that prompted his escape    116
4.3 Drawing by Tung, depicting his feelings about
    his place and future    120
6.1 Drawing by Val, depicting the things most important
    to her and related to her activism    161

# Preface

This book offers a comprehensive and in-depth analysis of over 200 contemporary slave narratives. The analysis is drawn from 196 contemporary slave narratives from autobiographies, nongovernmental organization (NGO) reports and collections, congressional testimony, and print narrative collections. The book also includes extracts from five additional new contemporary slave narratives gathered using cognitive interviewing methods to offer new rich testimony on survivors' own terms.[1]

Survivor narratives have informed our understanding of human abuse throughout time. Not only do narratives serve as a form of testimony and an opportunity to bear witness, but they can be a form of protest literature. They are a vital and underemployed resource, revealing unique first-person insights that can be weaponized to progress abolition. This book challenges the perception of narratives as historical "stories" of limited value. The historic and contemporary corpora comprise rich first-person sources that reveal weaknesses in systems and provide unique authoritative insights into risk factors, strategies for abolition, and the impact of slavery on survivors and their consequent recovery needs, having ramifications for the development of central and NGO support mechanisms.

Through their own voices, this book attempts a richer and deeper understanding of the needs of those who have been enslaved to help inform policy formulation for the prevention of slavery and for the support that is needed for those who have been liberated from slavery. By

---

[1] The full narratives range from 9,000 to 40,000 words and are therefore too long for complete inclusion in this book, but can be accessed in full at www.antislavery.ac.uk.

contributing to the number and discussion of contemporary slave narratives, and by analyzing these carefully, it is hoped that these important testimonies will affect the development of the antislavery agenda, identify gaps in existing strategies, and offer recommendations to deal with those gaps based on survivors' voices. Placing new narratives in the public field will also assist researchers and NGOs and will help expose the complexity of slave narratives and that of the experiences of enslaved women, children, and men, both during enslavement and in liberation.

## TERMINOLOGY

In writing this book, I have used the term survivor to refer to those with lived experience of slavery. However, I recognize that this is less than ideal. Some of those with lived experience of slavery do not always identify themselves as survivors, or they feel it is an inadequate and limiting term or expect negative consequences from identifying themselves as survivors.[2] However, in the absence of a succinct alternative, the term survivor has been adopted throughout this book but without any intention to minimize the lives or full personhood of those previously enslaved. If the word victim is used, this is typically in the context of prosecution and adopts the language of criminal law, but in some instances, it is also used to refer to those who did not survive their enslavement.

## A NOTE ON METHOD

In selecting narratives, I have taken a broad approach. Transatlantic chattel enslavement is the dominant image of slavery in contemporary discourse and has become the paradigm against which enslavement today has been measured. Images, records, and testimonies of transatlantic enslavement are often used to explain the conceptual boundaries of slavery as an institution, but such an approach presents a problem for defining the parameters of contemporary slavery in the absence of legality and fails to consider other historic enslavements over human history.[3]

---

[2] Alexandra Lutnick and Minh Dang, Researcher-Survivor-Ally Evaluation of the Mayor's Task Force on Anti-Human Trafficking Draft Final Summary Report, August 2018, Prepared for the National Institute of Justice, Washington, DC, 11–12.
[3] See Katarina Schwarz and Andrea Nicholson, "Collapsing the Boundaries between De Jure and De Facto Slavery: The Foundations of Slavery Beyond the Transatlantic Frame." *Human Rights Review* 21, no. 4 (2020): 391–414.

The complexities of defining the condition of slavery so as to capture the elements consistent over time are widely debated and do not account for survivors' own conceptions of enslavement.[4] While these debates on definition are important conversations to be had, most narratives do not provide sufficient detail to make a judgment as to whether survivors have been enslaved, whichever definition we might seek to apply. The archetype also inhibits survivors' own understanding of the nature of their exploitation; many do not associate their experiences with slavery until someone provides that label for their experiences. The consequence of the above is that rather than limiting the analyses only to those who explicitly identify as having been enslaved, I have examined narratives from a broad range of extreme forms of human exploitation. Some may fall somewhere along the scale between severe labor exploitation and slavery, but those wishing to consider the contents by archetype will certainly find examples within the corpus that meet the traditional framing of chattel slavery.

In order to engage with survivors' meanings, the five new narratives I gathered have been analyzed using interpretative phenomenological analysis, with constructivist grounded theory coding techniques employed for the typically shorter preexisting 196 narratives. A table of the narratives analyzed, including the survivors' names/pseudonym, their countries of origin and enslavement, the year of their narratives, and sources, is included in the appendix. The book explores the emergent categories over six thematic chapters on the value of telling, perceptions of freedom, the destruction and reconstruction of identity, trauma, recovery, and activism.

I endeavored to adopt interview methods that attempted to redress issues that have plagued narrative gathering across the genre and that were designed to address the power imbalance between researcher and participant. I tested emerging theory against a the larger corpus, comparing findings and revisiting the narratives countless times so that findings were, as far as possible, emulated across the majority of narratives. As Louise Kidder explains:

Qualitative researchers return home with hours of field notes, voices on tapes, intimate knowledge of communities under siege, [and] they grow uncomfortably aware of many incompatible responsibilities. There is a responsibility to

---

[4] Andrea Nicholson, Minh Dang, and Zoe Trodd, "A Full Freedom: Contemporary Survivors' Definitions of Slavery." *Human Rights Law Review* 18, no. 4 (2018): 689–704.

hear what informants are saying about their lives and the meaning of their experiences, and a responsibility to construct interpretations that may or may not conform to what informants have told us .... Whether we agree with the words of informants or not, whether we even like them or not, we have an obligation to surround their words with analyses for which we are the authors .... Partial, temporary and tentative, we have a responsibility to position ourselves in relation to our data, and our position will not necessarily be the same as our informants' (have no illusions – they will not agree with each other either).[5]

Where narrative extracts have been brought together on a theme, care has been taken to ensure that they have not been taken out of context or that important or contrary material has not been removed (and so misrepresentation avoided). Extracts from the other narratives analyzed have also been reproduced exactly, including punctuation, language, and spelling as provided by the publisher or author.

### RECOGNITION OF THE SURVIVOR STANDPOINT

During the years it took to research and write this book, I have had the privilege of meeting with survivors both as part of my research and as colleagues and activists. I have learned much from my connections and conversations with these individuals, in absorbing the research they have undertaken and the perspectives they have communicated. I am acutely aware that as a nonsurvivor my understanding will always be incomplete.

While the objective observer brings their own value to analysis, as Minh Dang eloquently explains in her epistemology of survival, I can never know the entirety of slavery, and the subjective brings insights that I will be unable to see.[6] I am acutely aware of my position as a nonsurvivor and the challenges this poses in interpreting survivors' narratives. As a nonsurvivor, my experience of freedom limits my understanding of survivors' meanings. Survivors' epistemologies are fundamentally different from those of nonsurvivors; survivors *know* differently from nonsurvivors.[7] Recognizing this is key to acknowledging the potential limitations of the book and a call to survivors to see in this corpus what I cannot. The contents are unlikely to describe every survivor's meaning or

---

[5] Louise H. Kidder and Michelle Fine, "Qualitative Inquiry in Psychology: A Radical Tradition," in *Critical Psychology: An Introduction*, ed. Dennis Fox and Isaac Prilleltensky (Thousand Oaks, CA: Sage Publications, 1998), 48–49.
[6] Minh Dang, "Epistemology of Survival: A Working Paper," 2021, 5. www.minh-dang.com/publications.
[7] Minh Dang, "Epistemology of Survival," 1.

perspective; indeed, it is impossible for them to represent every survivor. I am sure survivors will see things in the narratives that I have missed, and I welcome (and we need) further scholarship on contemporary slave narratives and the content here, particularly from survivors' perspectives.

In gathering my own narratives for the book, I have informally witnessed more than could be expressed in this research. Confronted with survivors' realities, their openness and confidences, I have been able to develop a deeper understanding of the effects of enslavement. It was impossible not to be deeply affected by their truths. As Kevin Bales notes in the conclusion to *Blood and Earth* – you cannot unknow what you know.

# Acknowledgments

I could not have adopted the interview method that proved so crucial to this book without the financial support of the University of Nottingham postgraduate fund that enabled me to undertake training in cognitive interview methods from an external specialist. My interview expenses were also supported by the Arts and Humanities Research Council Antislavery Usable Past project, and thanks also goes to the Rights Lab at the University of Nottingham for supporting a visiting fellowship, enabling me to finalize this work. I have been fortunate to have been encouraged in my work by a number of people, but of particular mention here are Celeste Marie-Bernier, Zoe Trodd, Todd Landman, and Kevin Bales. Thank you for your unerring support for this work.

My interviews would also not have been possible if it had not been for the support of governmental organisations and various NGOs who have fed back on ethics, taken the time to speak with their clients, offered or arranged private rooms for me to interview (in some cases, supplying unexpected coffee and biscuits), supported survivors through the process, and generally supported the research. In this regard, particular thanks go to Paul Fern and Paul Broadbent at the Gangmasters and Labour Abuse Authority, Jimmy Zachariah at Baca, Bronagh Andrew at Trafficking Awareness Raising Alliance, Diana Mankai at Dover Migrant Help, Yvonne Hall and all the staff at Palm Cove Society, Victoria Oji at Hestia, Jenette Carey and Atleu, and Phillip Clayton at City Hearts.

Last but not least, my heartfelt thanks go to all the survivors who have shared their stories, to the survivors unable to do so, to the survivors who did not survive to tell, and to the survivors who were willing to be interviewed: Tung, Pranus, Val, Keith, and Dwain. Without your testimony and activism, the antislavery community would be an impoverished space.

# Introduction

One winter's day in 1971, almost two years after arriving in the United States from Haiti, Jean-Robert Cadet was set an assignment in school as part of Black History Month. Given the task of making an oral presentation about the life of Dred Scott, he set about researching his subject. He recalls:

As I moved through this little research project, I often found myself wondering if Dred Scott had endured the same cruelties to which I had been subjected as a child slave on the impoverished island nation of Haiti. I wondered if his masters had passed around him to friends as mine had, with everyone living more easily off my labor. I wondered if he had ever gone to bed hoping never to awaken, to sleep forever. I wondered if slavery had stolen every moment of his childhood, as it had mine. I wondered if, like me, he had been taken away from his family as a toddler, never to lay eyes on them for the next thirty years. I struggled to interweave the history of slavery in the United States with my own background, because child slavery was then, and is *to this moment,* being practiced in all areas of Haiti ....

Each day during Black History Month, I listened to my classmates present the stories of Malcolm X, Booker T. Washington, Frederick Douglass, Harriet Tubman, and others. When my turn came to speak, I read verbatim what I had learned about Dred Scott. As I read my essay, I noticed the teacher nodding in agreement and smiling. For one of the first times in my life, I felt proud of my achievement. Even then, I could sense the irony of that moment. *Unknown to anyone in the room (except me), a modern-day slave was relating the pain-filled saga of a famous historical slave.*[1]

---

[1] Jean-Robert Cadet, *My Stone of Hope: From Haitian Slave Child to Abolitionist* (Austin: University of Texas Press, 2011), chap. 1, Kindle.

Identifying his experience as a child slave, a *restavec*, with the stories of historic survivors, Cadet wonders about their experiences and his own hidden history, something as yet unexpressed. While he wonders whether historic survivors' experiences were akin to his own, he at the same time finds some resonance and familiarity in the stories related; his then unspoken thoughts collapse artificial distinctions between historic and "modern" slavery to reveal the continuity of slavery to which he was subjected as a child. Cadet's two autobiographies, *Restavec: From Haitian Slave Child to Middle Class American* and *My Stone of Hope: From Haitian Slave Child to Abolitionist*, finally revealed not only his experiences in childhood but how they catalyzed his activism.[2]

While slavery and the slave trade are globally prohibited, it is estimated that 40.3 million people are living as slaves today.[3] Slavery remains an unchallenged and deeply embedded aspect of many cultures, with certain practices entirely consistent with chattel slavery. However, the "fourth wave" of the struggle against slavery that emerged since the 1990s constitutes a global social movement that has articulated its demands for the end to modern slavery in ways that have mobilized and raised awareness of policy makers, governments, NGOs, and intergovernmental organizations. This movement has identified modern slavery as a global problem, provided assessments of its nature and extent, its drivers, and possible solutions for ending it. These efforts have culminated in the promulgation of Sustainable Development Goal 8.7, which demands that states: "Take immediate and effective measures to eradicate forced labour, end modern slavery and human trafficking and secure the prohibition and elimination of the worst forms of child labour." Increased global recognition of the problem and the many ways in which key stakeholders address it are evidence that the movement has been successful to some degree. However, largely absent from the movement's discourse and policy prescriptions are the voices of those enslaved and survivors of slavery themselves, and a fuller understanding of the meaning of modern slavery from the very people who have experienced contemporary forms of slavery. Laws, policies, and strategies to assist survivors are being created without an accurate understanding of the emotional and physical realities, and effects, of enslavement. There is a tendency to focus on prevention (and on the perpetrator),

---

[2] Jean-Robert Cadet, *Restavec: From Haitian Slave Child to Middle Class American* (Austin: University of Texas Press, 1998), Kindle; Jean-Robert Cadet, *My Stone of Hope*.
[3] Walk Free Foundation, *The Global Slavery Index 2018*. https://downloads.globalslaveryindex.org/ephemeral/GSI-2018_FNL_180907_Digital-small-p-1540817680.pdf

rather than survivor needs following discovery, and there is a lack of consideration of the factors that can provide the conditions for survivors to assume agency and authority over the self.

For centuries, survivor narratives have comprised a unique and unparalleled resource for abolition and demonstrated the realities of slavery, exposing the dehumanization, abuse, loss, and alienation at slavery's core and presenting a strong moral argument for abolition. Cadet's and other contemporary accounts add to a corpus of historic slave narratives that have long been seen as a valuable tool in abolitionism, providing an unrivaled insight into the challenges faced by survivors on their journeys from enslavement to escape, and through to their post-enslavement lives. Short stories, editorials, art, speeches, and autobiographies by former slaves during the nineteenth century were central to galvanizing the abolitionist movement and effecting change, and these collections continue to inform our perspectives on slavery today.

Collectively, slave narratives offer the most extensive and influential revelations of the nature of slavery. Narratives also have documentary status, providing key testimony and adding representative, often excluded voices to the discourse on slavery. Every successful social movement has been "guided by those directly affected by the injustice [who are] best positioned to determine appropriate strategies and offer visionary solutions."[4] Public awareness can help to drive approaches to abolition,[5] and the stories told by those who have experienced slavery are important awareness raising accounts, unmasking the horrors of slavery as it existed then and continues to exist today. Their authentic voices expose the internal landscape of survivors, unearthing the subtle and complex facets of enslavement, discovery, and freedom while their accounts offering us access to the past through the perception of the slave's own reality.[6] Their testimony is "a means to exteriorize, while at the same time naming and validating the survivor's subjective experience," a written representation of their belonging, and engaging the expectations of religious

---

[4] Toban Black, Stephen D'Arcy, Tony Weis, and Joshua Kahn Russell, eds., *A Line in the Tar Sands: Struggles for Environmental Justice* (Oakland: PM Press, 2014), 3.
[5] Kevin Bales, *Ending Slavery: How We Free Today's Slaves* (Berkeley: University of California Press, 2007), 26.
[6] This paragraph includes brief exerts from a blog by the author: Andrea Nicholson, "Survivors' Solutions: The Value of Survivors' Voices in the Antislavery Movement," *The Rights Lab, University of Nottingham*, October 27, 2017. http://blogs.nottingham.ac.uk/rights/2017/10/27/walkfree8/

and political groups to "create cultural spaces in which the projection of self-representation takes place."[7]

Yet although history shows us the importance of slave narratives to abolition, contemporary slave narratives have not been utilized in similar and new ways when forming state antislavery strategies and structures. Only by turning to individual narratives, can we extrapolate the meaning, emotions, states of mind, and needs of each survivor. Currently, there are only a handful of writings about contemporary slave narratives. I have analyzed a corpus of over 200 contemporary slave narratives to explore how survivors describe their experiences and sought to understand what this tells us about slavery and recovery. Drawing on 196 existing contemporary slave narratives and an additional five new contemporary slave narratives I gathered through deep interviews, I have analyzed these narratives arriving at thematic chapters on the value of telling, perceptions of freedom, the destruction and reconstruction of identity, trauma, recovery, and activism, which emerged as a result of the analysis.

Throughout this book, I demonstrate that contemporary slave narratives reveal key insights and parallels that help to inform our understanding of contemporary slavery. By examining contemporary slave narratives, we move toward a greater understanding of the condition of slavery, the agency of individuals, movements toward liberation, and the effects of current law and policy on survivors. I unearth the continuities and distinctions presented in their narratives and meanings that will enable the antislavery community to usefully apply narratives to strategies and policies for survivor support. I also argue that through narratives, survivors can be empowered to engage in frontline efforts to tackle slavery and assist other survivors, bringing the survivor center stage in representing and freeing others. By making their testimonies heard, individuals' voices can be more usefully employed to determine concrete strategies toward abolition to analyze the role of governments and NGOs, and to identify procedural difficulties. For example, narratives can be excavated and applied to clarify debates on definition and to

---

[7] Katherine Angueira, "To Make the Personal Political: The Use of Testimony as a Consciousness-Raising Tool against Sexual Aggression in Puerto Rico," *Oral History Review* 16, no. 2 (1988): 72. Christopher Hager, *Word by Word: Emancipation and the Act of Writing* (Cambridge, MA, and London: Harvard University Press, 2013), 110. Philip Gould, "The Rise of the Slave Narrative," in *The Cambridge Companion to the African American Slave Narrative*, ed. Audrey Fisch (Cambridge: Cambridge University Press, 2007), 12.

identify gaps in survivor support.[8] Ultimately, my aim is to show what happens when we place the expressions of enslaved people at the heart of the antislavery movement. I hope to demonstrate that survivors' voices can impact on developments in the antislavery space and establish that narratives can influence the antislavery agenda, shape NGO approaches, and provide an argument for survivor-centric law and policy.

The analysis of the parameters of slavery is also key to determining issues that continue to challenge academics and governments around the measurement of slavery, definition, approaches to discovery, and processes for prosecution and survivor support. The availability of contemporary slave narratives, and their collection, sharing, and publishing, plays a valuable role in the antislavery agenda. But narratives of the past also have relevance today for our understanding of the nature of slavery. As part of the conceptual sociological and legal structuring of contemporary slavery, both historical and contemporary narratives provide a basis on which we can understand the nature of slavery. Thus, Chapter 1 explores the slave narrative genre, looking at historic and contemporary narratives to examine questions about the continuity of slavery over time, and to identify the impact of narratives on abolition and the problems with gathering and representation then and now. I ask, how do contemporary narratives compare to historical slave narratives, and what lessons have been learned from the past by the antislavery community in terms of how they approach these voices?

Today, survivors have access to technology and a variety of platforms that did not exist before the late twentieth century, and which can cost little to utilize. We have seen an explosion in platforms for survivor voices through social media, websites, journalism, NGOs, UN mechanisms, governmental panels, global conferences, human rights institutions, and social movements.[9] This means more sources for understanding, and an opportunity for survivors to voice their stories in full and explore their

---

[8] Andrea Nicholson, Minh Dang, and Zoe Trodd, "A Full Freedom: Contemporary Survivors' Definitions of Slavery," *Human Rights Law Review* (forthcoming). On the ethics of conducting survivor-focused research, see for example Alison Faulkner, *The Guidelines for the Ethical Conduct of Research Carried Out by Mental Health Service Users and Survivors* (Bristol: The Policy Press, 2004); Richard Hugman, Eileen Pittaway, and Linda Bartolomei, "When 'Do No Harm' Is Not Enough: The Ethics of Research with Refugees and Other Vulnerable Groups," *The British Journal of Social Work* 41, no. 7 (2011); Chris Newlin et al., "Child Forensic Interviewing: Best Practices," *Juvenile Justice Bulletin* (2015); and Ron Iphofen, *Research Ethics in Ethnography/Anthropology* (DG Research and Innovation of the European Commission, June 30, 2015).

[9] Paul Gready, "Introduction – Responsibility to the Story," *Journal of Human Rights Practice* 2, no. 2 (2010): 185.

own intellectual and emotional growth. In recent decades, thousands of first-person narratives have emerged, of which a number are authored by the survivor,[10] while others are written by amanuenses.[11] The majority of contemporary slave narratives are gathered by NGOs, journalists, and nondepartmental public bodies, or are a record of witness testimony in legal cases and national inquiries. There also exist several autobiographies and memoirs, some sponsored or supported by faith groups, some self-published, and survivors have utilized digital platforms, using blogs, videos, films, Twitter, and their own sites to voice their experiences. Only a few texts have sought out, faithfully reproduced and, importantly, analyzed some of these primary voices.[12]

The narratives I have analyzed come from my own interviews with survivors, from the above collections, NGO reports and websites, and congressional testimony, one of which includes Twitter testimony.[13] None

---

[10] See for example Mary Jordan, Carina Buckley, and David Mossop, *Destiny of Choice* (Southampton: Dolphin Marketing Press Ltd, 2014); Barbara Amaya, *Nobody's Girl: A Memoir of Lost Innocence, Modern Day Slavery & Transformation* (Pittsburgh: Animal Media Group, 2015); Sophie Hayes, *Trafficked: The Terrifying True Story of a British Girl Forced into the Sex Trade* (London: Harper Collins, 2012); Francis Bok and Edward Tivnan, *Escape from Slavery: The True Story of My Ten Years in Captivity and My Journey to Freedom in America* (New York: St. Martin's Press, 2003).

[11] For example, Mende Nazer and Damien Lewis, *Slave: The True Story of a Girl's Lost Childhood and Her Fight for Survival* (London: Virago, 2010); Zana Muhsen and Andrew Crofts, *Sold: One Woman's True Account of Modern Slavery* (London: Sphere Publishing, 2010).

[12] Laura T. Murphy, *The New Slave Narrative: The Battle over Representations of Contemporary Slavery* (New York: Columbia University Press, 2019); Kevin Bales and Zoe Trodd, eds., *To Plead Our Own Cause Personal Stories by Today's Slaves* (New York: Cornell University Press, 2008); Laura T. Murphy, *Survivors of Slavery: Modern-Day Slave Narratives* (New York: Columbia University Press, 2014); Rahila Gupta, *Enslaved: The New British Slavery* (London: Portobello Books, 2007). See also Laura Murphy, "Black Face Abolition and the New Slave Narrative," *Cambridge Journal of Postcolonial Literary Inquiry* 2, no. 1 (2015): 93–113; Laura Murphy, "The New Slave Narrative and the Illegibility of Modern Slavery," *Slavery & Abolition* 36, no. 2 (2015); Kelli Lyon Johnson, "The New Slave Narrative: Advocacy and Human Rights in Stories of Contemporary Slavery," *Journal of Human Rights* 12, no. 2 (2013); Kaelyn Kaoma, "Child Soldier Memoirs and the 'Classic' Slave Narrative: Tracing the Origins," *Life Writing* 15, no. 2 (2018).

[13] The narratives analyzed are not limited to the UK, but are global and constitute all the narratives that could be found during the study and which were available in English. Survivors' countries of origin and of enslavement are included in the Table of Narratives Analyzed in the Appendix. Of the five interviews I undertook, although these were held in the UK, only one participant was a UK national. The other four participants were from Africa, Vietnam, and Poland, and all had been enslaved in their home countries or trafficked from them, through Europe and into the UK.

were chosen based on the legal definition of slavery under the 1926 Slavery Convention, as this would require a judgment on the degree to which an individual was "owned" over which there is ongoing academic debate. Additionally, most of the narratives located were too brief to provide sufficient data for such a judgment.[14] Instead, I have adopted the social definition of "modern slavery" that encompasses a range of practices that may, or may not amount to slavery, but where narratives are presented as modern slave narratives in collections, through testimony, by survivors, and by amanuenses. I nevertheless encountered a number of difficulties in locating and selecting narratives. In the search for autobiographies and memoirs, distinguishing genuine narratives from fiction was challenging. On NGO websites, many stories are written about survivors and presented in the third person as "case studies" rather than as survivor narratives and so these too were excluded. A large number of texts exist that concern slavery-related practices, such as sex work, but which are not identified as a form of slavery, and many are fictional or are re-tellings of survivors' stories, but where the survivor has not been included as author. Equally, a number of texts touch on slavery, but were essentially concerned with race, gender, migration, or imprisonment (such as J. James' *New Abolitionists: (Neo) Slave Narratives and Contemporary Prison Writings*[15]). At the time of writing, I had identified thirty-one autobiographies, ten of which are coauthored with amanuenses, and three of which are only available in French and could not therefore be analyzed.

- Jean Robert-Cadet, *Restavec: From Haitian Slave Child to Middle-Class American* (1998)
- Henriette Akofa, *Une Esclave Moderne* (2000)
- Francis Bok with Edward Tivnan, *Escape from Slavery: The True Story of My Ten Years in Captivity and My Journey to Freedom in America* (2003)
- Beatrice Fernando, *In Contempt of Fate: The Tale of a Sri Lankan Sold into Servitude, Who Survived to Tell It* (2004)
- China Keitetsi, *Child Soldier* (2004)
- Ishmael Beah, *A Long Way Gone: The True Story of a Child Soldier* (2007)

---

[14] Article 1(1) Slavery is the status or condition of a person over whom any or all of the powers attaching to the right of ownership are exercised. For academic debate on the application of legal definition to "modern" slavery, see n. 2, 84.
[15] Joy James, ed. *New Abolitionists: (Neo) Slave Narratives and Contemporary Prison Writings* (New York: State University of New York Press, 2015).

- Faith J. H. McDonell and Grace Akallo, *Girl Soldier: A Story of Hope for Northern Uganda's Children* (2007)
- Sarah Forsyth, *Slave Girl – I Was an Ordinary British Girl. I Was Kidnapped and Sold into Sex Slavery. This Is My Horrific True Story* (2009)
- Timea E. Nagy, *Memoirs of a Sex Slave Survivor* (2010)
- Zana Muhsen and Andrew Crofts, *Sold: One Woman's True Account of Modern Slavery* (2010)
- Mende Nazer, *Slave: The True Story of a Girl's Lost Childhood and Her Fight for Survival* (2010)
- Emma Jackson, *The End of My World: The Shocking True Story of a Young Girl Forced to Become a Sex Slave* (2010)
- Rachel Lloyd, *Girls Like Us: A Memoir* (2011)
- Fatima Téigmoinage, *Esclave a` 11 ans* (2011)
- Jean-Robert Cadet and Jim Luken, *My Stone of Hope: From Haitian Slave Child to Abolitionist* (2011)
- Tina Okpara and Julie Jodter, *My Life Has a Price: A Memoir of Survival and Freedom* (2012)
- Sophie Hayes, *Trafficked: The Terrifying True Story of a British Girl Forced into the Sex Trade* (2012)
- Monluedee Lueche, *Child Sex Slave: A Memoir* (2012)
- Theresa Flores, *The Slave across the Street: How a 15-Year-Old Girl Became a Sex Slave* (2013)
- Katie Taylor and Veronica Clark, *Stolen Girl: I Was an Innocent Schoolgirl. I Was Targeted, Raped and Abused by a Gang of Sadistic Men. But That Was Just the Beginning ….This Is My Terrifying True Story* (2013)
- Sarah Forsyth and Tim Tate, *Slave Girl: Return to Hell. Ordinary British Girls Are Being Sold into Sex Slavery; I Escaped, but Now I'm Going to Help Free Them. This Is My True Story* (2013)
- Katariina Rosenblatt and Cecil Murphey, *Stolen: The True Story of a Sex Trafficking Survivor* (2014)
- Alice Jay, *Out of the Darkness: A Survivor's Story* (2014)
- Barbara Amaya, *Nobody's Girl: A Memoir of Lost Innocence, Modern Day Slavery & Transformation* (2015)
- Jinan and Thierry Oberlé, *Esclave de Daech* (2015)
- Lara McDonell, *Girl for Sale: The Shocking True Story from the Girl Trafficked and Abused by Oxford's Evil Sex Ring* (2015)
- Farida Khalaf and Andrea C. Hoffmann, *The Girl Who Beat ISIS: My Story* (2016)

- Anna Ruston, *Secret Slave: Kidnapped and Abused for 13 years. This Is My Story of Survival* (2016)
- Nadia Murad, *Last Girl: My Story of Captivity, and My Fight against the Islamic State* (2017)
- Vannak Anan Prum, Ben Pederick, and Jocelyn Pederick, *The Dead Eye and the Deep Blue Sea: The World of Slavery at Sea – A Graphic Memoir* (2018)
- Sammy Woodhouse, *Just a Child* (2018)

Academic analysis of these autobiographies and memoirs, as well as of the body of shorter contemporary narratives published by NGOs or as witness testimonies and speeches, has been very limited. There exists a wealth of resources analyzing and applying historic narratives across a number of disciplines, but in the few cases where contemporary narratives are considered this is done by a handful of researchers.

Murphy's excellent research reveals: that within survivor autobiographies there is a preponderance of the testimonies of formerly enslaved Africans that serve to associate their experiences with historic slavery to veil sponsors' crusade politics;[16] that survivors describe themselves in their narratives as human rights ambassadors; that today's narratives are often characterized by optimistic purposes; and that survivors retreat from graphic descriptions and bodily detail so these remain obscured.[17] However, I have found these findings are not emulated when the lens is widened to narratives from a range of sources, including the hundreds of narratives available through narrative collections, grey literature, congressional testimony, and the narratives provided by survivors on social media. In these typically shorter narratives, the characteristic of optimism is not present, with many survivors struggling to meet their basic needs in recovery, to live with the effects of complex trauma, having to confront feelings of shame and guilt, and finding themselves ostracized from their communities. Indirectly, the desire to bear witness for others lost to slavery and to make their experiences known can have the effect of promoting human rights, but an analysis of the corpus examined here revealed that the majority of survivors do not explicitly identify as human rights ambassadors. Further, graphic descriptions and bodily details are evidenced in some autobiographies, in many of the shorter narratives available, and were expressed by Tung, Dwain, and Keith in my own interviews with

---

[16] Laura Murphy, "Black Face Abolition," 97–98.
[17] Laura Murphy, "The New Slave Narrative," 393 and 399, respectively.

them. By way of example, Seba explains, "If I took food, she would beat me. She often beat me. She would slap me all the time. She beat me with a broom, with kitchen tools, or whipped me with an electric cable. Sometimes I would bleed; I still have marks on my body."[18] Christine Stark explains in explicit detail the degradations she endured, saying:

> These men gang rape us. They rape us with dogs. They rape us with knives and guns and beer bottles. They tie us down, chain us to bedposts and basement poles and each other. They make us eat shit and maggots and urine. They rape us with masks on their faces. They rape us in the name of Satan and Hitler and De Sade. They rape us in front of our mothers and grandmothers; they rape our mothers and grandmothers in front of us. They play games with us. They force us to choose who will live, which child or aunt, or grandmother will live and which will die. They hold mock executions.[19]

The use of narratives to support existing understandings of modern slavery is well established in key texts in the field, such as those by Laura T. Murphy, Kevin Bales and Zoe Trodd, E. Benjamin Skinner, Kathleen Barry, and Siddharth Kara.[20] Only Murphy has analysed autobiographical narratives in detail and touched on the ways in which narratives are used to pursue sponsors' agendas and few researchers have successfully engaged with survivors' meanings. None have undertaken a deep textual analysis across the breadth of narratives that have been excavated here, demonstrating the current vacuum in the excavation and theorization of contemporary slave narratives and the need for deep analysis to reveal the value of contemporary slave narratives to abolition.

---

[18] Kevin Bales and Zoe Trodd, *To Plead Our Own Cause*, 98.
[19] Kevin Bales and Zoe Trodd, *To Plead Our Own Cause*, 100.
[20] Laura T. Murphy, *The New Slave Narrative*; Kevin Bales, *Blood and Earth: Modern Slavery, Ecocide, and the Secret to Saving the World* (New York: Spiegel & Grau, 2016); Kevin Bales, *Disposable People New Slavery in the Global Economy* (Berkeley and Los Angeles: University of California Press, 2012); Kevin Bales and Ron Soodalter, *The Slave Next Door: Human Trafficking and Slavery Today* (Berkeley and Los Angeles: University of California Press, 2010), Kevin Bales, Zoe Trodd, and Alex Kent Williamson, *Modern Slavery: The Secret World of 27 Million People* (Oxford: Oneworld Publications, 2009); Kevin Bales, *Ending Slavery: How We Free the World's Slaves* (Berkeley and Los Angeles: University of California Press, 2008); Kevin Bales, *Understanding Global Slavery: A Reader* (Berkeley and Los Angeles: University of California Press, 2005); E. Benjamin Skinner, *A Crime So Monstrous* (Edinburgh: Mainstream Publishing, 2008); Kathleen Barry, *Female Sexual Slavery* (New York: New York University Press, 1979); Siddharth Kara, *Sex Trafficking: Inside the Business of Modern Slavery* (New York: Columbia University Press, 2009); *Modern Slavery: A Global Perspective* (New York: Columbia University Press, 2017). See also Julia O'Connell Davidson, *Modern Slavery: The Margins of Freedom* (Basingstoke: Palgrave Macmillan, 2015).

*Introduction* 11

BOOK SUMMARY

This book seeks to fill this gap. Analyzing over 200 contemporary slave narratives, I draw out survivors' meanings and analyze the reality of survivors' journeys through enslavement to liberation using interpretative phenomenological analysis (IPA) and constructivist grounded theory coding techniques. The majority of narratives are drawn from the websites and reports of nongovernmental organizations and from congressional testimony, but also from twenty-eight autobiographies (those available in English), as well as the three narrative collections by Bales and Trodd, Murphy, and Gupta, and the five narratives I gathered using cognitive interview techniques. Chapters 1–6 each address an overarching category that has emerged from this analysis and explores some of the areas that have not always been considered by the extant literature. Throughout, I argue for the value of narratives to both abolition and to survivors and show that survivors' voices have been neglected in terms of harnessing their power for abolition and survivor empowerment.

The first chapter sets the scene for contemporary narratives, including further comparisons to historic narratives, and explains the methods I employed for my analysis and interviewing. In this chapter, I argue that that a failure to look to the lessons of the past in the gathering and representation of narratives has limited the capacity for narratives to be employed effectively today and argue for my interview method as an important step in reconfiguring the way we gather narratives for the purposes of abolition and survivor growth. I explore the means by which contemporary narratives are gathered and presented, the roles and responsibilities of the interviewer and listener, and examine present challenges to the credibility of survivor accounts. I then move on to explore the power that narratives have for survivors and the value of the interview method for gathering rich testimony and allowing for the intellectual and emotional growth of survivors to be presented.

The five chapters that follow address survivors' perceptions of freedom, identity, trauma, recovery, and activism. Though it may seem a reversal of the chronology of a survivor's journey, in Chapter 2, I begin thematically with survivors' perceptions of freedom in order to explore how survivors perceive slavery as a physical reality and freedom as a relative concept, drawing out themes of resistance, death, and education as freedom. I argue that the binary of free and not free is artificial: Contrary to the belief that slavery is a constant, and that freedom is a joyous escape from enslavement, I make the case that micro freedoms occur and are assumed during slavery, and that conversely, slavery continues in the mind of the free, leaving individuals in a permanent state of survival and undermining the realization of meaningful freedom.

Chapter 3 explores survivors' constructions of identity during and post enslavement. In this chapter, I argue that the denial of personhood in slavery causes a destruction of identity, but that the giving of narrative plays a vital role in the reconstruction of identity. Here, I survey the ways in which slavery strips individuals of their cultural, political, and/or social identity leading to the formation of multiple identities in survival. Divorced from their past while at the same time defined by it, I expose the way survivors identify as the child, the parent, the sibling, the survivor, the hero, the victim, and as activist. I move on to show that the giving of narrative is one means by which survivors can explore and resculpt their inner landscape and their external presence, reduce their feelings of shame, isolation, and spectralization, while at the same time acknowledging these multiple identities for themselves and to the audience.

Chapter 4 analyzes the psychological and physical effects of slavery. In this chapter, I argue that we continue to place trauma within existing psychological frameworks but fail to understand the effect of ownership and objectification, which presents unique challenges to survivors of slavery and has ramifications for the support structures that are put in place. I argue that the need to bear witness, on both the part of the listener and the narrator, is therefore crucial to meaningful growth in light of current ill-suited support and allows us to acknowledge the truth of survivors' lives. This chapter in particular draws on autobiographies and my own interviews with survivors and maps their experiences to the psychological literature on trauma, exploring the need to bear witness as a powerful means of growth.

Chapter 5 focuses on survivors' experiences in survival and the challenges for recovery that are brought by freedom. I argue that survival exposes the interplay between agency and responsibility; where survival brings the potential for agency it also brings a corresponding responsibility for the self and for others. The paradox of this potential for growth is that at the same time these things – agency and responsibility – confront survivors with challenges *to* growth. There are no rights without responsibility, but the assumption of responsibility is complicated and impeded by misunderstanding and fragmented and incohesive support systems.

The final chapter explores the survivor as activist in the context of prevention, state mechanisms, and antislavery participation. I expose the antislavery strategies that survivors themselves suggest and reveal the challenges that survivors face engaging with the public sector to inform antislavery policy. The chapter includes an analysis of the extent of survivor participation in state processes and draws on analysis of the work of survivor activists.

The book's main argument is that survivors' voices are central to the success of the antislavery movement and cannot be abstracted from the strategies formulated in the fight to eradicate slavery by 2030. The in-depth analysis also revealed six key findings: (1) The observation that narratives continue to emulate historic slave narratives as a result of the failure of amanuenses to recognize the lessons of the past; (2) that freedom is more dependent on survivors' post-liberation condition than in the immediate aftermath of liberation; (3) that survivor identity post-enslavement brings a complex interplay between multiple identities which remain largely unacknowledged by the antislavery community and which have ramifications for prevention and support; (4) that community and belonging are fundamental to survivors' framing of their worlds and purpose, both in and out of enslavement; (5) that survivor participation in antislavery structures is hampered by a lack of attention to systematic change; and (6) that narratives ultimately have two fundamental roles: (i) They are a rich source for our understanding of "modern" slavery and the means by which we address it; and (ii) the giving of narrative can be a fundamental process in becoming for survivors, enabling an exploration and reformulation of the self as something other than victim and survivor.

The insights into survivors' meanings and experiences as they relate to the giving of narrative, their perspectives on freedom, the effects of slavery on identity and trauma, and the challenges of recovery and participation are merely the start of a conversation, an opening for further analysis and research. In my conclusion, I argue that the methods I have employed in the analysis of contemporary slave narratives has revealed that there is a need to develop and promote survivor-centric frameworks that consider survivors' lived experiences and meaningfully engage with survivor activism.

## METHODOLOGICAL APPROACH TO THE ANALYSIS OF CONTEMPORARY SLAVE NARRATIVES

The methods that have formed the foundation of my analysis have proven fundamental to revealing these findings. Employing IPA to analyze the five longer narratives that I have gathered myself using cognitive interviewing techniques. I have employed constructivist grounded theory coding techniques to analyze the remaining 196 narratives drawn from printed narrative collections, autobiographies, congressional, and other formal testimony, and from NGO websites. These approaches were chosen following an examination of the various methods of analysis available and their alignment to the aims of the research and were followed by detailed discussions with experts who undertake research with vulnerable participants. The combined use of IPA, cognitive interview techniques, and constructivist grounded theory coding allowed me to move beyond an examination of the typology of modern slavery, the statistical analysis of narratives, and the influence of amanuenses and sponsors, to bring a focus on the experiential concerns of survivors to examine how they see and make sense of their journeys, and their personal and social worlds.[21]

The use of IPA entailed a painstaking scrutiny of the narratives and is a particularly valuable method for revealing concepts and meanings, rather than simple outcomes and generalizations. Conducted on small sample sizes and using a detailed case by case study (typically between three and six case studies), I gathered five rich narratives from four men and one woman whose experiences ranged from sexual slavery, forced labor, forced criminality, domestic slavery, and forced marriage, and in some cases more than one of these categories applied to their experiences. I analyzed their narratives to explore survivors' meanings and draw out themes, later testing those findings against the remaining 196 narratives identified (and vice versa), looking for correlations to understand the meanings of survivors' experiences. The cognitive interviewing techniques I employed in my interviews also provided the rich text needed for IPA, enabling me to move beyond simplistic comparison and numerical outcomes. While there is no single way for conducting IPA, I took the approach suggested by Smith and Osborn which entailed first looking for themes, then mapping phrases that capture the essence of a section of text, or of a particular concept, feeling or meaning. These were then interpreted to allow theoretical connections that were grounded in the text.[22]

---

[21] For instance, see Helene Starks and Susan Brown, "Choose Your Method: A Comparison of Phenomenology, Discourse Analysis, and Grounded Theory," *Trinidad Qualitative Health Research* 17, no. 10 (2007): 1372–80; Deborah Biggerstaff and Andrew R. Thompson, "Interpretative Phenomenological Analysis (IPA): A Qualitative Methodology of Choice in Healthcare Research," *Qualitative Research in Psychology* 5, no. 3 (2008).

[22] Jonathan A. Smith and Mike Osborn, "Interpretative Phenomenological Analysis," in *Qualitative Psychology: A Practical Guide to Research Methods*, ed. Jonathan A. Smith (London: Sage, 2008).

A double hermeneutic is involved in the use of these methods: While survivors were trying to make sense of their world, I was also trying to make sense of how survivors try to make sense of their world.[23] The aim was therefore not to produce an objective view of the survivor's world, but to understand their subjective world, moving away from statistical and software-based analysis to ensure that the more complex and subtle expressions and meanings of survivor accounts are drawn out, and to identify what is important to them. While only the survivor can know exactly how they experience their world, the extraction of meaning and the nature of their reality as expressed was ultimately dependent on my own interpretation. This brings a complication to reflect the truth of survivors' meanings; it is impossible to remove myself from my analysis as my interpretation will inevitably be influenced by my own conceptions. However, this is a recognized and embraced aspect of IPA where my own conceptions were what was needed *in order* to interpret.[24]

To mitigate the effects of bias and misinterpretation, IPA requires strong self-reflexive practice which included writing post-interview reflections and memorandums (memoing). I also sense checked and proofed my interpretation by employing constructivist grounded theory, identifying where micro and macro themes were supported by the larger body of narratives accessed. Constructivist grounded theory as a method was particularly well suited to the analysis of such a large body of narratives that involved an analysis of the complexities of survivors' worlds, views, and actions. Using constant comparison to look for relations, connectors, and transitions in expression, I coded concepts and themes present in the narratives, the combined approaches of IPA and constructivist grounded theory enabling me to reach saturation and orient my analysis of such a large and varied narrative corpus. Constructivist grounded theory also involves an interpretive approach to qualitative research with a focus on theories developed that are dependent on my view as the researcher and which aligned well with the needs of the research. These combined methods gave me insights into the situations and relationships survivors experienced, placing the emphasis on the values, beliefs, feelings, and ideologies of survivors than on the methods of research, attended by gathering rich data, coding the data, and memoing.[25] As constructivist

---

[23] Jonathan A. Smith and Mike Osborn, "Interpretative Phenomenological Analysis," 53.
[24] Hubert L. Dreyfus, *Being-in-the-World: A Commentary on Heidegger's Being and Time* (Cambridge, MA: MIT Press, 1995), 107.
[25] Kathy Charmaz, *Constructing Grounded Theory: A Practical Guide through Qualitative Analysis* (London: Sage, 2006).

grounded theory did not minimize the role of myself as the researcher in the process it made a strong partner to the IPA employed for the five longer narratives I gathered through my own interviews.[26]

The process of analysis involved a number of steps. Initially, I read and reread the narratives I could find, noting themes, relationships, and meanings, and adopting a form of free association, loosely noting what came to mind as I read and reread in order to immerse myself in the data. As I undertook my own interviews, I employed IPA, reading and rereading the interview transcripts and listening to the audio recording together with my memos of the interviews. I then made some initial notes about what the survivor was saying, processes, places, and relationships they discussed, and language and initial thoughts on meanings that emerged from the text. With IPA, there are no rules as to what is commented on, and no requirement to divide the text into units. Instead, the aim is to come to analysis with an open and exploratory mind, which is later tested in the next stage. The text was then revisited to map more descriptive comments to the transcript, slowly developing a richer account of aspects contained in the narrative. Language is also noted, so that pauses, laughter, vernacular, and repetition were considered in context, and the past and future tense noted (and so it was vital that the transcript was reproduced accurately). I also undertook a more interpretative approach adopting conceptual thinking around aspects of survivors' stories in the context of the whole and taking into account their overarching feelings and narrative.

Categories started to emerge from both my own interviews and from the body of narratives, and inevitably the rereading, constant comparison, and reconsideration process had to be repeated several times across the corpus, with insights from the use of IPA on the richer transcripts from my interviews being tested against the 196 other narratives, and vice versa. Narratives were also revisited as each substantive chapter was approached and as my understanding and insights grew with analysis of each category. Smaller subjects or patterns were connected under larger themes that then formed the basis of each chapter.

At times, the primary focus on the truths revealed by narratives has proved challenging, particularly where other disciplines, such as trauma theory, have had a necessary influence on my understanding of survivor

---

[26] John W. Creswell and Cheryl N. Poth, *Qualitative Inquiry and Research Design: Choosing among Five Approaches* (London: Sage, 2018), 86.

expression.²⁷ As I progressed through the narratives, reading and rereading them to reflect on and explore their meaning, I manually coded over time, using two excel sheets to record extracts, notes, and adding thematic columns as the research progressed. I revisited my coding as more insights emerged from the research for each chapter and in light of the richer text gained from my own interviews which were carried out from February 2017 to May 2018. The key was to ensure the narratives were my primary source of interpretation; that what survivors expressed was applied to other disciplines to provide context, rather than applying existing theory to survivor narratives. In this way, survivors' voices have led the research instead of being led by it. The process of drawing out themes from the narratives for my analysis has also therefore been developmental.

Coding was carried out manually in two ways: on categories of meaning and on categories of fact. Where meaning was categorized, this included survivors' feelings of spectralization, indicators of the destruction of identity, the exercise of free will, the prevalence of violent domination, expressions of recovery, the influence of religious beliefs, perceptions of freedom, feelings about witnessing the enslavement or murder of others, and on other forced criminality (where applicable). It also included responses to renaming, indicators of shifting identities, feelings on education, indicators of psychological trauma, fear of recapture, self-destructive behavior, resistance strategies, concern for others, the importance of family, activist desires and abolitionist strategies, and feelings on labels (e.g. "survivor" or "victim"). Codes were clustered or connected and eventually these were reduced from the multiple to the few, to the umbrella themes that form the basis of each chapter. For example, findings on recovery (Chapter 5) encompassed survivors' feelings of responsibility, vulnerability, security, autonomy, labelling, and sense of freedom. That chapter also draws on survivors' perceptions on the primacy of systems over survivor needs, and feelings of stigma, isolation,

---

[27] Although it should be noted that there are those who critique trauma theory arguing the impossibility of having direct access to others' histories so as to make judgments. See for example S. P. Mohanty, "Us and Them: On the Philosophical Bases of Political Criticism," *The Yale Journal of Criticism* 2, no. 2 (1989); M. Balaev, "Literary Trauma Theory Reconsidered," in *Contemporary Approaches in Literary Trauma Theory*, ed. M. Balaev (London: Palgrave Macmillan, 2014); Irene Visser, "Decolonizing Trauma Theory: Retrospect and Prospects," *Humanities* 4 (2015); Kathryn Robson, "Curative Fictions: The 'Narrative Cure' in Judith Herman's Trauma and Recovery and Chantal Chawaf's Le Manteau Noir," *Journal for Cultural Research* 5, no. 1 (2001).

social acceptance, purpose, family, community, futurity, and activism. The thematic approach I have employed means that in one sense my findings are borne out by the large body of narratives examined, but also means that not all of the micro themes will necessarily apply to every survivor. This is in part because the data is limited to explore expression in some areas; the short nature of many contemporary narratives means there is little space for survivors to describe their lives and feelings beyond a description of their experience of slavery itself.

The second more factual form of coding involved classifying values such as types of slavery, ages, country of origin, country of enslavement, type and source of narrative, status, gender, and religion. It also included whether individuals were renamed or called slaves, use of the term master, profession in survival, means of escape, whether survivors discussed their pre- and post-enslavement circumstances, and how survivors self-described. This was done to test existing research and provide context to analysis.

# I

# A Narrated Self

## *The Slave Narrative Genre*

Historical slave narratives were "intensely political documents,"[1] contributing to debates, democratization, perspectives on freedom, and challenges to ideologies.[2] The act of speaking out was a way of confronting prejudice and racism, "an open act of rebellion ... a declaration of one's rights to speak,"[3] and their narratives were a form of protest literature used as proselytizing tools where language was used to "transform the self and change society ... functioning as a catalyst, guide, or a mirror of social change."[4]

Historic slave narratives not only critiqued an aspect of society but also suggested, "either implicitly or explicitly, a solution to society's ills ... striving to give voice to a collective consciousness, uniting isolated or inchoate discontent."[5] Narratives were therefore not just about moral suasion; they were also a move to political action, resistance, and revolt. For example, the abolitionist and survivor Olaudah Equiano used white men's belief systems and racial discourse to argue for abolition and "undermine the colonial narrative and reformulate that culture's notion

---

[1] Audrey Fisch, ed., *The Cambridge Companion to the African American Slave Narrative* (Cambridge: Cambridge University Press, 2007), 28.
[2] Audrey Fisch, ed., *The Cambridge Companion*, 29.
[3] Noreen Connell and Cassandra Wilson, eds., *Rape: The First Sourcebook for Women by New York Radical Feminists* (New York: The New American Library, 1974), 27–28.
[4] Lawrence Aje, "Fugitive Slave Narratives and the (Re)presentation of the Self? The Cases of Frederick Douglass and William Brown," *L'Ordinaire des Amériques* 215 (2013): 7; John Stauffer, "Foreword," in *American Protest Literature*, ed. Zoe Trodd (Cambridge, MA: Harvard University Press, 2008), xii.
[5] John Stauffer, "Foreword," xii.

of 'slave' and 'African'."[6] Former slaves used narratives "to indict both those who enslaved them, and the metaphysical system drawn upon to justify their enslavement. They did so using the most enduring weapon at their disposal, the printing press."[7] Narratives were not therefore just a record of someone's life in slavery but were "wielded as ideological weapons" to destroy slavery.[8] As such, narratives were more than a record of someone's life in slavery; they were a way of demanding accountability, of bringing rights into play, demanding recognition, and were a call for "civilized" nations to "live up to their moral responsibility."[9]

However, the well-known narratives of, for example, Frederick Douglass, Harriet Jacobs, John Brown, and Olaudah Equiano are exceptional examples of historic slave narratives. Their renown leads to the common misconception that historic slave narratives are few, rather than the hundreds that exist. While these are longer, more expressive, and carefully constructed narratives, the body of historic slave narratives is much more limited; they are typically short and demonstrate an "overwhelming sameness,"[10] using the sameness of configuration to reflect the effects of the dehumanizing environment of slavery upon its victims, rather than on their own individuality.[11] This was chiefly because their scope was defined by the audience and by the agenda of their sponsors, but it was also because of the drive to bear witness for others; both influences presented survivors with the problem of distinguishing between "the individual self and the community self and the desire to present the symbolic nature of one's personal experiences while maintaining one's own inimitability."[12]

The majority of historic narratives followed a familiar structure of the day-to-day minute detail of a life in slavery, their living arrangements, the physical and emotional abuse experienced, and more generally the transition from liberty to enslavement, and then to escape or emancipation. Foster identifies four chronological stages to historic slave narratives: the

---

[6] Samantha Earley, "Writing from the Centre or the Margins? Olaudah Equiano's Writing Life Reassessed," *African Studies Review* 46, no. 3 (2003): 4.
[7] Henry Louis Gates Jr., *The Classic Slave Narratives* (New York: Penguin, 1987), ix.
[8] Lawrence Aje, "Fugitive Slave Narratives," 5.
[9] Jeffrey Gunn, "Literacy and the Humanizing Project in Olaudah Equiano's *The Interesting Narrative* and Ottobah Cugoano's *Thoughts and Sentiments*," *Orality and History*, no. 10 (2007): 12.
[10] James Olney, "'I Was Born': Slave Narratives, Their Status as Autobiography and as Literature," *Callaloo* 20 (1984), 46.
[11] Frances Smith Foster, *Witnessing Slavery: The Development of Ante-Bellum Slave Narratives* (Madison, WI: University of Wisconsin Press, 1994), 5.
[12] Frances Smith Foster, *Witnessing Slavery*, 5.

loss of innocence in the realization that they are a slave, the realization of alternatives to slavery and the desire to be free, escape, and freedom obtained.[13] Within these stages, narratives revealed the quest for literacy and for freedom, and included details of lost family members and family ties.[14] They also revealed the shaming tactics used, the physical practices that undermined genderhood and sexuality, the complete disregard for age and capacity, the practice of renaming, the use of religious and cultural beliefs to manipulate those enslaved, and the use of disparaging language to undermine individuals' social and self-held beliefs as to what was "normal." Repeated motifs included abuse, objectification, alienation, and the author's strategic use of language to reformulate perceptions, exposing the master's hypocrisy and inconsistency, and making overt appeals to the imagination of the audience, using euphemism, simile, and metaphor, to express emotions and to relate brutal memories too painful to voice in graphic detail. However, as a body, narratives rarely described preenslavement birth and childhood, or the state of existence postemancipation, and they almost never told the "intellectual, emotional, moral growth of the narrator."[15] It is usually in the longer narratives and the autobiographies that we see these latter aspects emerge, something that has led to my choice of interview method and the methodologies adopted for this book (discussed in detail in Chapter 1).

The difference between longer texts and brief narratives is significant, as is the opportunity to tell free of influence. For example, the historic survivor Peter Bruner wrote his narrative in 1918 and was also interviewed by the Works Progress Administration (WPA) in 1936. While the WPA transcription was inaccurate, it was nevertheless clear that Bruner had both forgotten details and concealed aspects from his interviewers.[16] His 1918 narrative is fifty-four pages long, but his subsequent WPA narrative is only two and a half pages long and totals 830 words, providing the briefest outline of his journey from enslavement to freedom.[17] Consider also

---

[13] Frances Smith Foster, *Witnessing Slavery*, 85.
[14] Donna M. Campbell, *The Slave, Freedom, or Liberation Narrative*, Washington, DC: Washington State University. https://public.wsu.edu/~campbelld/amlit/slave.htm
[15] James Olney, "'I Was Born'," 51.
[16] John W. Blassingame, "Using the Testimony of Ex-Slaves: Approaches and Problems," *The Journal of Southern History* 41, no. 4 (November 1975): 491. See also Peter Bruner, *A Slave's Adventures toward Freedom. Not Fiction, but the True Story of a Struggle* (Oxford, OH: s.n., 1918). http://docsouth.unc.edu/neh/bruner/menu.html
[17] Federal Writer's Project, United States Work Projects Administration. *The Federal Writers' Project: Slave Narrative Project, Vol. 7, Kentucky, Bogie-Woods* (with combined interviews of others). Story of Peter Bruner, a former slave, pp. 88–90. www.loc.gov/resource/mesn.070/?sp=92

Douglass' second autobiography *My Bondage and My Freedom*.[18] Free of the influence of Garrison, this second narrative is twice the length of the first and reveals details such as his mother's literacy, tender moments between his mother and himself as a child, and that his father was white "or nearly white," details that would not have served abolitionist purposes in the first version. The second version is arguably a demonstration of the freedom Douglass found to express himself without constraint, to tell his whole unedited story, primarily serving himself but also allowing the audience the full truth of his story and feelings.

## A CULTURE OF DISBELIEF

Some of those longer narratives were also the most successful narratives because they were eloquent enough to persuade the audience of the veracity of their accounts. They confronted the audience with the author's capabilities and dispelled the belief that slaves were uncivilized and lesser. Yet their quality gave rise to a culture of disbelief. As survivors on the lecture circuit were re-conceptualized in the audience's mind from passive victims to intellectuals, activists, and agents for change, they were sometimes seen as too capable to be entirely believable. Douglass was told: "better have a *little* of the plantation manner of speech than not; 'tis not best that you seem too learned."[19] To persuade the audience, survivors had to understand the limitations of voice and strategically negotiate the bounds of propriety and the humility of self-presentation.[20] Therefore, while the abolitionist forum was a vital arena for expression, it also limited it. The audience's and sponsors' expectations led to survivors having to present themselves as the perfect victim, in other words as not too overtly clever, but sufficiently eloquent to persuade the audience of the wrong of slavery, painting a vivid portrait of the horrors of slavery, and bearing their backs as proof in order to authenticate their accounts, elicit sympathy, and motivate activism. Confined to this role, survivors were rarely employed for their expertise or given room to demonstrate their

---

[18] Frederick Douglass, *My Bondage and My Freedom*. Part I. Life as a Slave. Part II. Life as a Freeman (New York: Miller, Orton & Mulligan, 1855; New York: Penguin Group, 2003), 266. Citations refer to the Penguin edition. Frederick Douglass, *My Bondage and My Freedom* (New York: Miller, Orton & Mulligan, 1855).
[19] Frederick Douglass, *My Bondage and My Freedom*, 266.
[20] Philip Gould, "The Rise of the Slave Narrative," 20.

## A Narrated Self: The Slave Narrative Genre 23

intellectual growth. Douglass spoke of the fact that sponsors always wished to pin him down to his simple narrative, saying "give us the facts ... we will take care of the philosophy," but writes that "it did not entirely satisfy me to *narrate* wrongs; I felt like *denouncing* them ... I was growing, and needed room."[21]

It also took more than mere expression and the demonstration of physical injury to convince the broader American public of the authenticity of survivors' stories, particularly given that during the eighteenth and nineteenth centuries slavery was legal and the master's voice dominant. Expounding proslavery ideologies based on racism, paternalism, economic arguments, and religion, slavery was defended by the powerful: "it is not sinful to enslave the negro race, providing that it is done in a tender, fatherly and thoughtful manner, having the *fear* of God before our eyes, in a transaction of the kind, doing no violence to the bodies of or minds of such persons as slaves or servants, beyond proper and *necessary* correction."[22] The giving of narratives therefore provided those who had been subjugated the opportunity to reorder the power relations experienced in the master–slave relationship, to expose the falsehoods of slaveholders' reasoning, and to assume a right to voice and agency previously denied them.

As survivor accounts challenged the prevailing proslavery discourse, it was necessary for them to verify their narratives in order to preempt or dispel disbelief. Historical narratives added "proof" – letters or testimonials confirming their accounts. Survivors also had to represent themselves as morally equivalent – in part to emphasize the singularity of humanity but also to persuade the reader they were "worth" listening to. As a result, narratives also included testimonials, extolling the author's humanity and morality. For example, Lydia Maria Child in the first edition of Harriet Jacob's *Incidents in the Life of a Slave Girl* included a letter from Amy Post (a Quaker abolitionist, women's rights activist, and friend of Jacobs) who described Jacobs' appearance as "prepossessing, and her deportment indicated remarkable delicacy of feeling and purity of thought." She also recounted that Jacobs was "naturally virtuous and refined" and referred to her "sensitive spirit."[23] Narratives were also

---

[21] Frederick Douglass, *My Bondage and My Freedom*, 266.
[22] Josiah Priest, *Bible Defence of Slavery* (Glasgow, KY: W. S. Brown, 1852), 102–3. http://babel.hathitrust.org/cgi/pt?id=miun.aev3898.0001.001;view=1up;seq=7
[23] Harriet Jacobs, Lydia Maria Frances Child, *Incidents in the Life of a Slave Girl* (Boston, 1861), 304. http://docsouth.unc.edu/fpn/jacobs/menu.html

supplemented with photographs, declamatory addresses to the reader, letters, bills of sale, notices of slave auctions and escaped slaves, certificates of manumission, and birth, death, and marriage certificates.[24] And appendixes included official reports of legislatures, courts, governors, churches, and agricultural societies.[25]

Key autobiographies written by survivors also often explicitly noted the survivor as author, as "written by himself," primarily to illustrate the author's literacy and capability but also to assert the authenticity of the narrative. Ex-slaves also made a point of including their status, explicitly noting their status from slave to freeman, and using the adjective "fugitive."[26] However, in the eighteenth and nineteenth centuries, survivor literacy was low, and for the most part, ex-slave testimony was typically written by whites, with edits reflecting the author's education, religion, and attitudes to slavery. They were a "black message in a white envelope."[27] This caused such significant misrepresentation that the historian Ulrich B. Phillips remarked that historic ex-slave narratives in general "were issued with so much abolitionist editing that as a class their authenticity is doubtful."[28]

The questions raised over the authenticity of historic ex-slave narratives are no better exemplified than in the unethical way in which the WPA narratives were gathered and reproduced. The trustworthiness of this collection has been repeatedly brought into question,[29] but it serves as a valuable lesson for us today. The interview situation itself may not have been conducive to accurate communication. The interviews were limited in focus and so short as to be unhelpful in many cases, and the predominant use of white interviewers and class differences impeded honest communication. Comparisons between white and black interviewers' records show "an entirely different portrait of their [ex slaves']

---

[24] James Olney, "'I Was Born'," 49.
[25] John W. Blassingame, "Using the Testimony of Ex-Slaves," 477.
[26] Lawrence Aje, "Fugitive Slave Narratives," 2–3.
[27] John Sekora, "Black Message/White Envelope: Genre, Authenticity, and Authority in the Antebellum Slave Narrative," *Callaloo* 32 (1987): 482.
[28] Ulrich B. Phillips, *Life and Labour in the Old South* (Boston: Little, Brown and Company, 1929), 219.
[29] See the Works Progress Administration and the Slave Narrative Collection at www.loc.gov/collections/slave-narratives-from-the-federal-writers-project-1936-to-1938/articles-and-essays/introduction-to-the-wpa-slave-narratives/wpa-and-the-slave-narrative-collection/

treatment."[30] For example, white interviewers' records generally stated that ex-slaves spoke with "gratitude" of the "good old days," but the opposite view is revealed in the records of interviews conducted by black interviewers.[31] A premium was also placed by the majority of white interviewers on the "right" answers to questions such as "was your master kind to you?" and "was your master a good man?" with many interviewers refusing to accept the "wrong" answers. The racism and insensitivity present in this collection are also revealed by the language interviewers used to describe survivors, with interviewers using terms reminiscent of plantation practice. They called participants "darkeys," "niggers," "aunties," "mammys," and "uncles," which could only have reinforced the power imbalances of the relationship between white interviewers and black survivors of slavery.

In terms of the way these accounts were then reproduced, few were recorded verbatim. Portions were deleted, revised, and altered. Many interviewers deleted references to cruel punishments, runaways, blacks serving in the Union Army and voting during reconstruction, and they overwrote participants' expressions, replacing excellent English with stereotypical black slave dialect such as "de," "dis," "chilluns," and "folks," so that narratives were bruised by redaction and linguistic editing.[32] Further, the age of the participants impacted their memory; all of them were at least seventy-two years out of slavery, and many could not remember much of their childhood. In some cases, a large percentage of participants were black, but had never been slaves (e.g. 40 percent of the Arkansas collection consists of interviews with those born during or after the Civil War).[33] A detailed analysis of the collection undertaken by Blassingame in 1975 concludes that their uncritical use would "lead almost inevitably to a simplistic and distorted view of the plantation as a paternalistic institution where the chief feature of life was mutual love and respect between masters and slaves."[34]

---

[30] John W. Blassingame, "Using the Testimony of Ex-Slaves," 477–78.
[31] Ruby Lane Radford (Georgia Staff) – see George P. Rawick, ed. *The American Slave: A Composite Autobiography. From Sundown to Sunup the Making of the Black Community* (Westport, CT: Greenwood Publishing Company, 1972), xiii.
[32] John W. Blassingame, "Using the Testimony of Ex-Slaves," 477–78.
[33] John W. Blassingame, "Using the Testimony of Ex-Slaves," 488.
[34] John W. Blassingame, *Slave Testimony, Two Centuries of Letters, Speeches, Autobiographies and Interviews* (Baton Rouge: Louisiana State University Press, 1977), Lvi.

## THE CONTEMPORARY NARRATIVE GENRE

My analysis reveals that the nature of contemporary slave narratives in many ways continues to emulate what we have seen in historic narratives. Contemporary narratives are still concerned with resistance and portray the hardships of daily life. The details of survivors' lives preenslavement and in recovery are also mostly explored in the more detailed autobiographies and provided through my own interviews, but also occasionally, although not typically, in the shorter narratives. The majority of contemporary narratives available remain brief accounts, emulating the historic narrative journey of slavery to liberation. But today they also explore capture and trafficking in a way that many historic narratives did not, a sign of the illicit means by which individuals today are predominantly groomed into slavery. However, where historic narratives were employed to convince the global community of the wrong of slavery, today, at least theoretically, the moral argument has been won. However, factually, slavery is in many cases tolerated and employed even by states and communities despite its *jus cogens* status.

One key distinction between historic and contemporary narratives is that many survivors are today particularly concerned with exposing and persuading the audience of the continued existence of slavery. As a result of the historicization of slavery, today's slaves are in many respects "forgotten" slaves. The abolition of slavery means that it has become illicit or hidden, and there remains a question of "choice" that casts a shadow over the perception of the existence and prevalence of "modern" slavery. The issue of consent muddies the global community's perception of the existence of "true" slavery when compared to historic slavery. For example, where distinctions arise between smuggling and trafficking, where sex "work" is capable of distinction from sexual slavery, and where people are groomed and then trafficked. Slavery now exists in every country in the world, its victims drawn from a range of ethnicities, religions, and nations, and all within the same timeframe. With the many different types or practices with the potential to amount to slavery recognized today,[35] "modern" slavery no longer fits the perception of slavery in the public consciousness that has been built from what is known and taught of eighteenth- and nineteenth-century slavery. Slavery in all its forms no longer mimics the icon of the African slave in chains, even though the

---

[35] For example, forced sexual exploitation, forced labor, forced criminality, and cultural or religious systems falling within these, such as Trokosi and Restavec systems.

experience of slavery is in many cases entirely comparable. Survivors, therefore, face "a crisis of illegibility" as a result of the perception that slavery was permanently abolished in the nineteenth century.[36]

### THE WAYS IN WHICH CONTEMPORARY SLAVE NARRATIVES ARE GATHERED AND PRESENTED

I have mentioned in the introduction that many narratives provided on NGO websites are labeled "case studies" or similar. Rather than the verbatim reproduction of survivors' voices, these are typically told on behalf of survivors, denying the opportunity for the survivor and the global community to benefit from the process and outcome of narrative giving. Of over 150 survivor stories accessed via these websites, only 16 percent were reproduced in the survivor's own words, while a few other examples also included one or two short quotations from the survivor within the more general "case study" format. Often buried on the websites, through links at the bottom in very small font, or only accessible through several tabs via links to news, general resources, or blogs, accessing survivor narratives can involve the viewer having to navigate unclear pathways and in some cases sort through several years' worth of news or blog posts to pull out survivors' stories. Once accessed, the brevity of these accounts limits their structure to the familiar trope of slavery to liberation, providing only a snapshot of their experiences. Typically, survivor testimony is limited to short stories of between two and five paragraphs, told *for* survivors rather than *by* them. They are often accompanied by a picture of the survivor or a stock photo of circumstances or environments related to the type of slavery or the country in which slavery occurred. By way of example, two narratives from NGO websites are reproduced below:

*GRACE'S STORY*
Living in Africa, Grace experienced the horrors of an uprising and witnessed her husband and child being shot and killed in front of her. To make ends meet, she collected bottles on the street.

Desperate, she accepted a promise of a better life in the UK from someone she thought of as a family friend.

But when she got here, Grace was locked in a house and raped daily. She had no passport and couldn't speak English. Her trafficker profited from selling her

---

[36] Laura T. Murphy, *The New Slave Narrative: The Battle over Representations of Contemporary Slavery* (New York: Columbia University Press, 2019), 391.

for sex. Grace suffered horribly. But one day her trafficker didn't lock the door properly and she escaped.

Found by the police, Grace was brought to Unseen's 24-hour safe-house that's set up specifically for survivors of human trafficking. Her trauma had left her physically scarred together with Post Traumatic Stress Disorder and extreme anxiety. But, with Unseen's help, she received professional healthcare and psychological support, one-to-one sessions with specialist staff, and access to education and legal advice.

OUTCOME: GRACE HAS NOW LEFT THE SAFE-HOUSE AND JOINED UNSEEN'S RESETTLEMENT SERVICE, WHICH WILL CONTINUE TO SUPPORT UNTIL SHE'S ABLE TO RE-ESTABLISH HER LIFE – INDEPENDENT AND FREE FROM EXPLOITATION. SHE'S LEARNING ENGLISH, ATTENDING REGULAR COURSES AND IS NOW VOLUNTEERING IN THE COMMUNITY, WORKING WITH OTHER VULNERABLE WOMEN.[37]

**Benita Furaha: From Slavery to Dressmaking Trainer**
"My story is hard to tell," says Benita Furaha, a trainer at a dressmaking training center in Rubaya, Democratic Republic of the Congo. Benita's parents died when she was 13. Her older brother threatened to starve her or to send her out of the house if she couldn't contribute to household expenses. One option was to find a husband. Instead, she went to work in the mines.

"Every morning, I transported and sold sorghum juice to the quarry workers," Benita recounts. "I also transported minerals from the quarry. I worked from 6 a.m. to 6 p.m. and I hardly earned $1 per day." Benita was also a victim of sexual violence.

In 2012, Benita met community workers from the Free the Slaves partner organization ASSODIP. They encouraged Benita to leave her situation and join the group's dressmaking center in Rubaya. After several meetings including ASSODIP activists, Benita, and her older brother, Benita left the mine to learn dressmaking.

Since then, her life has changed. Benita spent three months in learning dressmaking skills. After the training, she joined the dressmaking workshop in the Rubaya market. At the same time, she took reading and writing classes. She mastered dressmaking skills and became a good seamstress. Benita explained that the dressmaking allows her to earn a decent and honest living.[38]

Benita was able to save enough money to buy two goats and eight chickens. Recently, ASSODIP hired her as the dressmaking trainer for survivors of gender-based violence at the ASSODIP training center in Rubaya.

These case studies essentially achieve three things: (1) they carry an educational purpose to expose the public to different "types" of slavery and elicit sympathy, (2) they are used as a marketing tool to promote the

---

[37] https://aesopagency.com/a-few-yarns/unseen-christmas-graces-story/
[38] www.freetheslaves.net/from-slavery-to-dressmaking-trainer-in-the-congo/

impact of the NGO in the field and encourage donation, and (3) they are a form of proof, with case studies repurposed for research and in evidence submitted to governments. In many cases, the provision of case studies is not about giving survivors a voice but is concerned with the organization's agenda and needs. The need to tell slavery as it is, the necessity to explain to the public audience what slavery involves, creates a rigid form that inhibits telling, and sponsor editing, or circumstances in the field restrict the opportunity for voice. However, there is also more variance today, in part reflecting the range of forms of slavery now recognized, and in part due to the growth in platforms for voice and the associated ease of access and representation.

By way of contrast to the above examples, a survey of first-person contemporary slave narratives shows that many survivors will choose to tell their stories differently and self-select varied aspects of their experiences and emotions. They will also locate their story within a wider, or a more selective space than is demonstrated on many NGO sites. For example, some survivors will focus the majority of their narrative on their escape, and some on their past prior to their enslavement, often trying to make sense of the circumstances leading to it. Others provide the briefest snapshot of enslavement, a paragraph only, and a number of survivors' narratives will detail their circumstances post enslavement. Those who do will discuss their improvement or lack thereof, describing their economic and cultural situation, or the strategies and leadership roles they have assumed. Although typically this latter aspect is only expressed where longer narratives have been made possible.

However, even in the familiar organization of the story, it is an oversimplification to reduce survivors' narratives to the convention of capture, slavery, and escape. Within these contemporary slave narratives, a number of aspects or themes emerge that expose how freedom is perceived, how self-identity is irrevocably damaged by enslavement, the effects of trauma, and what survivors value in liberation and recovery. The more detailed narratives, and those given more freely by survivors, explore how they seek explanation, understanding, and order in the turns of circumstance that have led them in and out of slavery, and how contemporary voices are affected, changed, and challenged. Slave narratives then and now expose the shifts and catalysts of personal development, with distinct contrasts played out between the highs and lows. They represent one part in the process of becoming and expose the many similarities to the way historical narratives were presented and received.

Despite the value of narratives to the antislavery movement and to survivors, it is clear that narratives are not gathered and employed as effectively as they could be. They are significantly edited in order to present a snapshot of practices, to serve the needs of sponsors or to capture public interest. While many organizations will make a choice to simplify and edit narratives to reach a wider public audience where awareness raising is the primary goal, or to establish facts to move forward with prosecutions and inquiries, full, free-told narratives also have a crucial place in current abolitionist efforts. As such, narratives do not always (and in the case of NGO websites rarely) expose the internalized behaviors and psychological insights that can be more completely revealed by full narratives where survivors are given the opportunity to tell in full, and do not engage with the imagery and symbolism survivors' employ, or with their memory and re-memory.

## THE CONTINUATION OF CHALLENGES TO THE LEGITIMACY OF SLAVE NARRATIVES

There is little evidence of a recognition in practice of past problems encountered in the gathering and presentation of narratives. Portions of narratives continue to be deleted to present digestible and informative short extracts, rather than sponsors facilitating and presenting survivors' full experiences as they wish to tell them. Language is also sometimes amended and there have been instances where narratives have been sensationalized to capture public sympathy.[39] Interview questions are also sometimes understandably devised to extract simple facts for a public audience, but I argue that these silence survivor expression by directing them to discuss limited aspects of their experiences. Shorter narratives typically amount to a few hundred words, whereas the longer narratives I gathered through deep interviews range from 8,400 to over 36,600 words, offering significant space for survivors to take their narrative beyond the restrictive parameters of a standard interview. It is significant that many of the contemporary narratives available are collected through traditional structured and semi-structured interviews and so do not present the opportunity for a full free-telling of survivors' stories.[40] The interview

---

[39] See for example the criticism of the publication of a collection of narratives by Jesse Sage and Liora Kasten, *Enslaved*, noted in the Introduction, n. 54.
[40] Nearly all the narratives analyzed, including some of the coauthored autobiographies, are constructed from interviews. The Appendix indicates the role of amanuenses and sponsors and whether a narrative was entirely self-authored.

techniques used, or particular aims of gathering these narratives can essentially redefine the telling, influencing the language used, the details given, and the overall narrative arc. The way in which other narratives are initially recorded and later reproduced is often clear in the language adopted; on occasion, the phrasing used indicates some leading of the story and in others, the narrative is touched with legal vernacular.[41] The narratives gathered, and the autobiographies and memoirs in particular, are built with a sense of the intended audience and so the audience informs the text. Where sponsors fashion survivors' narratives to meet the expectations of the audience, the lives of ex-slaves become in once sense "as much possessed and used by abolitionists as their actual lives had been by slaveholders."[42] Where control has finally been reclaimed in liberation, and in the ability to bear witness, the constraints and editing undertaken can frustrate new feelings of self-ownership and have the effect of silencing survivors.

I have stated that contemporary narratives have suffered similar questions over authenticity that plagued many historic narratives despite today's global acknowledgment of the wrong of slavery. While not subject to the problems of the WPA narratives on the same scale, contemporary narratives are still colored by the influence of sponsors and amanuenses. That influence continues to fertilize a culture of disbelief and has even led to attempts to discredit the veracity of, and motives behind, survivor accounts. Survivors therefore not only have to face their own disbelief in their survival of slavery, but through the giving of narrative are exposed to the audience's disbelief of the details of their testimony. A number of contemporary narrators feel the need to assert the authenticity of their narratives, stating "I am not lying, why would I lie?," and "people ask how can I remember? I'm telling the truth." Labov calls this the "reportability paradox" – the paradox of the survivor who has an extraordinary story to tell but who, "because of the sheer incredibility of the events of that story, bears an especially heavy burden in terms of narrative credibility."[43]

Contemporary autobiographies and memoirs also therefore adopt the authenticating strategies of the past. In place of bills of sale and notices of

---

[41] Best practice has been recognized in many states in the form of cognitive or forensic interviewing technique, see for example Chris Newlin et al., "Child Forensic Interviewing."
[42] James Olney, "'I Was Born'," 51.
[43] Joseph R. Slaughter, "Life, Story, Violence: What Narrative Doesn't Say," *Humanity* 8, no. 3 (2007): 471.

slave auctions they use statistics, scholarly works, family testimony, faith leaders, NGO leaders, and academics, to assert that the stories told are not fiction.[44] The veracity of their accounts continues to be declared in the titles of autobiographies and memoirs. Zana Muhsen's narrative is titled *Sold: One Woman's Heartbreaking True Account of Modern Slavery*, Ishmael Beah's is titled *A Long Way Gone: The True Story of a Child Soldier*, Mende Nazer's is *Slave: The True Story of a Girl's Lost Childhood and Her Fight for Survival*, and Shyima Hal's is *Hidden Girl: The True Story of a Modern-Day Child Slave*. Supporting testimony for Akallo's narrative is also provided by Adrian Bradbury, Founder and Director of the NGO GuluWalk, and starts with the assertion that *"Girl Soldier* is not fiction."[45]

In Mende Nazer's autobiography *Slave: A True Story of a Girl's Lost Childhood and Her Fight for Survival*, her coauthor Damien Lewis felt the need to demonstrate the authenticity of Nazer's account and address the accuracy of interpretation, describing in detail the rigor of the method used for interpretation. In the Afterword, he notes that when seeking help to escape, Nazer wanted a journalist to witness her rescue so that it was "on the record."[46] Lewis also explicitly recognizes the need to allow Mende the opportunity to tell all of her story from the heart, noting this was only achieved through the trust built between them. Working slowly in English, using an Arabic-English dictionary and various books on Sudan, the Nuba Mountains, and slavery, between them they were able to write her story as accurately as possible. Essentially the explanation in the Afterword achieves two things: it bolsters the reader's belief in Mende's testimony, and it is proof of the authenticity and accuracy of voice despite translation, thereby diminishing any challenges of sensationalism or invention.

The continued need to validate survivor accounts in this way is somewhat discouraging, but corroboration remains necessary where sponsors and amanuenses exert considerable influence, and where attempts to sift survivor testimony for fallacies are not uncommon. An example of the

---

[44] See for example the narratives of Timea Nagy, *Memoirs of a Sex Slave Survivor* (n.p.: Communication Dynamics Publishing, 2010); Theresa Flores, *The Slave across the Street: How a 15-Year-Old Girl Became a Sex Slave* (n.p.: Arrow books, 2013); and Faith J. H. McDonell and Grace Akallo, *Girl Soldier: A Story of Hope for Northern Uganda's Children* (Grand Rapids, MI: Chosen Books, 2007). For a more detailed analysis see Laura Murphy, "The New Slave Narrative."
[45] Faith J. H. McDonell and Grace Akallo, *Girl Soldier*, inside leaf.
[46] Mende Nazer and Damien Lewis, *Slave*.

latter can be seen in the response to China Keitetsi's autobiography of her childhood spent in the Yoweri Museveni's National Resistance Army in Uganda into which she was trafficked aged 9. The Ugandan President has denied Keitetsi's claims that young children were enlisted and abused, and a committee set up by the Ugandan government to investigate Keitetsi's case dismissed her as a hoaxer who joined the army aged 17, then deserted after involvement in a theft. The committee has said "there was never a policy of recruiting child soldiers" and claims the National Resistance Army simply cared for children left orphaned by combat. Keitetsi included a disclaimer to her memory in her narrative, saying, "I might have mixed the years, and the parents, in this first part, and for that I ask my readers to understand, as I was very young then,"[47] but has responded to the committee's assertions by releasing a photograph of herself in uniform when she says she was aged 13.[48]

Another well-known example of an attempt to discredit a survivor's account was seen in the systematic attack on Ishmael Beah's memoir *A Long Way Gone*.[49] Beah's narrative gives an account of his two years as a child soldier in Sierra Leone's civil war, but in a series of articles three journalists working for the broadsheet *The Australian* identified potential inconsistencies in his story.[50] They alleged Beah had only been a child soldier for two months and that some of his accounts did not bear up to scrutiny. Beah has vigorously defended his story, as have his agent and his editor, and made counter allegations of government-sponsored falsified evidence. In both cases, the authors of these survivor accounts were not just challenged by journalists and the public, but by the associated governments who were seeking to diminish testimony of human rights abuses they deny occur within their borders. The vitriol of the exchange between these parties lays bare the difficulty survivors can face in recounting their experiences, and exposes a culture of disbelief that continues to invade accounts of "modern" slavery. In other words, while narratives will always be open to challenge and may not always be precisely and accurately recalled, there

---

[47] China Keitetsi, *Child Soldier*, 51.
[48] Laura Smith-Spark, "Ex-Child Soldier's Path to Hope," BBC News online, Tuesday, May 25, 2004. http://news.bbc.co.uk/1/hi/uk/3733349.stm
[49] Ishmael Beah, *A Long Way Gone: The True Story of a Child Soldier* (London: Harper Collins Publishers, 2007).
[50] See for example Peter Wilson, "Beah's Credibility a Long Way Gone," *The Australian*, February 2, 2008. www.theaustralian.com.au/news/beahs-credibility-a-long-way-gone/news-story/44938c4253dcfa0600fc0750ad5c6da2?sv=550167032297c69bbb0fd3-fd6d384efb

is a fundamental truth at their core and the survivor's aspiration is to that truth where the story of a person's life is still essentially in their narrative.

The attacks on the authenticity of survivor accounts also take no account of the effects of trauma on memory. The giving of narratives involves "both a remembering and a forgetting"[51] and people sometimes recall what they can live with, rather than what happened. Survivors may not want to confront their trauma, they will forget or choose to conceal, and they may employ words and recall experiences to reflect their own agendas and their current circumstances, and/or the relationship with the listener, sponsors, and translator will also affect their telling. The inaccuracy of memory is well documented: "Memory is a great artist. For every man and for every woman it makes the recollection of his or her life a work of art and an unfaithful record."[52]

In this respect, there exists a body of work that examines the problem of memory for narrative as testimony, and the need for testimony's autonomy from history, arguing for the value of the subjective and a rejection of the need for historical truth, and advocating for the value of narrative truth.[53] Not all is false, and the materials of the lived, recalled past puts memory to use. Even where survivors' memories are unfaithful to the past, they can be a creative figuration of the living present and how it came to be.[54] Their narratives are essentially their subjective truth, a "recollective/narrative act which the writer, from a certain point in his life – the present, looks back over the events of that life and recounts them in such ways to show how that past history has led to this present state of being."[55] Olney argues for us to review our thinking and to reconsider the past, present and future in life writing as "a present of things past" (memory), "a present, of things present" (sight), and "a present of things future" (expectation).[56] And in *Metaphors of Self* argues "why not take memory for what it richly is – a function of present consciousness."[57] Where some accounts have been so severely doctored

---

[51] Michael Bernard-Donals, "Beyond the Question of Authenticity. Witness and Testimony in the Fragments Controversy," *PMLA* 116, no. 5 (2001): 1303.
[52] Andre Maurois, *Aspects of Autobiography* (New York: Appleton & Co., 1929), 157–58.
[53] James Olney, *Memory & Narrative: The Weave of Life-Writing* (Chicago: University of Chicago Press, 1998), 3.
[54] James Olney, *Metaphors of Self* (Princeton: Princeton University Press, 1972), 264.
[55] James Olney, "'I Was Born'," 149.
[56] See James Olney, "'I Was Born'."
[57] Christopher Hager, *Word by Word: Emancipation and the Act of Writing* (Cambridge, MA and London: Harvard University Press, 2013), 264.

that they frustrate this purpose, assessing the universal essences and consistencies present across the body of narratives nevertheless provide an authoritative and generally reliable exposition of the lived experience and effects of slavery.[58]

### RESPONSIBILITY TO THE STORY

In light of the challenges to the credibility of survivor accounts and the confined nature of many narratives, the importance of attending to the purposes of the interviewer and sponsor, as well as the purposes of the survivor, cannot be understated. Narratives are unavoidably influenced by the nature in which they are gathered and written, and even by the means by which they are intended to be shared. Much is revealed by what is said as by what is not, by who tells us and who does not, and by how we are told and how narratives are gathered. In considering narratives, researchers try to remain aware of the complex power balances in the relationship between the narrator and listener(s), and narrator and sponsor, which will naturally affect how narratives are told, heard, and subsequently employed.[59] Listeners or sponsors will not always have in mind these power balances when gathering and presenting narratives. I argue that in telling, both the narrator and the listener should be responding to the task of understanding and remembering, not just to acknowledge the needs of the audience and the experience of the individual, but also as a means of linking our survey of contemporary slavery to our understanding of slavery over time. The best and most effective approach to listening (whether interviewing, watching, hearing, or reading) is to be a survivor by proxy; in other words, the most meaningful way of witnessing is to take our minds and feelings through what survivors have been through and allow it in. As Caruth argues, it is the meeting of these two (survivor and proxy) not just the inactive listener that constitutes the witness.[60]

My findings are that while excavating narratives for insights into slavery today, we can also simultaneously acknowledge survivors' life

---

[58] John W. Blassingame, "Using the Testimony of Ex-Slaves," 478.
[59] Kay Schaffer and Sidonie Smith, *Human Rights and Narrated Lives: The Ethics of Recognition* (New York: Palgrave Macmillan, 2004). See also Lilie Chouliaraki, *Spectatorship of Suffering* (London: Sage, 2006).
[60] Cathy Caruth, *Listening to Trauma: Conversations with Leaders in the Theory & Treatment of Catastrophic Experience* (Baltimore, MD: John Hopkins University Press, 2014), 18.

telling as witness to their exploitation and abuse. Rather than seeking positive outcomes and happy endings, the reader might allow the discomfort that comes with understanding survivors' experiences to sit with them. As Minh Dang has written: "How prepared are people to hold the horrors of human trafficking? How prepared are people to hold the horrors while celebrating the joys?"[61] In this way, the researcher opens their mind to the realities and meaning of survivors' experiences and builds an empathic alliance with the survivor. This enables a building of trust that facilitates the survivors' narrative-giving to extend beyond short stories and familiar direction.

However, fears of accusations of voyeurism if graphic details are reproduced, the realities in the field and the often-limited time to gather narratives all inhibit the ability to generate longer, more expressive, and detailed narratives. Interview questions can be leading, and interruptions typically occur from between every seven seconds up to every four minutes. It is usually in the longer narratives and autobiographies that we really see the representation of the survivor as thriver, as activist, as professional. A lack of care and attention to the gathering and portrayal of survivors' voices can also affect the way these narratives are received, at times casting doubt on their authenticity and undermining the strength of the body of slave narratives as a whole. Observing the ethics of gathering can be challenging in complex and difficult circumstances and where the urgency of other needs take priority over the gathering of narratives it is "important not to make the perfect the enemy of the good."[62] In the face of the limitations placed on interviewers where the time to record lengthy narratives will not always be possible in the circumstances, a recognition of the problems known with historic narratives can lead to interview approaches today.

The research undertaken here seeks to generate a new understanding of how best to approach the question of survivor interviews, contributing to best practice criteria that can offer a set of guidelines to reframe the ways we work with survivors in gathering and presenting their narratives. For example, it is generally accepted that narratives should be presented verbatim and interview questions carefully devised so as not to lead, but consideration can also be given to the effects on survivors of constraining narratives, and interviewers remain conscious

---

[61] Laura T. Murphy, *Survivors of Slavery*, xvi–xvii.
[62] Paul Gready, "Introduction – Responsibility to the Story," *Journal of Human Rights Practice* 2, no. 2 (2010): 188.

of the influence of their own perspectives and agendas. Interviewers also need to be sensitive to the culture and beliefs of survivors, because "the very presence of interlocutors who no longer represent a world that was ignorant or indifferent ... motivates a sense of civic responsibility as interviewer and interviewee form a testimonial alliance aimed at making awareness and education a reality."[63] Where time allows and where possible, interviewers, sponsors and amanuenses can also ensure that survivors are provided with the option to exercise some control over the reproduction of their narrative and engage in any subsequent activism. Including survivors rather than simply representing them, so that they are seen as *more* than "just" a survivor and in the words of the Theresa Flores, as a "thriver."[64] Where a longer narrative sits behind the extract presented, access to the full narrative should also be provided. In these ways survivors are empowered, retain some control of their narrative, and the antislavery community avoids repeating the errors of the past.

With voice can come a sense of power; the lack of control over representation in human rights reports, advocacy and fundraising materials, the media or elsewhere, can mark a return to powerlessness. Ideally, interviewers and sponsors reflecting on the above might find ways to allow for a full free-telling of the survivors' story. However, they are often confronted with a conflict between the need to highlight awareness for a public audience that potentially has limited time to engage with long narratives, and the value to abolition and to survivors of unconstrained "free telling." Not all narratives can be lengthy, not all survivors will be able to participate. But we can attend to the ethics of storytelling to ensure that even in the briefest of interviews, we observe some fundamental principles. However, where possible, we should advocate for a fuller telling and allowing survivors to explore their memories, gain their own insights, employ the therapeutic effects of telling, and reveal experiences beyond the familiar narrative format. In so doing, we create and work within a "testimonial alliance" to facilitate a more detailed and nuanced narrative that enables the reader to engage with the survivor's emotion, trauma, desires, and suggestions. Details that we might consider sensationalizing or voyeuristic are actually important; the lesson is not the context, but our motivation for revealing it. Where time

---

[63] Geoffrey Hartman, "The Humanities of Testimony: An Introduction," *Poetics Today* 27, no. 2 (2006): 251.
[64] A descriptor adopted by the survivor Theresa Flores, see Theresa Flores, *The Slave across the Street*, 261.

allows, providing space for survivors to articulate their experiences and presenting their stories in their entirety are key to ensuring survivors have the opportunity to be heard in full, allowing them to participate in the creation of narrative. "Trust, painstakingly constructed and forged in the intimacy of safe spaces, such as interviews, can easily be violated within an ever-expanding public sphere, as the distance between narration and reception grows in time and space."[65]

## THE USE AND VALUE OF COGNITIVE INTERVIEW TECHNIQUES

The understanding of the issues encountered with the gathering of historic narratives, and the above reflections on the value of longer narratives outlined above led me to employ cognitive interviewing techniques when carrying out my own interviews with survivors. The cognitive interviewing technique, first introduced by Fisher and Geiselman in the late 1980s, is based on a significant body of widely documented psychological research on principles of memory and communication theory. Cognitive interviewing techniques are often chosen for interviewing witnesses in relation to particularly distressing events and have been used for public inquiries, such as the investigation into allegations of abuse in children's homes in Wales in the 1990s through to the Independent Jersey Care Inquiry concluded in 2017. Damien Lewis explains the need to build trust between translator and survivor for a full and true telling to be facilitated,[66] and cognitive interviews are well-suited to this end, being designed to build rapport and trust and putting the survivor's needs at the heart of the process. Everything, including the location, set up of the room and approach to the interview is designed, where possible, to put the survivor at their ease.[67]

---

[65] Paul Gready, *The Era of Transitional Justice: The Aftermath of the Truth and Reconciliation Commission in South Africa and Beyond* (Oxford: Routledge, 2017), 78.

[66] Mende Nazer and Damien Lewis, *Slave*, 320.

[67] This is in line with standard cognitive interview practice, which as a method is designed for interviews with vulnerable individuals. See Ronald P. Fisher and R. Edward Geiselman, *Memory-Enhancing Techniques for Investigative Interviewing: The Cognitive Interview* (Springfield, IL: Charles C Thomas Publisher Ltd., 1992). Such practice is also reflected in the Human Trafficking Foundation Slavery and Trafficking Survivor Care Standards 2018, in Section 1.2: "The Trauma-Informed Code of Conduct for All Professionals Working with Survivors of Trafficking and Slavery." These guidelines were created in collaboration with experts from across the antislavery sector. See Human Trafficking Foundation, *The Slavery and Trafficking Survivor Care Standards 2018*, 23–29.

In my interviews, I was often provided with rooms by NGOs where little could be done to make the surroundings more welcoming, but simple measures such as sitting on either corner of a table, rather than opposite each other, created a more conversational space. Making sure the survivor was positioned in a place where there were the least distractions (away from doors and windows) and removing posters assisted their concentration, and where possible I also arranged house plants, soft drinks, and biscuits to make the space less intimidating. Survivors had received an information sheet and support from the NGO beforehand, and were encouraged to ask questions before the interview to alleviate anxiety about the process and explore what was expected of them. The survivor dictated the pace and direction of the interview; I responded to, rather than directed, the information being received. Participants in cognitive interviews often refer to the cathartic nature of participating in this method. It gives them the opportunity to tell their story in their own way with an active listener and without interruption, allowing them to explain their story in more depth and for as long as it takes, while being gently guided through their account.

Cognitive interviewing rests on two principles: that memory has a network of associations that can be cued, and that memory will be more effectively retrieved if the context around events can be reinstated.[68] The full method involves four stages: *free recall* (where the survivors are given an undefined time to tell their story without questions or interruption); *varied free recall* (changing the starting point or perspective); *focused cognitive questions* (returning to points in the survivors' narrative to explore their senses, using survivors' own words and open questions); and *review* (final recall and clarifications). As the traditional technique typically takes several hours to unravel one short episode in time, and as the survivors I interviewed were available for a day to two days only and were attempting to recall years rather than hours, I omitted the second stage so as to manage time effectively and access the three core stages of the overall technique, although to some degree stage two was incorporated as questions where not asked in line with story chronology. In the first stage, it was vital that recall was not interrupted, and I tried to

---

[68] Brian L. Cutler, Steve Penrod and Todd K. Martens, "Improving the Reliability of Eyewitness Identifications: Putting Context into Context," *Journal of Applied Psychology* 72, no. 4 (1978): 629–37; Amina Memom and Ray Bull, "The Cognitive Interview – Its Origins, Empirical Support, Evaluation and Practical Implications," *Journal of Community & Applied Social Psychology* 1, no. 4 (1991): 291–307.

avoid making any sounds that would indicate the survivor had given the "right" answer. I also allowed silences to run, until the survivor indicated verbally that their telling had come to an end.

Interviews were audio recorded so that I could actively listen to them, avoid distracting them by writing, and to ensure that verbatim transcripts could be produced. This was an important aspect of facilitating recall, but also fundamental to the survivor's sense of being heard and helped to build the testimonial alliance between the survivor and myself during the interview. Once the survivor had finished speaking, I then moved to the focused cognitive questions returning to points in their narrative, restating their words to place them back in the context of that time, and asking questions concerned with their senses, such as what they could see, hear, smell, and feel. I found that most survivors responded to sight and emotion, but for one survivor smell rather than emotion was a significant memory trigger. He later confirmed he had been diagnosed with emotional detachment, one of the effects of the post-traumatic stress disorder he continued to suffer and so emotion as a tool to evoke memory was suppressed and unavailable to him. The final stage of the spoken interview involved clarifying questions, such as names, dates, and ages.

After the interview, I also asked survivors to create a drawing of something that was important to them in their journey, or of anything they wished to reflect at that time, and then recorded their explanation. Verbal language can inhibit the degree to which an individual's experiences can be expressed, and often visual narrative will display what verbal language cannot. Survivors were initially awkward about drawing (but had expected this final part of the interview process), and I left the room to allow them time to draw without scrutiny. The drawings are all very different. Val created a diagram that was a collection of colorful words, reinforcing the value she placed on education and the ability of language and negotiation to bring about change. Others, such as Dwain and Keith related more symbolic images, Dwain drawing multiple outline images in limited colors, representing himself as a box with an unseen side, as well as other images to represent his desires, fears, and symbols of freedom. Keith, whose eyesight was too poor to draw, explained visualizations he had explored with his therapist. In one of these, his trauma was represented by hands pushing to get out of a heavy safe, and in the other he related the image of a man like the Angel Gabriel, burning like a phoenix and breaking away from an invisible glass-like chain. Tung created a mountainous landscape, coloring the drawing with sweeping scratchy lines, and drew a small boat on a river, it's inside a deep crimson, explaining the boat was himself and the river represented his ongoing journey. Finally, Pranus depicted the most violent part of his story in a single dark grey pen, but that moment was also described by him as the catalyst for his decision to attempt escape. These pictures are analyzed in more detail in Chapter 4, but together with other survivor visual representations available warrant further analysis in other disciplines.

Two interviews were carried out with interpreters, which created challenges in using this method. Even though time was spent with interpreters carefully explaining the interview method, it was impossible to prevent them from making noises or interrupting survivors to seek clarification. They also had to summarize every ten to fifteen minutes, causing disruption to the flow of the narrative and making it difficult for me to know the exact words the survivor used. The available time to interview was also reduced as a result of the need for the interpreter to recount what was said, and as such the two shortest narratives came from this cohort. Another challenge came in identifying individuals willing to participate in such long interviews, particularly where they were now working and couldn't afford to give a day of their time. In two cases, the survivors wanted to extend the interview to a second day. In one instance this could be facilitated, but for the first survivor the NGO supporting them and providing a room for the interview wasn't able to make the room available the next day, and the survivor then moved on. The ability to maintain contact with two of the survivors was also prevented as a result of their unsettled immigration status. A final challenge in using cognitive interviewing techniques was the limitations of time; aside from adapting the four stages to three, I wasn't able to explore points in survivors' stories for as long as would usually be taken, and I also had to be selective about the parts of the narrative to explore.

Survivors were contacted a day or two after the interview to ensure they had not been traumatized by the experience, and transcripts were later forwarded to them to provide an opportunity to revise their narrative, redact material, and to approve any amendments made for anonymization purposes (such as the names of third parties). Despite the deeply personal nature of their stories, none have chosen to redact any material.

In terms of the way survivors expressed themselves and how much they felt able to discuss, I noted that where three survivors had been through prosecution processes this had influenced their narratives.

They each demonstrated a tendency to recount facts and dates as if giving evidence. However, the effects of this diminished over the course of the interview because the method enabled them sufficient space and time to elaborate and immerse themselves in their own narrative telling. In the cases of Pranus and Tung, the time available for them to move away from formulaic recounting was affected by the use of an interpreter and therefore their narratives, in particular, remain peppered with dates.

It also seemed to make little difference how long the survivor had been liberated in terms of the detail recounted. One survivor had been liberated for over twenty years, another had only been liberated from slavery for eleven months (although imprisoned for the first seven months of that period) and both were able to speak in detail of their experiences. Another had been liberated for over ten years, but struggled to recount the detail of her enslavement, focusing instead on her activism. However, this also demonstrated that survivors were free to control their narratives, select what was told, and relate more than the "facts" of their enslavement. Their reasons for telling were complex and, among other things, telling was as much about being heard as it was about processing trauma (while being heard itself is a means of processing trauma). Survivors choose what they feel is important to tell and will set out and determine the territory setting their boundaries. Given the right conditions, the telling of their stories is in itself a type of freedom.

### THE USE OF COGNITIVE INTERVIEWING TECHNIQUES TO ENABLE NARRATIVES TO FUNCTION IN NEW WAYS

The value of the methods I employed was striking. One survivor spoke for over two hours without interruption in the first stage, and the narratives were longer and more detailed and expressive than standard interview narratives. Importantly, the survivors I worked with retained control of their narratives and were reminded that I wasn't "looking" for particular material and that it was their opportunity to tell their story as they wished. The method meant survivors were not limited to "the facts" and were able to discuss their childhoods, their recovery, their feelings and emotions, and three of the survivors dedicated considerable time to their activism, or their desire to take an activist role.

Using this interview method, my finding was that survivors were facilitated to bring full and freely told stories into the narrative space, providing rich data, and ensuring they didn't feel tokenized or manipulated in the process of giving. Narratives almost never tell the "intellectual, emotional, moral growth of the narrator"[69] because the narrator is not provided with the conditions to do so. The interview method I employed addresses this. It is important to survivors and to the antislavery community that narratives convey the survivor's language and structure, the aspects of their lives they choose to present, and the significance of their experiences and of the self to the audience.[70] Survivors are not typically given the space to explore their recovery and activism or discuss abolitionist strategies. Once narratives are released from the form of edited fragments and are instead applied, made known, and analyzed in their full form, they can become powerful writings that represent some of the most important subjective expositions of what it means to be enslaved today. The method I employed enabled survivors to be fully heard, often for the first time, to explore their own feelings and memories, to choose what to reveal or conceal, and to identify themselves as more than just victims, but as an amalgamation of different identities. They gave the survivors a sense of freedom and a sense of activism. The giving of narrative in this way held measurable value for them, providing a means for them to locate their rights-based voice and discover therapeutic benefits in the ability to craft (or re-craft) their identities, assuming control over their bodies and lives.

## THE ABILITY OF "FULL" TELLING TO TRANSFORM

In longer narratives, survivors can explore their memories without the need to tell linear or chronological stories and can be freed of the constraints of having to only "tell the facts." With the opportunity for longer narratives, we can bring the two important aims together: narratives told for the self *and* to make survivors' experiences known to a wider audience. When asked what it meant to them to tell their story, Tung, one of the survivors, said "It was my secret and nobody knew .... I felt relieved as I can share my story"[71] and another, Dwain, said the opportunity to tell his story in his way "... means freedom."[72]

Telling their full, free-told stories can be a journey towards searching or sculpting out an alternative internal and external landscape where a

[69] James Olney, "'I Was Born'," 51.
[70] See Sterling Lecater Bland, *African American Slave Narratives: An Anthology* (Westport, CT: Greenwood Press, 2001), xiv.
[71] Tung, as told to Andrea Nicholson, February 9, 2017. With thanks to Palm Cove Society.
[72] Dwain, as told to Andrea Nicholson, November 3, 2017. With thanks to Atleu.

new self is created out of the very exercise of consciousness and memory. There therefore exists an intimate relation between narrative and self-knowledge; the telling is a form of self-discovery or exploration that provides an opportunity for survivors to grow beyond the parameters of the trauma that will continue to define them. It is the exposition of their universe through which they make sense of their own internal landscapes and the world around them, then and now. Part of the journey of recovery is in retelling, and survivors' stories have an important place in driving strategies for survivor growth. The giving of testimony can act as a form of rehabilitation, providing the survivor with a feeling of purpose, agency and identity, and facilitate the grieving process, providing an opportunity to grow and move forward in their lives. Narratives therefore reveal the possibility of addressing the tension between the legal, policy, and prosecutorial aims of the movement on the one hand, and the therapeutic aims of the movement on the other. With this adapted cognitive interview method, survivors were able to position their narrative within their own frameworks, express their emotions, discuss their need for belonging and acceptance, the need to recognize their humanity, the challenges that faced them in liberation, what freedom meant to them, and what was needed for survivor support and antislavery structures. Through these and other detailed narratives, there is potential to map survivor-informed antislavery strategies.

Through this interview method, survivors were enabled to recount their experiences despite the immense difficulty of using verbal language to describe their emotions and journeys, passing their stories on using every tool to be heard, using visual and literary paradigms to expose and reform identities through oral telling, writing, and imagery.[73] Narratives are self-facing and self-imaging[74], and in the free act of telling, survivors "create a significance in the universe that would otherwise not be there"[75] and create a record of a life lived and a personality achieved.[76] Thus, selfhood can become the very motive of creation. If a telling is in part a creation, it is also a recreation. In other words, in telling, survivors create

---

[73] Jeremy Hawthorn, *Narrative: From Malory to Motion Pictures* (London: Edward Arnold, 1985); Sherline Pimenta and Ravi Poovaiah, "On Defining Visual Narratives" (Bombay: Industrial Design Centre, 2010).
[74] Celeste-Marie Bernier, *Stories That Stick to the Skin: Quilting Traditions, Slavery's Stories and the Fight for Civil Rights* (University of Nottingham: Department of American & Canadian Studies [Lecture], 2016).
[75] James Olney, *Metaphors of Self*, 16.
[76] Christopher Hager, *Word by Word*, 140.

their own coherent, meaningful, and altogether self-oriented universe; there is value to the survivor in the mere telling of their experiences. In the motifs of slave narratives, we find patterns of the self where the life lived, and personality achieved, constitutes its own material. In this creative act, survivors seized the opportunity to acquire ownership of their stories and construct their futures, and in the ability to re-craft an identity and reclaim the body survivors have the opportunity through the giving of narrative to "write themselves into being."[77] The suppression and dehumanization experienced in slavery create a form of "unbeing" that can be resurrected through the giving of narrative. In so doing, survivors assert their rights and engage with the legal protection afforded to the state of being.

The act of narrating therefore has the potential to transform and reform. It provides a space for survivors to assert the self as deserving of humanity, of being human, of existing. Having known hostility, exclusion, and "personal impotence,"[78] survivors look to find meaning in their lives[79] and in more subtle ways facilitate change through their endeavors to reformulate our perceptions of them as human beings first and foremost, rejecting negative labels that have been attached to them and the powerlessness associated with the term "victim."[80] By voicing their humanity and by identifying as educators, carers, and activists, survivors at once identify both with a particular group of those previously enslaved and at the same time with humanity as whole. Their expressions are therefore fundamentally linked to their recovery and are an attempt at a conscious de-shaming. Their authorship confers a "mark of personhood that had been denied,"[81] bringing them closer to selfhood. The act of telling therefore has the potential to transform the survivor and offers the opportunity to present their experiences to the "court of world

---

[77] Charles T. Davis and Henry Louis Gates Jr., *The Slave's Narrative* (Oxford: Oxford University Press, 1985), xxiii.
[78] Frances Smith Foster, *Witnessing Slavery*, 11.
[79] For one of many examples, see the narrative of Chanta, who states "My life has had no significance, no value …. I hope that by sharing my story, my life will finally have meaning and prevent others from the deep sadness in my life." Kevin Bales and Zoe Trodd, *To Plead Our Own Cause*, 207.
[80] See for example the narrative of Dina Chan in Kevin Bales and Zoe Trodd, *To Plead Our Own Cause*, 103–6.
[81] Christopher Hager, *Word by Word*, 82.
[80] See for example the narrative of Dina Chan in Kevin Bales and Zoe Trodd, *To Plead Our Own Cause*, 103–6.
[81] Christopher Hager, *Word by Word*, 82.

opinion."[82] Through narratives, survivors can assert themselves as powerful agents for change and as more than the sum of their enslavement. It is a means by which survivors can be presented as more than victims of the past, and presents a portrait of the survivor as capable, literate, and independent. They are more than victims and more than just survivors, they exist also as mothers, fathers, sisters, and brothers; as capable, literate, independent individuals; as activists and experts. They are equals.

Where so many of those enslaved are "dehumanized" and treated as "other," the humanizing effect of narratives provides survivors with the opportunity to reclaim or recreate their identity. Just as the eighteenth and nineteenth century narratives such as those of Olaudah Equiano, Ottobah Cugoano, and Frederick Douglass sought to humanize the African slave, today the same applies for survivors who have been outcast and socially excluded due to mental health, age, illegitimacy, ethnicity, gender, and social status. Slaveholders then and now suppress victim's voices as a mean of maintaining control, so the act of narrating is in itself a type of freedom; it has therapeutic effects, creates a space for self-discovery, and allows survivors a voice that had been denied them during their enslavement. Through their narratives, survivors challenge societal preconceptions and align themselves with the activist community. The act of speaking out is an "open act of rebellion. It is a declaration of one's rights to speak."[83] It is a means of assuming agency, and a means of effecting change. The creation of narrative is a move from the passive experienced symptoms of their experiences to an active understanding and retelling of what happened,[84] and the commandeering of a new and purposive role.

As a witness to the enslavement, abuse and murder of others, survivors will also often carry a sense of responsibility to give voice and corporality to those unable to bear witness for themselves, expressing in their narratives a purpose and duty they feel for others. In the words of Shamere McKenzie, survivors act as a "the voice for those still enslaved, the voice for those perished while enslaved, and the voice for those who

---

[82] Kay Shaffer and Sidonie Smith, *Human Rights and Narrated Lives*, 3.
[83] Noreen Connell and Cassandra Wilson, *Rape: The First Sourcebook for Women by New York Radical Feminists* (New York: The New American Library, 1974), 27–28.
[84] Judith Herman, "The Politics of Trauma: An Interview with Judith Herman," in *Listening to Trauma: Conversations with Leaders in the Theory & Treatment of Catastrophic Experience*, ed. Cathy Caruth (Baltimore, MD: John Hopkins University Press, 2014), 141.

are free but have not the courage to speak up."[85] Narratives enable survivors to feel part of something and bearing witness becomes an "act of solidarity"[86] that enables a transformation of guilt to responsibility, which has enormous therapeutic value to survivors and can be an important means of reintegrating the fractured self in survival.[87] Survivors not only create narratives to have the audience bear witness to their experiences, but also narrate to bear witness to those lost or left behind, and to join with a community of survivors – in hearing the stories of those formerly enslaved, other survivors' stories "come out through theirs."[88] Their telling also acts as intergenerational witness, bearing witness to the trauma of their parents and families.

Narratives therefore offer an important opportunity for survivors to listen to trauma survivors in their own terms and in their own frameworks. Through their narratives, they share the secrets they were isolated and shamed into withholding, creating a metaphysical community of survivors, reducing their isolation, and starting to see themselves as powerful individuals that can influence the progress of abolition. The giving of narratives as a means by which survivors achieve these gains and find a sense of freedom exposes a core argument in the next chapter – that freedom is not only the moment of liberation from slavery, but is found and perceived in multiple and complex ways both in and out of slavery.

---

[85] Shamere McKenzie, in Laura T. Murphy, *Survivors of Slavery*, 53.
[86] Cathy Caruth, *Listening to Trauma*, 142.
[87] Cathy Caruth, *Listening to Trauma*, 13.
[88] Dori Laub, "A Record That Has Yet to Be Made: An Interview with Dori Laub," in Cathy Caruth, *Listening to Trauma*, 72.

## 2

## "I Was Free, I Still Wasn't Free"

### Defining Freedom

> From the beginning in my master's house I didn't realise I was a slave, I was confused; I wondered why I was here. Later on, my master was talking to her friend and she said two things that made me realise it. One, she mentioned she owned me. The other she called me 'abda' to her friend. She called me her slave. From that time on I understood who I am.[1]

Of the themes that have emerged from my analysis of contemporary slave narratives, one of the most unsurprising is the theme of freedom. Freedom and "unfreedom" are commonly expressed in faceted ways in survivor accounts. However, survivors' notions of freedom are not limited to the detail of their enslavement and liberation; their narratives expose the ways in which notions of freedom are perceived throughout their journeys, and the effect this has on their actions, well-being, and growth. Freedom can exist as a known, but also as an unknown, and abstract concept. Freedom is a relative concept and the binary of free and not free is artificial: contrary to the belief that slavery is a constant, and that freedom is a joyous escape from enslavement, micro freedoms occur and are assumed during slavery, and conversely, slavery continues in the mind of the free, leaving individuals in a permanent state of survival and undermining the realization of meaningful freedom.

Survivors' narratives are rich with examples of the way in which beliefs in, or concepts of, freedom are held, and, importantly, how they also shift

---

[1] Mende, in Kevin Bales and Zoe Trodd, eds., *To Plead Our Own Cause Personal Stories by Today's Slaves* (New York: Cornell University Press, 2008), 226.

and combine at any one time in the experiences of those enslaved and free. They highlight the difference between the way freedom is perceived during enslavement, and the way it is experienced throughout survivors' journeys. Their narratives expose the false binary between freedom and nonfreedom, with micro freedoms occurring within slavery, and slavery continuing in the mind of the free. Rather than the common perception that slavery is a state of continuous misery and absolute control, and that freedom is a contrasting joyous break from enslavement, slave narratives expose the freedoms won *within* slavery, both the hopeful and the dark means of attaining freedom *from* slavery and how it is experienced in liberation. My analysis has revealed two core themes that are explored in this chapter: freedom as it is projected during enslavement versus the reality of their slavery, and versus the reality of liberation.

Our interpretation of the notion of freedom, particularly as the antithesis to slavery, naturally influences how we formulate our views of the language and the structures of slave narratives and related concepts. Therefore, it becomes important to explore what is meant by freedom. One way to do this is to question our understanding by interrogating ancestral legacies – tropes, motifs, emblems, historic narratives, and contemporary accounts of slavery. In undertaking this exercise, we can attempt to more accurately appreciate narrative context and survivors' experiences. While a criticism could be raised that this is too large a body of material to compare, it is precisely this that enables us to draw out perceptions of freedom across time, and therefore to understand the commonalities and divergences between "old" and "new" slavery. By examining narratives in the context of freedom, we move toward a greater understanding of the agency of individuals, and movements toward emancipation, which may in some small part contribute to today's antislavery movement. Not only do these writings provide a contrast between the graduations of slavery and practices similar to slavery, but they also reveal the nuances of what freedom can mean to the survivor, both during their existence during enslavement, and afterwards in liberation.

## THE RELATION BETWEEN CONTROL AND PERCEPTIONS OF FREEDOM

The indoctrination of control by the slaveholder is fundamental to understanding the enslaved individual's perception and sense of freedom, the ways in which survivors view its possibility, and how notions of what constitutes freedom are nuanced and shift over time. Control is key to all suggestions for the definition of slavery, whether captured in the language of possession (The Harvard Bellagio Guidelines), alienation and powerlessness (Orlando Patterson), self-ownership (Julia O'Connell Davidson), or the loss of free will and personal liberty (Kevin Bales).[2] Contemporary narratives support these interpretations by revealing the degree to which individuals still reference feeling owned during their enslavement, where the language of master and mistress remains, and where there is regular reference to feeling dehumanized. While it has been pointed out that dehumanization is not physically possible,[3] it is the perception of dehumanization that is the context here.

For example, the account by Helia Lajeunesse says that her captor repeatedly stated she "was just an animal without any family,"[4] her slaveholder objectifying her as a resource and denying her the rights associated with a human being; she is something "other," less valued and deserving of humanity. Christine Stark's narrative expresses similar perceptions. Stark was born into sexual slavery in 1968 before gaining liberation in her 30s. She explains that "above all else they want us immobilized. They want to consume our lives, take our freedom with no resistance...we are their property, they own us."[5] In other words, the dehumanizing and controlling component to the treatment experienced by enslaved individuals, the "consuming" of lives, is to claim that individual's life for the slaveholder's purposes so completely as to tear down their personal identity and eradicate resistance, making freedom feel unattainable, as well as undeserved.

The level of control exercised by the slaveholder is often such that those enslaved are forced into criminality and in some cases, into those enslaved enslaving or harming others. This is common in the narratives of child soldiers and regularly mentioned by those forced into sexual slavery. Maria was kept in domestic servitude by the threat of black

---

[2] Members of the Research Network on the Legal Parameters of Slavery, *Bellagio-Harvard Guidelines on the Legal Parameters of Slavery*, 2012. www.law.qub.ac.uk/schools/SchoolofLaw/FileStore/Filetoupload,651854,en.pdf; Orlando Patterson, *Slavery and Social Death: A Comparative Study* (Cambridge, MA: Harvard University Press, 1982), 13; Orlando Patterson, "Trafficking, Gender and Slavery: Past and Present," in *The Legal Understanding of Slavery: From the Historical to the Contemporary*, Jean Allain, ed. (Oxford: Oxford University Press, 2012), 329; Julia O'Connell Davidson, *Modern Slavery*, 63; Kevin Bales, "Professor Kevin Bales's Response to Professor Orlando Patterson," in *The Legal Understanding of Slavery*, Jean Allain, ed., 371.
[3] Julia O'Connell Davidson, *Modern Slavery*, 51.
[4] Laura T. Murphy, *Survivors of Slavery: Modern-Day Slave Narratives* (New York: Columbia University Press, 2014), 63.
[5] Kevin Bales and Zoe Trodd, *To Plead Our Own Cause*, 101.

magic, conditioned into acting without volition and became an accessory to murder, as she "didn't know anything else but to follow commands."[6]

It is also worth considering here the narrative of Oumoulkhér, who states "I have been a slave all my life. I was a good slave. A slave who obeys her master is a good slave. I am still a slave; I am looking for my freedom."[7] In one respect, Oumoulkhér clearly saw her value and worth in her obedience, in her being a "good" slave, but there are conflicts in her narrative illustrating the confusing states of existence in and out of enslavement. When she was younger Oumoulkhér tried to run away, and in liberation she states she is still a slave. However, she also places slavery in the past tense and states that she can now "rest" (having been rescued by her daughter). There is some indication she stayed because of her children, but that she did not want to leave once her children had died or escaped. She only finally agreed to go with her remaining child Selek'ha when the slaveholders were insulting to her daughter and Selek'ha started to cry. Perhaps she believed, like Dina, that she could not divorce herself from her enslavement because "life has become this way now."[8]

It is important to recognize that the control exercised over individuals therefore extends beyond the period of enslavement, inhabiting the survivor in freedom and essentially rendering them "not free." In her escape from slavery, Selek'ha (Mauritania 2004) articulates that her brother, who had been formally freed by their master, told her she would go to hell for exercising her legal rights by leaving; she explains that her "*brother is an ally of my master – because he was freed.*"[9] Her brother's freedom exposed the complicated state of being in liberation after years of control. Despite his understanding acutely the value of freedom, it was precisely the preciousness of that freedom that led him try to persuade his sister to return to slavery, despite driving her back to that which he could not bear again for himself. That he would participate in persuading his sibling to return to that situation betrays something of his self-identity after emancipation, and the extent of control that remained over him even in freedom. In Selek'ha's case, she had become aware that her enslavement was not legal and had witnessed the emancipation of her brother, but for many enslaved individuals, liberation from enslavement seems little more than a dream.

---

[6] Kevin Bales and Zoe Trodd, *To Plead Our Own Cause*, 168.
[7] Kevin Bales and Zoe Trodd, *To Plead Our Own Cause*, 174.
[8] Kevin Bales and Zoe Trodd, *To Plead Our Own Cause*, 106.
[9] Kevin Bales and Zoe Trodd, *To Plead Our Own Cause*, 173.

## THE DESIRE FOR FREEDOM

Nevertheless, there is a shared and natural perception of freedom of the person as inherently desirable, something that the poet Albery Allson Whitman describes as the "lullaby of freedom"[10]; something both elusive but intrinsically basic and vital to human nature. We see this in countless narratives both "old" and "new." An example here comes from Lunsford Lane who wrote: "I used to lie awake whole nights thinking of it. And oh, the strange thoughts that passed through my soul, like so many rivers of light; deep and rich were their waves they rolled...."[11] A modern example comes from Salma, who expresses that freedom was a thing that was "necessary" and something "all the others dreamed of."[12]

My findings indicate that it is not necessarily the severity of the slave's treatment that dictates their concept of freedom, with narratives reflecting the historic testimony of the Rev. William T. Allan: "it is slavery itself, and not cruelties...that make slaves unhappy...The slaves in my father's family are almost as kindly treated as slaves can be, yet they pant for liberty."[13] The need for freedom is innate, and is felt deeply despite varied circumstances and/or whether freedom has been experienced before or not, although it is more tangible to, and conceptualized more by those who have been "flogged up."[14] For those born into slavery, slavery is of the moment, it is their current and ongoing existence for which they may have no real or remembered experience of freedom, so freedom emerges as something particularly abstract; an unknown or unlikely existence. There are also still many who are born into slavery or brought into it at a young age and therefore do not know or recall a different existence, but for whom, once revealed, freedom becomes necessary.[15] Efforts by nongovernmental organizations to free entire villages

---

[10] Ivy. G. Whitman, ed., *At the Dusk of Dawn, Selected Poetry and Prose of Albery Allson Whitman, by Albery Allson Whitman* (Boston, MA: NorthEastern University Press, 2009), from "The Octoroon" Part II, 227.

[11] Lunsford Lane, *The Narrative of Lunsford Lane, Formerly of Raleigh, N.C. Embracing an Account of His Early Life, the Redemption by Purchase of Himself and Family from Slavery, and His Banishment from the Place of His Birth for the Crime of Wearing a Colored Skin* (Boston, MA: J. G. Torrey, 1842), 14. http://docsouth.unc.edu/neh/lanelunsford/menu.html

[12] Kevin Bales and Zoe Trodd, *To Plead Our Own Cause*, 225.

[13] Theodore D. Weld, *American Slavery as It Is: Testimony of a Thousand Witnesses* (New York: The American Anti-Slavery Society, 1839), 47.

[14] Henry Bibb, *Narrative of the Life and Adventures of Henry Bibb, An American Slave, Written by Himself* (New York, 1849), 14. http://docsouth.unc.edu/neh/bibb/bibb.html.

[15] There is also a correlation here with those that have not experienced any formal education either prior to, or during enslavement.

from hereditary slavery demonstrate this acutely, with survivors having initially no notion of a different existence and having to be slowly introduced to processes toward liberation. Kevin Bales explains that in this situation liberation has to be done:

> Very subtly, like community workers, organizers, and say, "How long have you been like this? Oh, you all work for the same man? Where's the school? There's no school? Oh," and then, in time, begin to say, "You know, there's a village down the road that used to be just like this one, but they have their own school now, and they work for themselves," and slowly open up the idea of freedom for families who haven't known freedom for generations. And the beautiful moment is when that group of families and the village take the collective conscious decision for freedom. And then we stand with them as they step out to freedom and hit that moment of crisis, when the slaveholder is ready to use violence to keep them in their place.[16]

This view is supported by the narrative of Choti who states that after being visited a few times by the NGO Sankalp, "slowly...things began to sink in, and we came to realise we were doing all the work...they made us realise that we were being exploited and that we were under the control of the slaveholders....they made us aware there was something we could do about it."[17] These individuals are born into a denial of freedom, into an environment consisting of hostility and maltreatment, and into a culture of slavery.

The significance of the difference between those born into, and those brought into, slavery is fundamental to understanding contemporary slavery in its myriad forms, the means by which survivors can be supported, and by which they can be participants in the anti-slavery movement. Where a survivor has a sense of identity prior to enslavement, they are more likely to identify as something other than a "slave," and this helps in their being able to envisage and establish a new life. Individuals who are unable to recall an existence outside of enslavement are more likely to identify themselves as slaves, as the identity of the self is more tightly bound up with their only known state of existence. While my analysis of the narratives reinforces the above, it also reveals that the difficulty of divorcing from a slave identity is also not confined to those born into slavery. There is evidence of individuals struggling with nonslave identity

---

[16] Kevin Bales and Amy Goodman, "The Slave Next Door: Human Trafficking and Slavery in America Today," Democracy Now, September 9, 2009. www.democracynow .org/2009/9/9/the_slave_next_door_human_trafficking

[17] Laura T. Murphy, *Survivors of Slavery*, 236.

despite having known a different existence, and to some degree, there are individuals in both categories who do *not* see themselves purely as slaves. Many will also identify as something other than a slave, for example as a mother or father, brother, sister, aunt, teacher, or carer. Although, where survivors discuss their past identity, it is often related in terms of their position in the family and their relations with them.

For those who began or remember their lives as free individuals, there is understandably a greater sense of "non-slave" identity and an understanding of what freedom resembles. However, while freedom might be recondite for many, the differences between those born into and those brought into slavery are eroded when the smallest sight of it is gained. Once unveiled, survivors voice their natural right to freedom; their narratives revealing there is a shared perception of freedom as inherently desirable, something that is elusive, but intrinsically basic and vital to human nature. Once experienced, whether seen or understood (even at the smallest level) freedom becomes something that cannot be forgotten. When a notion of freedom becomes a part of the individual's consciousness, it is an awakening, a natural state of being to which they sense they are entitled, serving to emphasize the darkness and injustices of enslavement and which can act as a catalyst for resistance and a reclaiming of the self.

This yearning for freedom is just as apparent in those born into the kind of slavery that permits little concept of freedom. Christine Stark was born into sexual slavery in 1968 and she did not experience the world outside of her enslavement until her liberation some thirty years later. While she explains that she often wished for death, she also speaks powerfully of her drive to survive, identifying the state of slavery as essentially a loss of the self and speaking with a forceful feminist quality. In her narrative, she states: "we stay alive because there is something we want, something we seek. We may not even know exactly what it is; we may not have ever experienced it. Or we may have known it only for a moment... We stay alive because we are women in search of our lives; we are women in search of freedom."[18] By voicing that she is a woman in search of her life, Christine not only touches on issues of gender and the vulnerability of women and girls to slavery, but she also implies that slavery is not life, or a life, and that in freedom, she is searching for the parameters of her self-knowledge, her authority and autonomy, which had all been denied to her. Christine's narrative also moves into the present tense, implying

---

[18] Kevin Bales and Zoe Trodd, *To Plead Our Own Cause*, 101.

she believes her freedom has yet to be found despite her liberation. In fact, there is a consistent confusion of past and present tense throughout many contemporary narratives that is telling of the state of existence for survivors. That the search for freedom continues beyond discovery is an important consideration in the understanding of survivor trauma, identity, and recovery (addressed in detail in Chapters 3–5).

Further, in trying to gain an understanding of what freedom is, Christine must also reconcile the abstract with the reality, and her seeking is inherent, despite her having no prior experience of freedom. Freedom can be perceived as a fantasy and/or an ideal; it is an imagined state of being that provides a deep contrast to their existing state of enslavement. Another example comes from Salma who was born into slavery in Mauritania. She states: "for me, liberty was a thing that was necessary, that all slaves must dream of. I always thought about liberty. The other slaves were afraid of being free...I always believed that I had to be free, and I think that helped me escape."[19] Salma's comments on freedom are felt deeply and expressed in almost utopian terms, as if she held an innate sense of something "other" despite her being born into slavery. These extracts are typical of the state of existence in slavery and of the perceptions of those enslaved. Their narratives reveal that while a more tangible notion of freedom is held by those brought into slavery, freedom is nevertheless an instinctive and desired state of existence, and that it is slavery that must be learned. Equally, it is also correct to say that for many, freedom as a natural state does not mean that freedom is a *known* state, and it too must be learned (or learned anew).

## MICRO FREEDOMS WON AND PERCEIVED WITHIN THE STATE OF SLAVERY

It is tempting to repeat the binary of free and not free, that slavery is a constant state of "unfreedom" and that liberation gives immediate rise to "full" freedom. However, the reality is that survivors do express the means by which small freedoms are gained during enslavement, including moments of relief and periods of joy. Some enslaved individuals also have the ability to retain personal and intimate relationships within their families and with persons of their choice. Others have opportunities to earn a separate income, or to walk outside of the confines of their

---

[19] Kevin Bales and Zoe Trodd, *To Plead Our Own Cause*, 225.

workplace or homes without chaperone or monitoring. In these cases, survivors find solace in the time they have to spend with their children or in the freedom to move between houses and locations without interference (although not necessarily without monitoring or threat). Mende Nazer notes that she particularly valued the little freedoms she experienced when her slaveholders thought she wouldn't escape: "just to leave the house and walk down the street was a joy in itself."[20]

In my interview with Keith, he explained how he was generally free to carry out a romantic relationship, even staying overnight at his girlfriend's flat until he attempted escape from his exploitation one time too many and was then more tightly controlled. Some survivors also express relief in the relationships and communities created with others with whom they are enslaved. While these micro freedoms are essentially not true freedoms, as ultimately, survivors were still subject to the control of their exploiter they are forms of freedom perceived on a micro level. In gaining these small freedoms, enslaved individuals are able to conceptualize liberation. This realization serves as a source of resistance and reveals to them the power that they can start to draw for themselves, which in turn starts to erode the state of their existence as a slave. The ability to move unaccompanied and gain some income can act as the catalyst for escape or cultivate the realization of a larger concept of freedom, whether that be an abstract or concrete notion.

However, there is a divergence between the historical and contemporary where the capability to gain some level of economic freedom is involved. In contrast to a number of historical accounts that relay the carrying out of small enterprises that enabled the establishment of skills and businesses, which in turn led to economic freedom both during and following slavery, there are few contemporary accounts of slavery where earnings can be kept. The only means by which Keith was able to gain income was to steal from the businesses he attended to collect construction materials, stealing additional materials from collection depots, and covertly selling them on. Debt bondage is a common means of enslavement and ongoing debt impacts on perceptions of freedom as something unattainable, so liberation becomes even more difficult. In my interview with Tung, he explained that although he had opportunities to escape, and indeed did manage to escape on one occasion, he was drawn back to his slaveholders because of the threats to his family in Vietnam over

---

[20] Mende Nazer and Damien Lewis, *Slave: The True Story of a Girl's Lost Childhood and Her Fight for Survival* (London: Virago, 2010), 194.

repayment of the family debt. Equally, debt has an impact upon the ability of survivors to build a new life in liberation, and this again brings us back to the distinction between those born into, and those brought into slavery. Those brought into it will have a greater sense of the possibilities of, and support available in, liberation. Again, recognizing these issues is key to our understanding of how to assist survivors' transitions into a new life, and consequently to prevent them being drawn back into slavery.

## THE SEEMING IMPOSSIBILITY OF FREEDOM

Freedom in one sense is often expressed by survivors as something broad and nebulous, as freedom from the state of slavery as a whole. In other words, it is conceived as simply a completely different state from their current existence, one that remains undefined, but which involves autonomy, privacy, and a lack of physical and emotional abuse, an essentially optimistic imagining of an alternative existence. However, where "full freedom"[21] is felt to be out of reach, the inability to view freedom as a reality, or the contrast of micro freedoms won during enslavement against the everyday hardships of slavery, results in the destruction of the self. This is related through accounts of substance abuse, attempted suicide, and/or deliberate and defiant behavior knowing the consequences could have resulted in their deaths. Narratives where such acts are recounted openly express such anguish that the overall tenor of their expression brings a sense of fatality to their accounts.

The yearning for freedom and the innate sense of freedom, whether consciously defined by the survivor or not, can also cause those enslaved to feel more acutely the misery of their existence in slavery. This in turn highlights the contrast between hopeful and positive perceptions of freedom on the one hand, and the darker, destructive means of assuming and coping with freedom on the other. In enslavement, the destruction of the self, of the commodity that has been made of their bodies, is the one thing over which they retain some control and is a way of ending the sufferings of slavery. And these seemingly contradictory states of the positive and the destructive, the light and the dark, can and do coexist in resistive behaviors and in the minds of those enslaved. For example, statistics relating to survivors in the Congo expose that one in every six survivors

---

[21] Frederick Douglass, "Give us the Freedom Intended for Us," *The New National Era*, December 5, 1872.

had attempted suicide,[22] and suicide and attempted suicide appear frequently in contemporary slave narratives.

However, more commonly, survivors will employ strategies that might alter the condition of their enslavement, but where there is a real risk of death. In other words, they might relinquish themselves to the possibility of death, rather than make an active attempt to take their own lives. For example, those enslaved will deliberately detach from reality knowing this will lead to their being considered an economic drain and likely resulting in their being sold on, moved, or in some cases murdered. These are clear attempts at freedom from their current state of enslavement, whether through the potential for an end to their suffering through death or dissociation, or for a change that may bring release from their existing state of existence, or from their existing slaveholder. Survivors seek release, both physically and psychologically. Maria was trafficked into sexual slavery as a teenager and states:

> I always dreamed. I dreamed that I was in a tunnel and the little dot of light was freedom to me. Every time I had that dream, I knew that was my freedom...A lot of times I wanted to die, just die. That was my only way out. I didn't want to provoke my own death, but I wanted to die. I was just living one more day. Either he was going to kill me or I was going to die.[23]

While Maria's hope for freedom prevented her from committing suicide, it did not prevent her from welcoming death.

Where attempts at suicide and the suicide of others are recounted, individuals will take any opportunity to end their situation when freedom seems an impossibility, or where freedom itself is too challenging. In my interview with Keith, he explained his need to find self-worth in survival, describing the antithesis of self-worth as follows:

> it's the feeling. You are stripped of every humanitarian feeling. You're not allowed to, er, love. Yeah it's more the feelings 'cause you're stripped of everything. How to love, feel, and even now I struggle showing my emotions. Whether even fear, sadness, stuff like that.
>
> ...So probably about 7 to 10 years I drank heavily, I smoked a lot of drugs trying to block the pain. If you're, like, trying to, trying to rehabilitate myself, clinging on to any type of humanity that I could get hold of. Desperately wanted a family and it [the case against his slaveholders] was only when it is carried into the Press, which sent me over the edge of it, and I did try to commit suicide.

---

[22] Kevin Bales, *Blood and Earth: Modern Slavery, Ecocide, and the Secret to Saving the World* (New York: Spiegel & Grau, 2016), 34–36.
[23] Kevin Bales and Zoe Trodd, *To Plead Our Own Cause*, 167.

...I see myself, you know what I mean, as a survivor, a veteran with similar to a soldier. No, I haven't lost a limb, but I've lost a chunk of my life which I'll never get back, so it is almost like losing part of my body.

And describing an incident with his friend with whom he'd been enslaved he said:

I feel so sorry for him when I can see the sadness in his eyes when I talk to him, the emptiness. That's what it is. He's just a shell. He just needs like, even someone there to just hold and without doing nothing and maybe cry on your shoulder. It's hard having, say, a protected person, police around you and maybe social workers, maybe even doctors. It's that personal touch that will only get you through...So, it's like my friend, I sent him up and I just knew to phone him one night and I video called him, and he was in the last stages of taking an overdose. And he begged me not to phone anyone. It was so, so difficult; I knew what he was talking about, I knew how much he was suffering, and it was so, so, difficult not to go for his wishes.

Keith explains the risk of suicide even in liberation, and perhaps, as a result of it. He discloses the feelings and sense of self that have been stripped away in slavery and which are difficult to recover, leaving survivors as "shells" of their former selves, and the escape he found in drugs and alcohol. At the end of these extracts, he relates his internal struggle with his friend's suicide attempt, recalling his own experience of attempted suicide and its potential for release from the difficult existence in liberation.

The consequences of failed suicide attempts can include individuals overdosing on drugs, being disappeared when they have displeased their captors, being killed for subordination or slow work, being disfigured, and in one well-known incident, the survivor Beatrice jumped from a fourth-floor balcony in an attempt to gain freedom or die in that attempt.[24] Beatrice is clear that her intention was to gain freedom, not to commit suicide, but acknowledges that death could have resulted from her actions, with escape or death preferable to her continued enslavement. Thus, the two are combined; as an alternative to the continued existence of slavery, hope for freedom and hope for death often interconnect and are one, just as death can mean freedom itself. The narratives that are precise in their descriptions of the conditions of slavery serve to highlight the contrast between slavery and freedom; the greater the contrast is conveyed the more slavery and freedom are portrayed as extremes. However, it is also clear that while self-destructive acts may be an attempt at freedom

---

[24] Kevin Bales and Zoe Trodd, *To Plead Our Own Cause*, 162.

through the psychological or physical death of the self, many of these attempts are also acts of rebellion and resistance, and therefore a form of gaining authority or ownership over the self. Where the body is a commodity exploited by the slaveholder, in dissociation or attempts to end their lives survivors' bodies become a powerful tool for dissent.[25]

The tortures of slavery described in narratives do not only relate to the violent practices inflicted on slaves, but also to the torture of their existence and the bleak realization that liberation is unlikely. The physical and psychological harm suffered during enslavement is so abhorrent to the individual that having lost any hope of freedom they would subject themselves to further suffering to end their situation. Freedom becomes so improbable that such release becomes their only hope. They cannot quite bring themselves to end their lives themselves but find ways of "accelerating" the perceived inevitability of their death. Often this occurs at a point in their narrative where those enslaved were experiencing a severe traumatic dissociation from their circumstances and is expressed as a desire for death to occur at the hands of the slaveholder, or as an eventual consequence of their situation.[26] In death, power over the self is returned to those enslaved and ensures the separation of the body from the soul, removing the body's senses from the existence of slavery and offering consolation in mortality. Not only does this form of release remove the power of the slaveholder over the body and mind of the enslaved, but it demonstrates a form of resistance that assumes the proprietorial right to the self that has been until then exercised by the slaveholder.

In my interview with Val, a Masai woman who had been forced into marriage at a young age, she explained she had come to the point where she felt she had no option but to assume her freedom despite the potential consequences. Describing that moment, she said:

I'd had enough. Absolutely had enough and by then the rage was too much, because I was feeling if I don't, if I don't do something nothing will change. I'll continue being in a situation where I am controlled by someone else. And this man was must have been more than 30 years older than me and I think I just absolutely had enough. So, at the point I was like whatever happens, it happens, and I went and ripped the little thing he had given me to put on my neck. And that was it – for me that was really symbolic.

---

[25] See for example, Raffaela Puggioni, "Speaking through the Body: Detention and Bodily Resistance in Italy," *Citizenship Studies* 18, no. 55 (2014): 562–77.
[26] See for example, Jill Leighton, "My Life as a Slave in America" in Jesse Sage and Lidra Kasten, *Enslaved*, 75.

## "I Was Free, I Still Wasn't Free": Defining Freedom

So, I couldn't care anymore, and it took really long before I would even talk about that with my family but when he left the village I was so glad that I, I never saw him again because .... I know I've moved on, but I don't know how I would feel if I was to see him again. But, yeah, that was it. For me, it was "that's it – end to it," and that chapter was closed ...

... and it was a powerful moment where I felt at least I had control of things and how I wanted my life to be. And looking back sometimes I actually laugh about it because it was just that moment where you feel like 'whatever it is, if I'm going to die let me die. I'm not having it anymore.'

I remember, because all the beads are all over the place (laughs). I think he was in front of me and he was saying "follow me, follow me." and I said "I'm not following you" and just grabbed it and threw it away and I ran away, so that's the thing I can remember from that moment.

Interviewer: How did it feel seeing all the beads scatter?

It felt amazing. I think for me it was, that was the moment of liberation. That was it.

Val switches from the past to present tense particularly when describing the symbolic act of tearing the beads from her body, which she had been required to wear by her "husband" as a mark of their marriage: "I remember...he was saying" and "all the beads are all over the place." She notes her conflicting emotions, her rage, her determination to end her enslavement, and the need to gain control and make her life what she wanted it to be. Her full narrative reveals some of the violence she experienced, and she notes that for her, liberation or death was the only remaining solution to her situation.

### THE PSYCHOLOGICAL AND SOCIAL BARRIERS TO, AND IN, LIBERATION

While Val and many other survivors have been pushed to the point of risking or attempting death in order to gain liberation, the complexities of liberation and of escape are expressed by others as insurmountable, particularly given the potential consequences if caught. These complexities alter enslaved individuals' views on the value of freedom, leading some to retreat from liberation and seeking surety in what is known (enslavement) than what is unknown (liberation). Many narratives betray a fear of the consequences of freedom. Despite the abuse, those enslaved have a measure of food, accommodation, and in some cases a small income. They are also aware that an unsuccessful escape would likely result in harder labor and/or severe punishment, and in some cases their murder. Salma explains that the women with whom she was enslaved were afraid of freedom and that they "didn't know where to go, who they could safely talk to, or what to do once free."[27] Many individuals are trafficked into a different country and so have no knowledge of the culture or language, nor any associations that they can run to. Munni Devi states "I can't run away. How will I run? Where will I run? What will I run towards? I'm here. I spend my whole day here."[28] Munni's narrative indicates that she did not understand what escape (and freedom) would entail, so she remained in a situation that was at least a known existence. Not only did her fear extend to the means of escape and a lack of knowledge of her environment, but more fundamentally she did not know what life she was running towards.

Further, as a result of the practices they were forced to carry out, particularly where sexual slavery has occurred, survivors are often shamed in liberation and ostracized from their families and communities as a result of their enslavement. Survivors express how aware they were during their enslavement that they would be considered "dirty" and "despised."[29] Equally, many survivors knew that once free, they would struggle to feed and home themselves or to find work. The state of slavery was more secure than potential liberation, even while they were desperate for it. These fears are legitimate, and they are reinforced by slaveholders as a way of their exerting emotional control over those enslaved.

Narratives also show that survivors can internalize slaveholders' dogma in liberation, remaining in the same profession because they are unable to conceive of a different future. For example, Dina remained in prostitution following her discovery, because in her words "life has become this way now…there is no turning back."[30] The power that is exercised over the enslaved individual by their slaveholder(s) is therefore instrumental in creating a fear of freedom, and that fear often originates from the psychological manipulations of the slaveholder. However, this power is not demonstrated solely between master and slave but must also be considered in the context and time of slavery in question. Cultural and social mores can set the foundations for a power imbalance such that a sense of nonentitlement, worthlessness, lower standing, and duty are felt beyond the parameters of the master–slave relationship. These can be a deeply embedded part of the culture and environment of those enslaved and liberated, particularly where related to gender, religion, or caste. In many cases, it therefore matters little

---

[27] Kevin Bales and Zoe Trodd, *To Plead Our Own Cause*, 225.
[28] Kevin Bales and Zoe Trodd, *To Plead Our Own Cause*, 48.
[29] Kevin Bales and Zoe Trodd, *To Plead Our Own Cause*, 101.
[30] Kevin Bales and Zoe Trodd, *To Plead Our Own Cause*, 106.

that the law grants rights or forbids discriminatory behavior; ultimately, freedom cannot be realized where a society or community creates conditions for ongoing discrimination and maltreatment. Survivors find themselves ostracized from their communities, find cultural or social restrictions on their liberties, or may even be murdered for offending community values, and the prejudice, discrimination, and racism that is evidenced in historic narratives continue to echo today for many survivors of slavery.

In Christine Stark's narrative, she states that in liberation she felt "Our voices are non-existent...we are dirty, ruined, despised...The intensity of my emotions does not match up to a normal life."[31] When Christine describes her voice as nonexistent, this interacts with earlier testimony where she describes herself as silent and numb. It is as if her "nonexistence" not only relates to her ability to give voice or testimony but also relates to her self-identity or her humanity. Christine's view of herself is created by her slaveholders and by cultural perceptions, which are transposed to her consciousness. She is a construct of indoctrination by her captors from birth, and post enslavement to societal attitudes to the acts she was forced to carry out, so she believes she is "dirty, ruined, despised." There are no soft edges to these words; in freedom, Christine must fight to overcome cultural perceptions and her own ingrained self-perception in order to forge a more positive identity for herself. Therefore, the trauma of slavery, the realities of freedom, and the risk of re-establishment into slavery (whether actual or perceived) destabilizes survivors' feelings of freedom in liberation.

## THE CONTINUAL CAPTIVE: SURVIVOR IDENTITY IN LIBERATION

The tenor of Christine's narrative is repeatedly affirmed in contemporary narratives and exposes the contrast of freedom in fact versus freedom in form. The complexity of freedom for survivors extends far beyond the release from the condition of slavery. The reality of freedom is often far from its imagined state and is tainted by their trauma. Salma states with straightforward clarity: "I was free, I still wasn't free,"[32] and Jill explains that she was she was so emotionally stunned and lost in her own world that she "didn't exist as anything more than a slave, except [she] was an escaped slave."[33] In both these examples, the message is essentially the

---

[31] Kevin Bales and Zoe Trodd, *To Plead Our Own Cause*, 101.
[32] Kevin Bales and Zoe Trodd, *To Plead Our Own Cause*, 223.
[33] Kevin Bales and Zoe Trodd, *To Plead Our Own Cause*, 175.

same; freedom is not freedom where the psychological harm of slavery and the realities of freedom mean the survivor cannot experience freedom as we would. Jill's identity remained thoroughly tied to that of a slave, but now as an "illegitimate" slave, as someone that has not been fully liberated, for whom recapture was a very real prospect, and who felt her freedom to be illicit. Despite there being no legal foundation to her enslavement, cultural attitudes to her situation meant that for Jill, it was her freedom that was unsound, not her enslavement. The consequences of freedom for Jill were homelessness, depression and anorexia, shame, fear, and self-destructive behavior.

For many, their liberation is therefore a "bittersweet experience."[34] In *Child Soldier*, Ishmael Beah expresses how these things affect him in liberation. He states that:

Even with all this freedom, I still have the fear that I had to carry every day of the desperation that I saw in almost every soldier. That desperation often betrayed the innocent, as everyone struggled to find favours among the superiors. This is my final humiliation to speak of myself about shameful abuse and inferiority, because that's the only way I can save my friends. I was there, and I don't need to imagine their pain. I know it, and I still feel the abuse, the humiliation, scars which my body and soul will carry forever. My fear seems to be permanent, and it feels as a mark for life.[35]

Survivors may never recover fully from their experiences, and so they often remain psychologically bound by their enslavement. The fear, shame, and humiliation they carry, the psychological scars and internalized behaviors and beliefs constructed by their slaveholders and their experiences indicate survivors will never be free of their slavery.

As a young girl, Mende Nazer was trafficked and enslaved following a raid on her village in Sudan. In liberation, she was able to contact her family, only to discover they had been told she had been kidnapped and converted from Islam to Christianity and that she had changed her name to Caroline. She had to explain to them that she had instead escaped to the UK. She relates the moment that she called them and on hearing their voices realized her parents were aging, that her father sounded weaker and discovering that her mother had lost her hearing as a result of being beaten around the head in the raid. She expresses worry for their safety and concerns about her own future and security.

---

[34] Ishmael Beah, *A Long Way Gone: The True Story of a Child Soldier* (London: Harper Collins Publishers, 2007).
[35] Ishmael Beah, *A Long Way Gone*, Part Four: "A New Life – A Time to Be."

She states "the nightmare of my years in slavery didn't end as soon as I escaped. It was just the nature of my suffering that changed."[36] She also states:

> I had never anticipated how difficult it would be for me to change my mindset from being a captive to being a free person, or how complicated life could get in the process. Many people in my life thought I should be happy for what I had, happy simply for my freedom, but it wasn't that easy. Happiness is not a switch people can turn off and on. Not that I wasn't happy...for many years I had thought I would be happy if I could only see my family. Now I knew that was just a fantasy, and that happiness and disappointment can be tightly intertwined.[37]

Nazer goes on to state:

> It is now two years since I escaped. In that time, London has become my new home and the place where I have tasted my first years of freedom. How has it been for me? To me freedom is so precious, and I would not give it up for the whole world....it remains a beautiful, epical experience...But for me, this freedom is also a terrifying thing. I was captured when I was still a child. I spent my teenage years and my early adulthood in slavery. For all that time, I had no freedom. I was a non-person.[38]

She also goes on to describe the everyday difficulties of coping with her freedom. After years of being controlled and finding herself an adult for whom came to a liberated life as a newcomer, she found she had to learn everything from scratch, such as how to manage money, open a bank account. She had to learn basic social etiquette and how to be served by others at a restaurant, but "most difficult of all, I had to learn now not to be afraid anymore."[39] She was:

> Overwhelmed with everything about my new life...I have no other word to describe how emotionally overloaded I was. It was still hard for me to believe that simple freedoms – such as being able to sleep later than daybreak on a weekend morning, OR sitting down at a table to eat rather than serving the meal – were mine...I had more time to myself. That was a new concept for me: personal time. I had no idea what I should do when I wasn't responsible for something or someone else...I ended up spending most of my free time alone in my room.[40]

---

[36] Mende Nazer and Damien Lewis. *Slave*, 299–300.
[37] Mende Nazer and Damien Lewis, *Slave*, 114–15.
[38] Mende Nazer and Damien Lewis, *Slave*, 292–93.
[39] Mende Nazer and Damien Lewis, *Slave*, 297.
[40] Mende Nazer and Damien Lewis, *Slave*, 9–95.

## THE IMPORTANCE OF BELONGING TO THE SENSE OF FREEDOM

Narratives also reveal what survivors feel is important to them in survival, what it is they value in freedom, and what progression in freedom looks like. Often these relate to seemingly small changes in their circumstances, like peace, privacy, and freedom to speak, but are intimately related to the things denied to them during their enslavement. In my interview with Pranus, he said:

> And now here I am a free person. I can do what I want. I can go to school. At the moment I haven't got a job, but I hope that soon I will manage to find a job. So, no one is controlling me now, and I know that no one is going to assault me … freedom is when a person can go anywhere they like, freedom to say anything you like. Freedom to express yourself. Freedom is freedom. When you are not locked in prison. If you want you go there and there. No one is following you. When no one tells you what to do. Of course, there are limits.[41]

Keith revealed freedom to him was a feeling of positive growth, the ability to learn, to have voice and to be his own person:

> It's a bit like a horse, when you first let a horse out of the stables into the fields they'll all run, you know what I mean? And it's like for me to actually even just sit in my lounge just like being allowed to just take that [sigh] deep breath and say, yeah, I'm happy, I'm happy. Do you know what I mean? I can do what I want, when I want. Erm, I had freedom when I was on the streets, but I didn't have responsibilities. Erm, now obviously I've got responsibilities, but I've also got that freedom where I'm my own person and I feel myself getting better and better by each month. Every month I feel so much empowered, so much, the more knowledge I pick up the more I don't know, the more I read about things on the internet the more I hear. I just feel I'm just, I'm just thriving, you know what I mean? Like a tree, I'm being fed water, do you know what I mean? I'm just growing, and my mind is just growing so much it's, it's quite an amazing feeling, you know, to be able to speak out, have that voice and there, do you know what I mean?[42]

And Shyima Hall realized that although she had been physically free for a period of time, she was also emotionally freer: "My small freedoms of being able to go to school and make choices about my spare time at home did wonders for my state of mind"[43] and that she could

---

[41] Pranus, interview by Andrea Nicholson, January 20, 2017.
[42] Keith, interview by Andrea Nicholson, May 17 and 19, 2018.
[43] Shyima Hall and Lisa Wysocky, *Hidden Girl: The True Story of a Modern-Day Child Slave* (New York: Simon & Schuster Books, 2014), 115.

"worship and pray to a God in any manner that I chose."[44] Reflecting on her childhood prior to her enslavement she also values the freedom she had then to move around the neighborhood, to play games, and to make choices.[45] Farhia Nur states that in liberation:

> It was nice and clean everywhere. When we went out to buy milk, we were not scared walking the streets. When you see all this peace you feel relaxed. I slept well after a long time. I cannot explain what freedom from fear feels like. For so long I had worried about who was going to come knocking on my door. I was lucky I didn't go mad I used to shake and drop glasses sometimes. I am no longer like that I don't remember breaking in any glasses in England.[46]

And Tung said, "Freedom is not to be kept prison and can travel freely. And to get all the basic human rights for example going to school. And to be able to do whatever one likes as long as it's not illegal and have a life and privacy; not being watched, not be tightened up by anything."[47]

In addition to these, there are larger aspects to survivors' perceptions of the value of freedom, and my analysis reveals, survivors' need to reconnect with communities and families, and importantly how this relates to acceptance, belonging and their sense of futurity. For example, Shyima Hall places focus on how much she valued finding a church which was "open and accepting of me"[48] and explains that, for her, her freedom crystallized when she became a citizen of the United States. She was "finally as free as everyone else." Citizenship allowed her to make "real plans to begin helping others find theirs" and was also a symbolic, physical and psychological rejection of Egypt, her country of origin and the country in which she had been enslaved. She states that "to become a United States citizen I had to renounce my citizenship to Egypt. I was no longer obligated to have anything to do with that country, and I felt as if the last tie that bound me to it had been cut."[49]

In November 2017, I interviewed Dwain. Dwain had been "adopted" by his community and used as a child domestic slave as soon as he was

---

[44] Shyima Hall, *Hidden Girl*, 101.
[45] Shyima Hall, *Hidden Girl*, 63–64.
[46] Rahila Gupta, *Enslaved: The New British Slavery* (London: Portobello Books, 2007), chapter 1: "Faria Nur, No Refuge."
[47] Tung, Interview by Andrea Nicholson, February 9, 2017. With thanks to Palm Cove Society. See also Amber Lobepreet who states that the condition of slavery meant she was accompanied everywhere; she had no real freedom of movement and little privacy: Rahila Gupta, *Enslaved*, chapter 5: "Amber Lobepreet: I had Nowhere to Go."
[48] Shyima Hall, *Hidden Girl*, 152.
[49] Shyima Hall, *Hidden Girl*, 209.

able to work, trafficked through Europe to the UK and only escaping his enslavement in his late teens. Dwain explained that on meeting the sons of William Wilberforce recently they asked him what he wished for. His reply was "my passport, recognition, acceptance, and I can make a decent woman of my partner, and I can take my kids on holiday. That's all." Having explained to me the difficulty and frustration he had experienced trying to obtain a passport and to be acknowledged as a UK citizen (currently denied), I asked what freedom meant to him, he replied:

In a simplistic way then it's just to be able to travel, you know, er, if you go to that travel agency and say "can I get a flight to Tenerife please"? And the following week I'm there. That would be freedom to me. I've been stuck in your country for this long .... So they...said "... come back with your mum and dad's birth certificate and marriage certificate" and I thought 'yeah, right, fat chance that's going to happen, I don't even know me Dad.' Anyway so I took myself gingerly out of the room thinking 'whoa, that was more serious than I probably let off.'

Interviewer: So really you're identifying the ability to travel, which is linked to them giving you a passport, as really symbolic of a lot more.

Oh yes, it is. You've read it. It really is. It's so symbolic that I probably keel over and cry in front of anybody because what that's shown me is finally what I've strived for forever, which is acceptance. I didn't choose to be this way, it's just what's happened. What I've tried to do is live with the Achilles that I have, if it is that. But because I'm living with it, why can't anybody just respect that and work with me on it rather than against me? Or like someone said in that Summit you know people like me are treated like criminals. How can I be a criminal? I didn't choose this, I didn't choose to come into a country that I didn't even know I was coming into illegally. So, because of that why am I still being punished? I said to someone recently if the system wanted to punish me because I came in illegally then that's fine. But after 40 years don't you think that's far too much? It's enough's enough. But it's still going. And us as humans are letting it happen by not changing either the statues or the legislation surrounding it. Because it stinks.

It's not ever been easy for me to regularise myself ever. The amount of institutions I've gone to, the amount of people I've been to, the amount of documentation I've provided, it's still kept me here. So of course, I'm going to put all my eggs into this situation knowing that, oh well, it's going to be pushed across to the channels that are interested in things like this will they turn it over will they look into, this into that. Nonetheless I still don't have that physical book that I probably would need for myself anyway. Because all of a sudden by next weekend I'm saying 'you know what, I'm fucking off out of the UK for a while and find my head, fund myself, I've finally been accepted so that whole notion has to – I've got to get accustomed to – because it's the first time ever.' You couldn't imagine that.

So it would take a lot. It would wind me probably, it would take all the wind out of me, but positively. Because then the new wind that would come would be a positive energy, a more vibrant, optimistic, looking forward to the future you know, because I feel like I can make a difference in my future now rather than, I suppose, sleeping on it. And of course, anyone that cares for me to know that I'm sleeping on it, is frustrating. But I'm now limited to what I can do, if I don't sleep on it what do you want me to do? Scream on it? Because if I scream on it I'll get put inside prison or some mental institution. I'm trying to keep my sanity so that when the good times do come I can actually recognise it as good times, rather than [laughs] think "hold on I need a fix." You know, "inject me with something please" and that that's where it's at; I'm absolutely tired.[50]

Freedom for Dwain is not only tied up with belonging, but even in twenty years of liberation he continues to hold a projected conception of freedom, one that is "vibrant, optimistic" and "full of positive energy." It is this projection that keeps him sane, keeps him from falling into self-destructive behavior, but is an elusive, and perhaps unattainable, concept of freedom. Dwain recognizes that his freedom is inhibited because in the denial of citizenship, he remains "unacknowledged" by society. He has no birth certificate, no papers, and no passport. He continues to exercise a responsibility for himself that has been a feature of his life since childhood, throughout his enslavement, and now long into his liberation. The onus is still on him to make a place for himself in this world while at the same time both acknowledging and continuing the constant repression of his trauma and its effects.

It is therefore fundamental to recognize that liberation itself is not freedom, that survivors will hold different and moving concepts of freedom over their journeys. It is not the case that the contrasts touched upon in this chapter appear separate from one another, but often exist in the same narrative, in the same person's experience. It is not accurate to say, for example, that an abstract concept of freedom is the only descriptor of a particular individual's perception, rather it can vary. They may experience feelings of freedom within the state of slavery and feel as if their identities are still inextricably bound up with slavery in liberation. Contemporary narratives show a conflict in this sense; there is a bleeding and blurring of the boundaries of concepts of freedom in the mind of the enslaved individual. Theirs is a very complex state of existence, which is not conducive to clean categorization, as perceptions of freedom will shift over time for each individual.

While freedom is felt as something inherent once understood, the effect of slavery on survivors is to render the experience of freedom as something limited, tainted, illicit, or illegitimate. The reality of liberation often doesn't live up to survivors' perceptions of what freedom would

---

[50] Dwain, interview by Andrea Nicholson, November 3, 2017.

entail and its reality affects their potential to envisage a different future, leaving them struggling to attain "full" freedom. The view that slavery and freedom are absolute rather than relative concepts is therefore illusory, as across these works survivors stress that these are states of existence that bleed together. Further, the enslaved individual's perspective and actions will be altered by smaller freedoms felt during slavery, their projected understanding of what eventual "total" freedom could entail, and the subsequent reality of that freedom.

Ultimately, where liberation can't be won through escape, the body remains a final source of power and resistance. A different kind of freedom can be gained by denying the slaveholder their commodity through death or destruction of the self, while at the same time achieving a corporeal and psychological freedom from the pain of slavery. But in survival, the effects of their enslavement, of these survival and resistance strategies, and the contrasts in freedom as it is perceived in bondage, then experienced in liberation, have profound effects on survivors' identities both in and out of slavery. Chapter 3 explores these effects in more detail, examining the ways in which identity is destroyed and reconstructed as a result of slavery, the need for survivors to divorce from it in liberation, and the impossibility of doing so.

# 3

# The Construction and Reconstruction of Survivor Identities

> I had to hide essential parts of my identity .... My parents and perpetrators forced me into the boxes of bad daughter, prostitute, whore, hurtful child, and on and on. In order to fit those boxes, I was made to contort myself into unfamiliar forms and to put on a mask as disguise. In my healing process, I have come to adorn new masks and to hide in new boxes, primarily those of victim and survivor.[1]

In analyzing the corpus of narratives for perceptions on freedom, it became clear that survivors' identities were deeply affected by their experiences of freedom and its denial. The dogma and violence to which they were subjected in order to maintain their submission, and the complex psychological effects of liberation, have ramifications for the reconstruction of identity. The third chapter of this book explores survivors' constructions of identity during and post enslavement.

The term identity has the potential for multiple meanings; it can be used to express categorical attributes, such as race and gender, it can have reference to our location in a social and political space, social movements, and/or have relation to solidarity or "groupness."[2] In the context of this chapter, the term identity is predominantly used to mean a core aspect of "selfhood," the fundamental condition of social being, something "deep,

---

[1] Minh Dang in Laura T. Murphy, *Survivors of Slavery: Modern-Day Slave Narratives* (New York: Columbia University Press, 2014), xiv.
[2] Robert Brubaker and Frederick Cooper, "Beyond Identity," *Theory & Society* 29, no. 1 (2000): 7–8.

basic, abiding and foundational" to the self.³ However, in stating this, it should be recognized that states of identity shift, and as such the aim here is not to try to determine a discoverable "essence" of identity, but to adopt a realist approach, embracing the multiple and fluctuating identities that are reflected in the hundreds of contemporary slave narratives analyzed.

The self is the product of multiple and competing discourses, which can be fluctuating and fragmented in nature.⁴ In other words, selfhood is not continuous, instead, we change with experience.⁵ Identities are therefore constituted differently in each individual and formed in different historical contexts so that identity is neither stable nor internally homogenous.⁶ This is particularly the case for survivors whose experiences in and out of slavery result in multiple identities that pose challenges to self-identity, and their recovery in liberation. The themes and correlations that emerge from survivors' lived experiences throughout the corpus of contemporary slave narratives provide unique insights into the psychological and physical impact of slavery on their self-esteem and their physical well-being. They also reveal the role of narrative giving in making sense of their fractured identities.⁷ The complexities and subtleties of "multiple" identities that are often assumed or chosen for complicated subjective reasons can be objectively evaluated.⁸ Such an evaluation is particularly valuable because identities form the basis of the associations we develop and our views on societal structures that affect our life chances and self-authority. Examining the correlations that appear while recognizing internally the relative, subjective nature of those experiences can therefore unmask important considerations for survivor growth.

## THE VALUE OF TELLING TO THE FORMATION OF IDENTITY

The self is a fragile thing. In our framing of the self, threat events – our traumatic experiences, our extremes of pain are known to have greater effect

---

³ Robert Brubaker and Frederick Cooper, "Beyond Identity," 7.
⁴ Robert Brubaker and Frederick Cooper, "Beyond Identity," 8.
⁵ Christopher Hager, *Word by Word: Emancipation and the Act of Writing* (Cambridge, MA, and London: Harvard University Press, 2013), 24.
⁶ Paula M. L. Moya and Michael R. Hames-Garcia, *Reclaiming Identity: Realist Theory and the Predicament of Postmodernism* (Berkeley and Los Angeles: University of California Press, 2000), 1.
⁷ Mardi J. Horowitz, "Self-Identity Theory and Research Methods," *Journal of Research Practice* 8, no. 2 (2012): 6.
⁸ See for example Paula M. L. Moya, *Reclaiming Identity*.

on our construction of the self than our positive experiences.⁹ Survivors of slavery are therefore inescapably molded by their trauma and are "too likely to suffer the mutilation of their distinctive shape and identity by the swarm of external reality."¹⁰ In their narratives, we see survivors seeking explanation, understanding, and order in the turns of circumstance that have led them in, and out of slavery. There is value in the mere telling and "a life lived, a personality achieved, constitutes its own material."¹¹ The act of telling enables survivors to forge a fundamental link between the world and themselves. Through telling, survivors impress their image and allow themselves to connect what is known of the world to the unknown, establishing new relational patterns and organizing the self into a new entity.¹²

However, the means by which we interpret and understand our experiences is formed from often incomplete or constructed memory and remembering. The cynic in us may therefore question the accuracy of memory following trauma (on which there is a vast literature and which is addressed fully in Chapter 4).¹³ As discussed in Chapter 1, memory provides an unfaithful record and can be a work of art, but the lived and recalled past is still valuable and a reconstruction of how the present came to be.¹⁴ It is precisely the subjective, not the objective, that is of value in contemporary slave narratives, as the subjective can reveal important truths about the present.¹⁵ While there are few means by which we can assure ourselves of the accuracy of memory in telling, it serves little to deny the authority of survivor narratives. The acceptance of survivors' narratives as given, the subjectivity of their narratives, the experiences they have had, and their interpretation of events as they are internally formulated and externally communicated, is valuable precisely because of that uncertainty. It is being in their skin, "looking from within and with human eyes"¹⁶ that we seek. Essentially narratives are a representation of how survivors felt then and now, and how their experiences

---

[9] José Augusto Pinto-Gouveia and Marcella Matos, "Can Shame Memories Become a Key to Identity? The Centrality of Shame Memories Predicts Psychopathology," *Applied Cognitive Psychology* 25, no. 2 (2011): 282. See also Christopher Hager, *Word by Word*, 25.
[10] Christopher Hager, *Word by Word*, 15.
[11] James Olney, *Metaphors of Self* (Princeton: Princeton University Press, 1972), 140.
[12] Christopher Hager, *Word by Word*, 31–32.
[13] Martin A. Conway and Emily A. Holmes, *Guidelines on Memory and the Law: Recommendations from the Scientific Study of Human Memory* (Leicester: The British Psychological Society, 2008).
[14] André Maurois, *Aspects of Biography* (New York: Appleton & Co., 1929), 157–58.
[15] Christopher Hager, *Word by Word*, 264.
[16] Christopher Hager, *Word by Word*, 21.

are remembered.[17] The listener is acknowledging the experience of the individual and engaging with the narrator's feelings, emotions, instances of anger, denial and hope, the trauma they experience, are revealed, and in the telling.[18]

In the interpretation of narratives, I have argued in Chapter 2 that there is a tendency for us to seek linear stories and happy endings which should be resisted to allow for an authentic analysis of survivors' narratives. Similarly, when analyzing narratives in the context of identity, there is a need to depart somewhat from the common psychoanalytical aim of seeking out only those aspects that indicate well-being and recovery.[19] I excavate narratives for insights into survivor identities with a conscious attendance to what is being told, and by simultaneously acknowledging their life telling as it is. This allows the discomfort that comes from an understanding of the difficulties of the destruction and construction of identity forms a more authentic, representative analysis, rather than analyzing with the sole aim of seeking solutions.

The multiple theories on identity formation could lead the reader to apply a particular theory to narratives, which would naturally reformulate what is understood. However, I argue that in order to understand survivors' lived experiences, it is more valuable to identify where the body of narratives reflects those theories. Such an analysis tells us that each person is unique and will construct their identity fluidly and over time, and that trauma has a fundamental impact on identity, choice, and actions. However, what this means for survivors, how slavery causes disruption to the self, whether identity can be recovered, and how it is remolded in survival can only be ascertained from their narratives.[20] I have stated that given the right conditions, survivors will choose what they feel is important to tell and will set out and determine the territory of their narratives. What survivors choose to tell, or not to tell, can therefore be revealing when unravelling the shifting identities that are constructed over such timeframes.

---

[17] For example, see further on this Frances Smith Foster, *Witnessing* Slavery, xxii.
[18] Leela Ghandi, *Postcolonial Theory: A Critical Introduction* (Edinburgh: Edinburgh University Press, 1998), 7–9.
[19] Sam Durrant, *Postcolonial Narrative and the Work of Mourning: J. M. Coetzee, Wilson Harris, and Toni Morrison* (Albany: SUNY Press, 2004), 9.
[20] See for example Henry Greenspan, *On Listening to Holocaust Survivors: Beyond Testimony* (St. Paul, MN: Paragon House, 2011).

## THE CREATION OF THE SLAVE: HOW IDENTITY IS REFRAMED DURING ENSLAVEMENT

In my interview with Dwain, he disclosed that during his childhood enslavement he felt he had, "no identity. You don't really belong to anybody, but you're someone's possession."[21] When an individual is subjected to slavery their worth is essentially reduced to their economic or physical value, rendering the enslaved individual a "non-person"; a mere possession. In slavery, the authority over the self is denied in such profound ways it has ramifications for the success and degree of survivor recovery; it affects not only who they are, but how they "become." Their experiences will, therefore, also affect their agency and consequently their ability to participate in and lead the antislavery agenda. This is particularly true for those born into hereditary slavery who are unlikely to have a concept of themselves that is not derived in one way or another from their natal slavery. Having known no other existence and having no exposure to other environments they are unable to frame a different reality. By contrast, those brought into slavery have a stronger sense of who they are and of their enslavement and are able to perceive a comparison of culture and freedom.

Once enslaved, a number of aspects or themes emerge from contemporary slave narratives that expose how self-identity is irrevocably damaged by enslavement. These include the objectification and alienation of the individual, the practice of renaming, the use of language to reformulate perceptions, and shaming tactics. They also include using religious and cultural beliefs to manipulate individuals, physical practices that undermine genderhood and sexuality, and the use of minimizing language to undermine individuals' social and self-held beliefs as to what is "normal."

The objectification of individuals is well known as part of our understanding of historical slavery but is more problematic as a determinate criterion of slavery where ownership of another is now illegal. Without the legitimacy of legal ownership of another, the antislavery community continues to debate the parameters of factual ownership amounting to slavery. Objectification and alienation are two such criteria, and while it is difficult to demonstrate in every case, there are nevertheless many instances of individuals being treated as if they were sub-human. Survivors have had to sleep on floors, in outbuildings or cattle pens, or outside on the ground. Many are only fed from left-over food and only when it is available, receive no healthcare and are beaten and tortured. They are called "animal,"

---

[21] Dwain, interviewed by Andrea Nicholson, November 3, 2017.

"slave," they are treated as if they are worthless; they are "disposable people." Survivors explicitly reference feeling owned and dehumanized. The alienation, isolation, and attempted dehumanization of individuals is therefore a common theme throughout the body of slave narratives, both historical and contemporary. As Christine Stark explains: "above all else they want us immobilized. They want to consume our lives ... we are their property, they own us."[22] Helia Lajeunesse asserts that her captor repeatedly stated she "was just an animal without any family,"[23] her slaveholder essentially objectifying her as a resource and denying her the rights associated with the human being. She is something "other," someone less valued and deserving of humanity. Kavita states she "was tied and thrown into a room like a piece of furniture ... almost like I didn't exist. I was nothing."[24]

At the age of 12 or 13 (her birthdate is unknown, as is customary among her people), Mende Nazer was abducted following a slaving raid on her village. She was sold into slavery to a woman in Khartoum who stripped her of her name, locked her up, and made her sleep in a shed. She was required to serve an Arab family for six years where she was forced into hard labor and was subjected to physical abuse. She was repeatedly called a "yebit," meaning "one worthy of no name," and "abda," meaning "slave."[25] She says:

From the beginning in my master's house I didn't realise I was a slave, I was confused; I wondered why I was here. Later on, my master was talking to her friend and she said two things that made me realise it. One, she mentioned she owned me. The other she called me "abda" to her friend. She called me her slave. From that time on I understood who I am.[26]

Nazer also explains that her treatment had "completely destroyed my sense of my own identity and own self-worth" and that she was "no longer valuable as a human being. I lived in a complete state of terror. To rebel against all that, to rebel against the woman whom I called 'master' and who called me 'slave,' had become unthinkable."[27] The strategies used to divorce Nazer from her previous identity, to adopt terms that are reminiscent of and create a purposeful association with historical slavery,

---

[22] Kevin Bales and Zoe Trodd, eds., *To Plead Our Own Cause Personal Stories by Today's Slaves* (New York: Cornell University Press, 2008), 101.
[23] Laura T. Murphy, *Survivors of Slavery*, 63.
[24] Kevin Bales and Zoe Trodd, *To Plead Our Own Cause*, 138.
[25] Mende Nazer and Damien Lewis, *Slave: The True Story of a Girl's Lost Childhood and Her Fight for Survival* (London: Virago, 2010), 133.
[26] Kevin Bales and Zoe Trodd, *To Plead Our Own Cause*, 226.
[27] Mende Nazer and Damien Lewis, *Slave*, 189–90.

set the foundations for an understanding of her changed position and reformulate her knowledge of herself and her place in the world. "Some people say I was treated like an animal" reflects Nazer, "But I tell them: no, I wasn't. Because an animal – like a cat or a dog – gets stroked, and love and affection. I had none of that."[28] Not only does she raise the distinction between human and animal treatment to highlight the mistreatment that denies her personhood, but she goes further to imply she was not even afforded a value equal to that of an animal. She was irrelevant and dispensable. The dehumanizing and controlling component to the treatment experienced by enslaved individuals, the "consuming" of their lives, is to claim that individual's life for the slaveholder's purposes so completely as to shape their identity and eradicate resistance. Such experiences parallel historical slave experiences in that, "Slaveholders think nothing of [slaves]. Because they regard their slaves as property, the mere instruments of their convenience and pleasure. One who is a slaveholder at heart never recognises a human being in a slave."[29]

Many survivors express similar experiences, exposing the deep degradation they experienced at the hands of their slaveholder(s), and the disregard shown for their age and capacity. These experiences force survivors to redefine their self-worth, their slave environment becoming "a world within itself."[30] The attempt by slaveholders to reframe enslaved individuals' perceptions of themselves in this way is achieved in a number of other ways. For example, the confiscation or destruction of identity documents might seem innocuous in comparison to the other experiences survivors describe. This act not only assures the slaveholder that the victim has no means of escape, but it is also used to threaten enslaved individuals with their illegal status, making discovery a fearful rather than hoped for event. However, it also affects how the enslaved individual views themselves: "Until your passport is in your hands, until it has the right stamps on it, you are doomed to remain at the mercy of those who wave it in front of your eyes … you are a non-person, or an 'unperson'."[31]

---

[28] David Cohen, "My Life as a London Slave," The Evening Standard, Wednesday, January 21, 2004. www.standard.co.uk/news/my-life-as-a-london-slave-7298724.html

[29] Testimony of Angela G. Weld in Theodore Dwight Weld, *American Slavery as It Is: Testimony of a Thousand Witnesses* (Chapel Hill: University of North Carolina Press, 2011), 149.

[30] Henry Turner, Arkansas. Collected by the Federal Writers Project, Works Progress Administration, Interviewer Watt McKinney. Phillips County, Arkansas. Published in George P. Rawick, ed., *The American Slave: A Composite Autobiography* (Westport, CT: The Greenwood Press, Inc., 1979), Supplement Series 2, v.1, 135–41.

[31] Rahila Gupta, *Enslaved: The New British Slavery* (London: Portobello Books, 2007), 3.

By stripping individuals of their formal identity documents slaveholders remove the agency attached to that identity. An enslaved individual feels they are no longer a "legal" person capable of holding and exerting their rights, nor are they the person they once were. The act of destroying or removing identification documents is a symbolic removal of the past and of the transition from free to not free.

Another tool used to sabotage pre-enslavement identity is the renaming and labelling of individuals and their purpose. "To have a name is to have a means of locating, extending and preserving oneself in a human community, so as to be able to answer the question 'who?' with reference to ancestry, current status, and particular bearing, with reference to the full panoply of time."[32] By labelling individuals as slaves or outcasts, and/or by requiring the terminology of master and mistress, language is used to isolate and undermine identities. By placing a new identity on their captors, slaveholders gain security through their captive's new anonymity and use this practice as a means of divorcing their victims from their previous existence. Sometimes names are chosen purposefully in order to deny them any remaining association with their home culture or religion. The psychological manipulation that occurs with the renaming of individuals is therefore used as a means of enforcing a slave identity. It is an attempt to strip away cultural origins, thereby exacting submission to their new state of existence.

Nevertheless, individuals' identities are never fully eradicated. Indeed, renaming can have the opposite effect in that it can drive individuals to cling to their identity all the more, remembering their birth name as a form of escapism or as an act of defiance, as was the case with Mende Nazer. This defiance can even extend to their progeny, for example, Ajok was born in Sudan and enslaved following a raid on her village, then "given" to a soldier as his sexual and domestic slave. Renamed Howah by her slaveholder, when she gave birth to his child, he named the boy Ahmed. However, Ajok continued to call her son by a different name: Thiop.[33] Ajok uses the very same tactic that her slaveholder used on her, renaming her son in an attempt to annihilate the identity given to her child by him. Where names carry cultural significance, Ajok's use of a different name for her child was not only a means of retaining his sense of self, but it was also a symbolic act signifying a lack of right of ownership over them. The adoption of different names in survival is explicitly

---

[32] Quoted in Sigrid King, "Naming and Power in Zora Neale Hurston's *Their Eyes Were Watching God*," *Black American Literature Forum* 24, no. 4 (1990): 683.
[33] Kevin Bales and Zoe Trodd, *To Plead Our Own Cause*, 35.

recounted by survivors as an attempt to reject their enslavement. It is a means of reformulating their identity in liberation and creating a psychological divorce from their enslavement. For example, while Patience does not reveal what name was given to her in slavery, or whether she retained her birth name during her enslavement, she states "I want now to be called Patience. This will be my new name because I want to forget about all my past and start a new identity in life."[34]

## THE DENIAL AND MANIPULATION OF CULTURAL IDENTITY AND BELIEFS

Aside from renaming, slaveholders also use other tactics to dismantle individuals' cultural identities, forcing them to observe different belief systems, or shaming and deprecating them for their origins, religion, or ethnicity. Nazer states: "I tried to hide anything of my Nuba identity. I never spoke my Nuba language. I never sang any Nuba songs. And I never, ever mentioned my past life."[35] Nazer was ordered not to pray, but she retained one set of prayer beads and daydreamed about her past life, which she expresses in a way that implies she felt her past self was an alternate reality. When her slaveholder found the beads, he denigrated her saying they "stank like black people" and were "only worn by savages."[36] Thus, attacks by slaveholders on ethnicity, cultural and religious beliefs are used to marginalize, discriminate, dehumanize, and undermine spiritual identity and ideologies.

Many survivors are also made to convert to a different religion, for example from Christianity to Islam,[37] or their religious beliefs are used to manipulate and control them. Patience was ten years old when she was brought across the border from Togo into Ghana to become a *trokosi*. This is a form of ritual servitude where (typically) young girls are enslaved in traditional religious shrines in payment for services or in religious atonement for alleged misdeeds of a family member. In Patience's case, she was eventually informed that she had been delivered to the shrine to atone for the death of a relative involved in a land litigation case. The dispute resulted in her relatives being cursed by the shrine for trying to

---

[34] Kevin Bales and Zoe Trodd, *To Plead Our Own Cause*, 67.
[35] Kevin Bales and Zoe Trodd, *To Plead Our Own Cause*, 165.
[36] Kevin Bales and Zoe Trodd, *To Plead Our Own Cause*, 166.
[37] See for example the narrative of Marco in Kevin Bales and Zoe Trodd, *To Plead Our Own Cause*, 38.

possess land that did not belong to them. As a child *trokosi*, she was left to fend for herself and spent her days farming and selling charcoal for the priest. She was not allowed to earn for herself and was dependent on the priest for food, clothing, and soap. As she reached adolescence she was given to the priest's brother, raped and beaten, forced to live with him, and bore his children. She was eventually liberated from the shrine in 2002. It is clear from her narrative that the priest manipulated her fears and imagination with the concept of the family curse to ensure her continued servitude: "When life became tough for me, I decided to run away from the shrine for a while. The priest heard this and cautioned that the curse I came to redeem from my family would follow me. Misfortune would follow me and I would fall sick and die."[38]

Spiritual beliefs are also plundered for similar purposes. In order to enslave Joy, a survivor of forced sexual exploitation for commercial purposes, her traffickers made her drink blood. She was made to eat a sheep's eye and place her hand on the juju (possibly an amulet or other representational object). At this point, she believed she was under the power of juju and she was told that the juju would kill her if she tried to run away or told anyone of her circumstances. At age 16 this would have exercised a powerful and fearful control over her, a fear that may carry into her survival.[39] Maria was also similarly controlled through her belief in witchcraft. She was led to believe that her slaveholder was a witch. She believed she was going to a cleaning job, but was then brainwashed to believe that she was cursed and she was so instilled with fear that she was unable to leave:

She took me to the place, and it felt like it took forever. I didn't know the area – I just knew how to get to my niece's school and to the store. She took me all the way to Azusa. I was living in Sierra Madre, so it was a long drive.

When we got there, I met this old man. Probably he was sixty-five or seventy, I don't know. When I met him, he had a big smile …

… The third day in the house he told me he had bought me, that I was his slave, that he paid $200 for me. I didn't have a mind of my own. I was controlled by his witchcraft. He told me he was a witch. I was afraid of him. I was terrorised by him – He beat me, he raped me; every day he abused me mentally, physically, emotionally, spiritually. I was not in touch with my family because I was afraid of saying something to them that he disliked or making him think that I was going to escape. I lived in fear. When I fell asleep because I was so tired, I'd get woken up by him putting things on my face, and telling me, "you have the curse and you cannot leave this house" …

---

[38] Kevin Bales and Zoe Trodd, *To Plead Our Own Cause*, 68.
[39] Kevin Bales and Zoe Trodd, *To Plead Our Own Cause*, 171.

## The Construction and Reconstruction of Survivor Identities 81

... Once in a while I thought, how can I get out of here? But then I changed. I was afraid to think that. He told me he knew what I thought. He had me believe that he saw everything in his crystal ball. So I believed him ...

... By then I hadn't seen anything. I didn't know anything. I was just sixteen. I wanted to be with my family the way I was before, and my dreams were crushed. Crushed. They never let me bloom, like a rose. They never let the rose grow up to be a rose. That's how I felt ...

... The way I ended up in prison was that he had another place in back of the house. He rented to a young couple and tried to pursue the wife. He was trying to do witchcraft on them, and one day the young guy killed him. I heard the noise and came out. The victim was on the ground. The only thing I remember is that he told me to grab the stick and put it under the house. I did that. He put it in my hand and I did it. I put the stick under the house. I didn't know anything else but to follow commands. I didn't even know if I called my family or how my family got there, but my sister came and took me with her.

... I was like a zombie. I didn't talk. I didn't want to eat. I couldn't sleep, and I was very fearful, thinking he was going to come and get me.[40]

It is telling that Maria continued to fear her slaveholder would recapture her, despite her having seen him killed. Maria also shifts from talking about her slaveholder as "he" to referring to him as "the victim." The use of the word "victim" here could simply be an automated reflection of police and court language but could also indicate complex and conflicting emotions that are evidenced in many narratives. The desire to seek reason for their enslavement and humanity in their traffickers is a form of self-preservation, a means by which survivors try to make sense of their experiences.

### THE WAYS SLAVEHOLDERS INCULCATE A NEW "NORMAL"

Language is also used in many circumstances to reframe victims' perceptions of what is normal or respectful, or to manipulate compliance with cultural norms. Recounting how she came to be in a forced marriage, Val states:

... this old man who from when I can remember was constantly told that I was his wife. Because part of the culture is that someone can just have a conversation with an elder and say, you know, "we have a girl child and this will be your wife." And it starts from simple jokes, and for me I was, you know I was really innocent, I didn't know what was going on, but erm in my head because it was constantly repeated, it became apparent that someone's, that I was someone's wife. This man was a bit, he was a bit awkward, because he would say things and

---

[40] Kevin Bales and Zoe Trodd, *To Plead Our Own Cause*, 166–68.

say "you are a child, I need to look after you," I don't know, "you need to do this and this." for me I was really confused because I couldn't have conversations with my parents about it, because I'm like "ok, no I have heard this conversation is happening and people are saying being married off at a younger age." But he could do whatever he wanted to do with me, and he lived within the same homestead which made it even more difficult for me.

But erm that year was one of the most difficult ones, because a lot of people were telling me "why do you have to fight to get an education, because you can get married like many other girls?" And some of the girls who were married at the age of nine or at the age of ten, and for me I could tell that is not the path I really wanted to take; I wanted something different and I could see the life my mum was living where she would wake up so early in the morning, go to the farm and do all this, you know, hard labour. And I was thinking "this is not what I want" you know for my mother and for my siblings. So I had to find a way of really getting an escape route.

From a very young age these are things I grew up hearing "oh your husband" – you know in some instances sometimes people make it as a joke and for me I thought it was a joke until the more I grew up I was like "oh right, so this is serious."

... people would just make comments and you know he would come and say "my wife" and up to now that still happens. But in most cases, it's in a light way where ... because traditionally in the Masai culture people could even "reserve" a girl before she was even married. Let's say for example if you had a son, and maybe I'm pregnant, if we are close family members, maybe your husband might say "ok, if it's a girl who will be born, they will be married to my son" or even then they will say "if you give birth to a girl, they will be my wife." And people will make jokes around that and for me it was a joke until when it started being, you know, getting really serious. I was young and didn't really know exactly what was going on and I believed, it came to a point I completely believed, because it's what people are saying – I would be chased by other children saying "oh, so your husband ..." It would upset me, but I wouldn't say anything because everybody's saying it, whether some of those were saying it as a joke, or whether they knew exactly what was really going on. And it started really gradual until it came to a point where it just happened like that and you don't really know how. I didn't even realise how much it escalated, because it's things you would hear over and over from people and family members.

I think I started realizing things were getting out of hand from the age of 15 or 16. And then when I kept being thrown out of school because of school fees, and then people put me under pressure because there is no money and people were saying "just accept it, remain married or get married" – whatever people were saying. So, it was a combination of things. But reflecting on it now, part of me sometimes feels like someone like my Mum couldn't really have done much because either, maybe with the situation at home, there was nothing much she could have done to change the situation, and maybe she was under pressure as well. But it's just that constant, you know, anger. Because as a result of the abuse from this man and the fact that he was actually living within the homestead where we lived, it made it even worse because I couldn't talk about it that closely with my family. And you know part of me was thinking is everyone ignoring it or is it the normal thing? Now after I grew up and started talking to my Mum and knowing how old she was when she was married off to my Dad, you know it started kind of making sense.

While Val initially did not understand her arranged marriage, thinking it a strange joke, or child's play, she nevertheless carried a discomfort when her "husband" was mentioned. Throughout her childhood, her community and family attempted to normalize her impending forced marriage to a man thirty years senior. Their references to her future "husband," the tone and manner in which references to her impending marriage were casually were a (unsuccessful) means of reframing her perception of what was morally right. Her community and family essentially manipulated her emotions and framing of her world from a very young age in order to ensure her submission to marriage.

### THE MANIPULATION OF SHAMING

Slaveholders' manipulations also include shaming, and conditioning individuals to believe they are stupid, devaluing their sexuality and gender, calling them "girls" or "boys" to undermine their adulthood, and shaming them so that they believe themselves to be worthless or socially deplorable. For example, Anita was trafficked from Nepal to India and then sold to a brothel. They cut her hair to mark her as a prostitute and which indicated in her culture that she was a "wild woman."[41] Her captors refused her any writing materials when they learned she was literate, called her "ignorant" and used minimizing language in an attempt to convince her that she was making more of her circumstances than was necessary, as if it was simply a case of adjusting to her new circumstances and denying the trauma of them. In this sense, she was told she would "get used to it" and they told her that "being a prostitute is not that bad. All of my food, housing and clothes were provided. All I had to do was sell my body."[42] Her trafficker also insisted she refer to him as her "brother" and at the brothel she was told the women in the house were her "sisters" and they had to support each other.

Anita was travelling home when she was offered a drugged drink and subsequently trafficked into forced drug smuggling and later sexual slavery. When her slaveholders cut her hair, she knew then that she "could

---

[41] Kevin Bales and Zoe Trodd, *To Plead Our Own Cause*, 109
[42] Kevin Bales and Zoe Trodd, *To Plead Our Own Cause*, 110.

not leave the brothel without everyone identifying me as a prostitute."[43] She explains:

> When I first went home to my family it was very uncomfortable. The people in the village laughed at me. In my culture, a woman is scorned if she is missing for just one night. I had been missing for two months. It was very hard for my family, especially since we are members of the Brahmin caste. So today I live in Kathmandu. I work as a domestic servant in the city. I am still without my children since they went to live with their father when I was taken away. I am told my husband's new wife is very cruel to my children, but my husband does not want my children to be with me because of where I have been.[44]

In survival, Anita continues to identify strongly with her culture. However, the level of her social standing prior to her enslavement means that her new circumstances potentially create a deeper sense of shame. Where caste is such an intrinsic aspect of Indian culture and directly relates to individuals' social standing, as a result of her enslavement Anita has potentially "lost" the protection and opportunities afforded to belonging to her caste, recounting how her village laughs at her, which establishes a form of exclusion and isolation and reiterates her shame. The effect is greater when placed in the context of the findings in this book, and which is discussed further in Chapter 5, that belonging, community and acceptance are key to meaningful recovery. Further, we see that her enslavement, her community's views, and her family's views have also deeply affected her view of herself as a mother. If we reframe her words, she essentially states: "I, who have returned and wanted my children/family, am still without my children because I was forced into prostitution and cannot now be accepted within my culture as a mother." In other words, her enslavement has affected her choices in freedom as well as her identity as a mother.

Shame memories, whether externally imposed or internally felt create an association with the self as someone defective, worthless, and powerless. Where this is internally perceived, it becomes externalized and will eventually relate to how they are perceived by others.[45] Shame can have a profound effect on selfhood. Memory of trauma or negative emotional events can become central to one's life story and generate future expectations, narrowing life narratives to certain events in life and becoming emblematic. When surveying the body of narratives, it is striking that

---

[43] Kevin Bales and Zoe Trodd, *To Plead Our Own Cause*, 109.
[44] Kevin Bales and Zoe Trodd, *To Plead Our Own Cause*, 112.
[45] José Augusto Pinto-Gouveia and Marcella Matos, "Can Shame Memories Become a Key to Identity," 281.

the most common instances of survivors remaining in the profession for which they were enslaved is in prostitution. This occurs in countries and to individuals where culture is less influential and betrays the degree to which trauma resulting from sexual slavery can reformulate the sense of self. It may be that to continue in prostitution is the only way survivors know to earn and they aren't in a position economically to do other work. However, in some cases, they will have little alternative due to an inequality in rights and societal perceptions of women's perceived roles.

Sina Van notes that:

> Sex work is two-fold ... one is sex slavery – they are forced; they are tricked into it. And sex work is what they do when they have problems in their life. And their life is ruined, and they have no other options. If, even when they think of going to work in garment factories, they have to bribe [someone] in order to get the job.[46]

In one study, women trafficked for sexual purposes were less stable, more isolated, had higher levels of fear, more severe trauma, and greater mental health needs than other victims of crime.[47] In my own interview with Tung, he resisted attempts to be forced into prostitution until it became apparent that he was still not earning enough to repay his family debt. Tung was a fifteen-year-old Vietnamese boy when he was trafficked to the UK in order, so he was told, to reunite with his father. Over a period of six years, he was forced in and out of domestic slavery, working nineteen hours a day, seven days a week and sleeping on the floor with six others behind the kitchens of a Chinese takeaway. Later he was forced to manage cannabis farms, being trafficked around the country and left alone for weeks at a time with limited food and strict instructions to remain inside the premises. Eventually he was pressurized into sexual slavery.

Speaking of the moment when he eventually capitulated, Tung became introverted and spoke painfully about his treatment. He revealed the acts he was required to carry out, his declining health, and the time soon afterward when he was held down as they undertook genital surgery to "make him like a sex toy." No doubt the humiliation and trauma of this and of his forced prostitution will have affected Tung's concept of his gendered self.[48] He had no means of fighting the degrading features of

---

[46] Laura T. Murphy, *Survivors of Slavery*, 240.
[47] Tiffany Dovydaitis, "Human Trafficking: The Role of the Health Care Provider," *Journal of Midwifery & Women's Health* 55 (2010): 462–67.
[48] Barbara J. Risman, *Gender Vertigo: American Families in Transition* (New Haven: Yale University Press, 1999), 7.

his enslavement, and, being isolated, he was not in a position to realize his masculinity through friendships and other social practices. Where our bodies are the primary site of social control and regulation,[49] the inability to retain mastery over his body will have deepened his feelings of humiliation, degradation, and emasculation.[50] Survivor narratives expose how individuals struggle to reconnect with their state of being as adult women and men, and sexual slavery affects the qualities or characteristics culturally and personally associated with gender, with men struggling with homosexuality and masculinity issues as a result.[51]

## THE INABILITY TO DIVORCE FROM A SLAVE IDENTITY

In the act of telling, those who choose to disclose their circumstances after enslavement, often frame and become a different self, one at once divorced yet defined by their past. In their survival, they transform the mere fact of existence "into a realised quality and possible meaning."[52] They can never divorce from the past, so while there is a conscious effort to exclude the past, it is impossible, and their enslavement will form the basis of reformulation. The paradox is that in telling survivors seek both to recall the past while at the same time attempting to lay it at rest.[53] In the act of telling, in the recording of narratives, the mere fact of existence is asserted and assured. Survivors can work to stabilize their new identity and are able to universalize their experience in the subjectivity of their telling. The ability to record their story can empower survivors to speak and force us to confront realities unlike our own, requiring a recognition and adoption of responsibility on the part of the listener.[54]

During enslavement, survivors' previously held identities are irrevocably altered, and they continue to bear that loss in liberation so that there is no real transition from slavery to freedom. Instead, their enslaved consciousness continues in their freedom. In order to survive this, they become multiple selves and so narrative becomes a form of survival in

---

[49] Victoria Pitts, *In the Flesh: The Cultural Politics of Body Modification* (London: Palgrave Macmillan, 2003), 6.
[50] Sergio A. Lussana, *My Brother Slaves: Friendship, Masculinity, and Resistance in the Antebellum South* (Lexington: University Press of Kentucky, 2016), 55.
[51] David Lisak, "The Psychological Impact of Sexual Abuse: Content Analysis of Interviews with Male Survivors," *Journal of Traumatic Stress* 7, no. 4 (1994): 525–48.
[52] Christopher Hager, *Word by Word*, 44.
[53] Sam Durrant, *Postcolonial Narratives*, 9.
[54] Sam Durrant, *Postcolonial Narratives*, 3.

## The Construction and Reconstruction of Survivor Identities 87

itself where survivors achieve meaning, become visible, and expose the conflicts they continue to wrestle with.[55]

The struggle to craft their identity post enslavement is very clearly expressed in slave narratives. The inevitable conflicts between acknowledging and owning their history and creating a new self to divorce from trauma and imposed identity will be the same things framing that new self-creation. Identifying with slavery, placing a label on what has happened to them is very important to survivors. Identifying with a body of individuals who have also emerged from enslavement, to have a community of survivors, diminishes their isolation. The ability to share or locate their experiences with other survivors reduces feelings of shame and grows a realization that their circumstances are not their fault. Their experiences, choices, and actions are placed in context. Further, by labelling what has happened to them, there is an external acknowledgement of the harm they suffered, they are no longer ghostly, but of the world and have presence.

This issue of labelling also has ramifications for our interpretation of what we mean by slavery in law and the lines we try to draw between slavery and practices *similar* to slavery. One survivor acknowledged to me they have felt insulted by others who label their experience slavery where the survivor felt there was no comparison to the circumstances and harm they had suffered. They see freedoms enjoyed that they did not have and contrasts in abuse that render some others' experiences to appear "less" than slavery. What this means for definition is that there is an argument to contract its scope to ensure we reflect these perceptions.

While survivors' experiences shape their internal landscape and they cannot dissociate from their experiences, many do manage to grow beyond them. There is, however, an internal tendency for the reader to look for growth, an element of our search for happy endings. However, for a smaller number of individuals, their condition in slavery is all they know, or they are so irreparably harmed that they are either drawn back into slavery or they remain "free" but in the same profession. In other words, for many, the psychological effects of enslavement mean they are still enslaved, as they are unable to gain emotional freedom or identify as anything other than a free slave. For example, Alina was forced into sexual slavery. She was subsequently deported having been imprisoned for prostitution and on return to

---

[55] Michel Foucault, *The Archaeology of Knowledge*, trans. A. M. Sheridan Smith (New York: Pantheon, 1972), 216.

her home country was unable to extract herself from her previous circumstances: "I came back without any money ... everybody was treating me as if I were a prostitute, saying bad words. My life has changed since that time. Now you see me here in the street. I have become a real prostitute."[56] Alina chooses the word "real" to distinguish between her enslavement and her working as prostitute, implying the latter involves choice and that she retains some income and has some freedom and control over her life and choices. However, to what degree do we see this as genuine choice? Cultural attitudes to her were that she was essentially a ruined woman; her role in freedom was established for her by her community. The brief opportunity for her to create an alternate reality was quickly eradicated by societal labelling and she was therefore unable to divorce herself from some aspects of the identity imposed by her enslavement.

Slave narratives repeatedly evidence the consequences of strong prejudice, discrimination, and racism, which are still echoed today for many survivors of slavery. The trauma of slavery, the realities of freedom, and the risk of re-enslavement (whether actual or perceived) destabilize the feeling of freedom and confine the space for identity reformation. In several narratives, there is a link between slavery and spatialization. In this respect, survivors can feel as if they are a ghost population during their enslavement and in liberation.[57] The freedom to tell their story, to conceptualize a different or greater story rather than just that of their enslavement, can provide the opportunity to locate and assert a pre-enslaved identity. It acknowledges the effect of trauma on a newly constructed identity, enabling survivors to reject and accept what has gone before and dispel idealized expectations about who they are.[58] In effect they are exercising control over their life story; a freedom that could not be realized during enslavement, or even in many cases over their past. It is a means of asserting their presence in the world so that they are no longer spatialized.

Christine Stark states that post discovery she felt that "Our voices are non-existent ... we are dirty, ruined, despised .... The intensity of my emotions does not match up to a normal life."[59] There is so much expressed within this short sentence. When Christine describes her voice

---

[56] Kevin Bales and Zoe Trodd, *To Plead Our Own Cause*, 126.
[57] Abigail Ward, "Servitude and Slave Narratives: Tracing 'New Slaveries' in Mende Nazer's *Slave* and Zadie Smith's *The Embassy of Cambodia*," *Wasafari* 31, no. 3 (2016): 45.
[58] Alexandra Lutnick, *Domestic Minor Sex Trafficking: Beyond Victims and Villains* (New York: Columba University Press, 2016), 97.
[59] Kevin Bales and Zoe Trodd, *To Plead Our Own Cause*, 101.

as nonexistent, this interacts with earlier testimony where she describes herself as silent and numb. It is as if her spatialization, her "nonexistence," not only relates to her ability to give voice or testimony but also relates to her self-identity or her humanity. Christine's view of herself is created by her captors and by cultural perceptions which are transposed to her consciousness. She is a construct of indoctrination by her captors from birth, and, after enslavement, to societal attitudes over the acts she was forced to carry out, so she believes she is "dirty, ruined, despised." There are no soft edges to these words; in freedom, Christine must fight to overcome cultural perceptions and her own ingrained self-perception in order to forge a positive identity for herself. The tenor of Christine's narrative here is echoed over and over again in contemporary narratives. Here lies the contrast of freedom in fact versus freedom in form. The complexity of freedom for survivors extends far beyond the release from the condition of slavery, and the reality of freedom is often far from its imagined state and tainted with trauma.

It is known that our location in our community is important to our individual identity.[60] When survivors are rejected and stigmatized by their community it can have serious consequences for their growth and to their ability to grasp freedom in full. Jill explains that she was so emotionally stunned and lost in her own world that she "didn't exist as anything more than a slave, except [she] was an escaped slave."[61] Jill's identity therefore remained utterly tied to that of a slave, but she now sees herself as an "illegitimate" slave, one that has not been fully liberated, for whom recapture was a very real prospect, and who feels her freedom to be illicit. Despite there being no legal foundation to her enslavement, the cultural tenor of her situation was that it was her freedom that was unsound, not her enslavement. The consequences of freedom for Jill were homelessness, depression and anorexia, shame, fear, and self-destructive behavior. Survivors may therefore never recover fully from their experiences, and so they remain psychologically bound by their enslavement. This is emulated where individuals remain in their profession post enslavement. For example, Dina "chose" to remain in prostitution because "life has become this way now."[62]

---

[60] Jill Marshall, *Human Rights Law and Personal Identity* (University of Leicester School of Law Legal Studies Research Paper Series, Research Paper No. 14-30, November 11, 2014), 168.
[61] Jill Marshall, *Human Rights Law*, 175.
[62] Dina in Kevin Bales and Zoe Trodd, *To Plead Our Own Cause*, 106.

## THE EFFECT OF SURVIVOR GUILT
## ON THE RECONSTRUCTION OF THE SELF

The issue of survivor guilt is a serious one and comes across in countless narratives, as so many survivors lose families, children, and friends. In many cases, they have witnessed the murder of their siblings and parents, or their abuse before losing contact with them completely. Survivors carry the guilt of watching others succumb to slavery, of being impotent to protect them, or of being forced to enslave others,[63] reiterating and perpetuating the "sisterhoods" created between those enslaved. They also feel guilt for surviving where others have not. All these sorrows are difficult to reconcile with life and are carried with them in freedom.[64] The potential for individuals to therefore categorize themselves in survival as weak, powerless, morally uncertain, damaged, and undeserving is clear.

Where survivors speak of their plans for the future, it can be seen that survivor guilt plays a significant role in their choices going forward. The loss and guilt create a need to construct new families from friends or work, or to find families even where those families were abusive. The survivor as carer is also a common outcome of enslavement, with individuals working with other survivors, supporting and educating children, working as teachers, with NGOs, and working as counsellors – roles that afford a way to deal with internal pain and guilt, and offer them a valuable and meaningful place in the post enslavement world. For example, Kavita's slaveholders tried to break her bond with her sister and isolate them from each other. Tied in corner she witnessed her ten-year-old sister's torture, unable to protect her or talk to her. She does not know what happened to her sister and has lost contact, but now cares for child survivors at a shelter, helping to educate and support them. Despite the fact she is aware she had no physical way to help her sister, the role she has assumed is as much a way to deal with her internal pain and guilt, as it is to find a valuable place in the post enslavement world.[65]

---

[63] See for example the narratives of Nu, Tamara, Alana, and Milena in Kevin Bales and Zoe Trodd, *To Plead Our Own Cause*, 91, 128, 131, and 132, respectively.

[64] Theodor W. Adorno, *Meditations on Metaphysics from Negative Dialektik*, trans. Simon Jarvis (Frankfurt: Suhrkamp, 1966), 4–5. https://readinggroupcork.files.wordpress.com/2012/07/simon-jarvis-translation-of-tw-adorno-_meditations-on-metaphysics-word-97.pdf

[65] See for example the narratives of Rita and Kavita, Kevin Bales, and Zoe Trodd, *To Plead Our Own Cause*.

Sina Vann's narrative exposes the complexities of assuming a different identity and of the drive to care for others very well. In her narrative she states:

> This is not Sina from childhood, but a different Sina. This is different Sina, that people have helped me to become who I am ... like I said earlier, the previous Sina has died. This is a different Sina; the brothel owner has shaped me. My childhood dream has been destroyed. There is only hurt and revenge.
>
> My hurt has become [the] strength for me to help others to not fall victims like me. Up until now I cannot forget my past. No matter how far I go, it cannot be separated from me. So that is something that I get advantage of to help others. When I help a victim, I feel happy.
>
> I am very happy that they are free. I'm very happy that I have destroyed the work of those people.[66]

Education can also be a catalyst for personal development and the realization of freedom. Salma states to learn things and go to school is "liberty" for her,[67] and Helia recounts a brief encounter with schooling whilst enslaved in therapeutic terms, associating her three days of schooling with her slaveholders' absence, and twice describing the school as "under the little shade house,"[68] a phrase which is naïve in its imagery, and which conjures a sense of a protective embrace in a cool and calm environment. Education is widely accepted as coexisting with the rights of communities and of unlocking the ability to enjoy all other human rights. Depriving individuals of education and denying them their literacy ensures they remain unable to read any support information available and makes it difficult for individuals to conceive of a different life, thereby ensuring their continued submission.

The ability to engage with education gives survivors power over the self and reveals the lack of rights of others to exercise such a denial over them, which itself is symbolic of the denial of their natural right to freedom. This realization is expressed and implied in many narratives and supported by the repeated accounts of survivors' motivation post enslavement to gain an education for themselves or for their children. In seeking out an education, survivors recover their autonomy, self-confidence, and the means to create a life after slavery. Not only does this provide an avenue for participation in the antislavery agenda, education essentially affords a stronger sense, and form of freedom,

---

[66] Laura T. Murphy, *Survivors of Slavery*, 238 and 242.
[67] Kevin Bales and Zoe Trodd, *To Plead Our Own Cause*, 223.
[68] Laura T. Murphy, *Survivors of Slavery*, 63.

perhaps to the extent that any abstract or idealistic view of freedom is more likely to be realized.[69] In many narratives, survivors are driven toward education in the hope of preventing their re-enslavement, of providing the basis for a different future, and of educating others at risk. Education is also therefore a means of resistance and activism, a rejection of the circumstances that led them into slavery, and a means of recording and making known what was done to them. To Val, education was key.

### REFORMULATED IDENTITIES AND PURPOSE: SURVIVORS AS LEADERS AND ACTIVISTS

Acts of self-appraisal as are carried out when providing a life story can reiterate shame and guilt, but also pride and self-esteem,[70] as survivors' disclosure of trauma serves to educate others and empowers them to transition from the passive to active survivor.[71] By associating with and asserting themselves as survivors rather than victims, individuals at once assume a dominant and purposive role. It is a means of claiming agency and a form of resistance and activism. Often their experiences have created a sense of permanent survival post enslavement, which can galvanize resistance and activism.

Shamere McKenzie is a well-known survivor activist who was simply trying to find a way to pay her college tuition when she met her trafficker. He promised her she could make money dancing, but instead he forced her into sexual slavery. In her narratives she says:

> It took me five years to start speaking about my experience. As I travel throughout the country and speak to various people on the issue, I now realize that I went through the trauma not for myself, but for someone else .... I believe I am the voice for those who are free but have not yet the courage to speak up. We all have a story. What are you doing about yours. I am determined to use my story to make a difference in the life of someone else, leaving a legacy in this world.[72]

---

[69] On the value of education to the eradication of slavery, see for example Marion Weiner, "Child Labour in Developing Countries: The Indian Case," *International Journal of Children's Rights* 121, no. 2 (1994); and Amartya Sen, "More Than 100 Million Women Are Missing," *New York Review of Books* 37, no. 2 (1999).
[70] Mardi J. Horowitz, "Self-Identity Theory and Research Methods," *Journal of Research Practice* 8, no. 2 (2012): 5.
[71] Linda Alcoff and Laura Grey, "Survivor Discourse: Transgression or Recuperation?" *Journal of Women in Culture & Society* 18, no. 2 (1993): 262.
[72] Shamere McKenzie in Laura T. Murphy, *Survivors of Slavery*, 53.

Christine Stark explains this in terms of fighting a war, and as a battle of life and death, and her narrative clearly portrays the points made in the above chapter and how she has been driven to action in survival:

> It is only recently that I have been free from their sexual and physical abuse, and to be honest, I don't always know what to do with myself. I was beaten and raped, or at least verbally assaulted, virtually every day of my life. The intensity of my emotions does not match up to a normal life. Other survivors talk about this, too. Even though we escaped, we live in the pimp's world. We have flashbacks and night tremors ... our world view is one of war, constant rapes, and beatings. We may escape but we will always be isolated, we will never be part of society. We know too much, we have seen too much. The world does not want to acknowledge the truth of women's lives ....
>
> I escaped the pimps. It took me twenty years to do it, but I did it .... I want to be free, and I want my sisters to be free. And I will be free, and I will help women and girls escape or I will die trying. I have been in a sort of exile myself, on the run, surviving, remembering, waiting for them to kill me, gathering my strength. I have been outsmarting them, and speaking out to help other woman and girls ...
>
> It is difficult to know what to do with yourself when all you have known is chaos and destruction and the streets. You're not good company, you're not polite or talking or thinking about socially acceptable things. You're talking about your life. You're talking about the lives of other women and girls who are still kept captive, who are still being hurt, who may not survive. You feel an urgency, a bond deeper than blood to the very women and girls they tried to make you hate ...
>
> There are many women, strong women, brave women all across the world who are rising up to meet and to end the tidal wave of male violence against women. We escape, we organise and we educate and we go back down into the trenches to pull out our sisters. This is war, a battle of life and death. A battle that women must win ... the pimps do not know state or national boundaries; women in battle must not know them either. We must be on the lookout for each other. The brothels of the world house all the women in the world. We must go into those brothels, search one another out. We must break down the doors, beat back the pimps, and get out the girls and women held in cages. As I go back, back into brothels and porn houses, I will be on the lookout for you. I hope I will never find you there, but if I do you have my word I will lend you a hand.[73]

Through her narrative, she controls how she is seen, and how she is represented, and utilizes her writing as call to activism. The conflicted and dissociated self-concepts of survivor and victim, slave and free are laced throughout, and her narrative is an important site of struggle.

Again, Christine also reflects on her enslavement in the present tense, saying "And I will be free" reflecting the emotional enslavement that

---

[73] Christine Stark in Kevin Bales and Zoe Trodd, *To Plead Our Own Cause*, 102.

continues in survival and which has been highlighted in other chapters. She also associates with and creates for herself multiple communities, so while she still feels isolated and unable to be part of society, she associates with sisterhoods (plural). She clearly conceptualizes a community of girls and women either in or survivors of sexual slavery, while at the same time drawing on women worldwide as an activist community.

Slavery is the denial of selfhood affecting who those enslaved are and how they become. In liberation, and after years of control and denial, survivors have to suddenly frame a new reality and construct a new identity. Unable to reconcile their pre-enslavement construction of the self with who they are after their enslavement (or where individuals held only a slave identity having been born into it), survivors are left with significant challenges to selfhood that can destabilize freedom and inhibit recovery. The othering they experience in slavery – the renaming, shaming, labelling, destruction of documentation, denial of cultural origins, and prohibition of faith practices – leave survivors adjusting to a liberation where what is "normal" is no longer known. Enslavement brings with it a double shame. The shame of slavery while in it (submission, impotence, the loss of identity, of genderhood and childhood, shame for acts they were forced to carry out), and shame of slavery in liberation (feelings of worthlessness, the projection of social perceptions of what is shameful onto survivors, and survivor guilt). Again, there is no clean transition from slavery to freedom. The binary does not exist, because there is no emotional freedom in liberation, and the construction of the new and liberated self cannot be built without the emotional marks of their experiences in slavery.

One means by which survivors reconcile these complex issues surrounding identity is through narratives. Narratives are a way for survivors to present a reconstructed self to the world. They are a means by which survivors can place their experiences in the past while at the same time acknowledging their impact for the future. And a means by which they can gain control over their story and how they are seen, presenting more than what is shameful or sensationalistic, asserting themselves as survivors rather than victims, and as more than passive individuals, but as activists, educators, liberators, and carers.

# 4

## Bearing Witness

### *Trauma in Contemporary Slave Narratives*

Trauma: Origin. Late 17th century: from Greek, literally "wound."

Woven through the body of existing survivor narratives, and in my interviews with survivors, the repeated desire is for survivors to have voice, to be heard, to make people understand what has been done to them, and to galvanize action. Being heard, however, is not simply to communicate as accurately as possible the experiences and effects of enslavement. For survivors, there is an urge to have their stories witnessed, and to bear witness to other survivors' trauma and deaths. The need to bear witness, on both the part of the listener and the teller, has also been proven over decades of trauma studies to be crucial to meaningful survival. Telling moves the survivor from passive experienced symptoms to an active understanding and retelling of what happened.[1] Growth requires individuals to confront their grief, and a fundamental part of that process is bearing witness to their experiences and having them witnessed by others.

In his personal narrative, James Kofi Annan reveals that: "One of my greatest challenges is getting people to gain insight into what it means, practically, to be a victim of trafficking. No matter how crafty and skilful a writer or an artist may be, nothing on paper can parallel the experience for its length, intensity and emotions."[2] So while it is virtually impossible

---

[1] Judith Herman, "The Politics of Trauma: An Interview with Judith Herman," in *Listening to Trauma: Conversations with Leaders in the Theory & Treatment of Catastrophic Experience*, ed. Cathy Caruth (Baltimore: John Hopkins University Press, 2014), 141.

[2] James Kofi Annan in Laura T. Murphy, *Survivors of Slavery: Modern-Day Slave Narratives* (New York: Columbia University Press, 2014), 191.

for survivors to completely express the immensity and consequences of their experiences, it is only by enabling a full telling and engaging with the detail that we can most achieve that understanding. The most meaningful way of witnessing is to take our minds and feelings through what survivors have been through and allow it in. It is the meeting of survivor and proxy, not just the inactive listener that constitutes the witness.[3]

Reading people's life stories, engaging with the detail and the complexity of these narratives, is to place their experiences in our consciousness and ask us to attend to the meaning and effect of survivors' experiences. The material of the lived, recalled, and surrendered past puts memory to use both as a technique and a subject. Even where it is unfaithful to the past, it can be a creative refiguring of the living present and a summary reconstruction of how the present came to be. It is a subjective truth that we can take for what it richly is – a "function of present consciousness."[4] Through the detail of their telling, survivors' experiences are made visceral, connected to our known world. They compel our empathy, drawing out our own emotional memories of grief, loss, pain, humiliation, discrimination, and abuse. They also force us to understand slavery as more than a summary of "types" and sorrowful practices that are so easily abstracted or far removed from our own experiences.

### EXPRESSING THE DETAIL OF TRAUMA

During their enslavement, survivors have suffered inhuman treatment and have in many cases been treated like (or worse) than animals. Ajok, forced into sexual slavery, talks of being passed between soldiers, being forced to live together with other women "like cattle" and being made to live in a cattle pen, reinforcing her belief that she was disposable.[5] Many survivors are denied food and only permitted to eat leftovers. They are forced to sleep outside or with livestock, or to sleep on floors, in storage rooms, and in cupboards. The physical mistreatment they suffer often leaves them with lasting psychological and physical trauma. Many of the effects and behaviors discussed above are symptomatic of complex

---

[3] Cathy Caruth, *Listening to Trauma: Conversations with Leaders in the Theory & Treatment of Catastrophic Experience* (Baltimore: John Hopkins University Press, 2014), 18.
[4] Christopher Hager, *Word by Word: Emancipation and the Act of Writing* (Cambridge, MA, and London: Harvard University Press, 2013), 264.
[5] Kevin Bales and Zoe Trodd, eds., *To Plead Our Own Cause Personal Stories by Today's Slaves* (New York: Cornell University Press, 2008), 34.

posttraumatic stress disorder (C-Ptsd). complex posttraumatic stress disorder differs from the recognized definition that currently appears for posttraumatic stress disorder, as C-Ptsd addresses the circumstances of multiple traumas throughout the lifetime rather than a single acute trauma. Symptoms are wide ranging and not all survivors will experience the full range, however, an analysis of the body of narratives demonstrates the following: Emotionally, survivors experience profound sadness, anger, depression, resentment, severe anhedonia (loss of interest in previously rewarding or enjoyable behavior), fear, and hopelessness. Cognitively they can experience a dulling of memory, hysteria, mental breakdowns, regression, flashbacks, "operative thinking" (an emphasis on the mundane and severe impairment of capacity for wish-fulfillment), and dependence, symptoms that are common in those with C-Ptsd.[6]

Physically, survivors suffer broken limbs, scarring, chronic pain, anorexia, malnourishment, genital mutilation, and an inability to bear children. Trauma studies of other groups, such as holocaust survivors and survivors of armed conflict, also reveal effects such as twitching, hypertension, an increased risk of heart disease, and a high mortality rate that will likely apply to survivors of slavery, but which aren't revealed in the narratives. In addition to these, I have observed in my own interviews the effects of isolation, alienation, feelings of spectrality, and an inability to regulate emotions, which is displayed as a persistent shifting back and forth between sadness and forgiveness, to anger, aggression, frustration, and emotional detachment within the same interview.

Some survivors will also have developed a substance dependence that complicates survival; addiction can be purposefully created as a means of control by the slaveholder, leaving survivors to deal with addiction in the aftermath. However, some survivors turn to substance dependence as a form of self-medication as a way of coping with the pain of their trauma, either to numb their misery, or from self-loathing. My findings evidence that sexually exploited women in particular take to gambling, alcohol, and/or drugs during their enslavement in order to cope with the trauma of repeated rape and the hopelessness of their situation (often encouraged and provided by their slaveholders because it makes them

---

[6] See generally Judith Herman, *Trauma and Recovery: The Aftermath of Violence – From Domestic Abuse to Political Terror* (New York: Basic Books, 2015), and Henry Krystal, "Trauma and Aging: A Thirty-Year Follow-Up," in *Trauma: Explorations in Memory*, ed. Cathy Caruth (Baltimore and London: The John Hopkins University Press, 1995), 79.

more pliable). In survival, they can develop or will maintain these addictions in order to numb the trauma of their experiences. For those forced into sexual slavery, there are the additional consequences of genital mutilation (both male and female) and disease (including AIDS, pelvic inflammatory disease, hepatitis, gonorrhea, syphilis among others). Genital mutilation and untreated disease can lead to severe physical and psychological consequences for the survivor, including an inability to bear children in the future. Many enslaved individuals also suffer forced abortion, self-abortion, and have been made to abandon children born during their enslavement.[7]

In the effort to control their world, to escape their past, survivors struggle with the difficulties of maintaining constructive patterns of behavior. Nu was brought up by distant relatives in Thailand, but on reaching puberty she was raped and pimped out by the son of the family she lived with. She ran away at age 15 and started working as a prostitute. She was not earning enough money and went to an agent who promised her waitressing work in Japan. On arrival, she was told she had incurred a heavy debt, that her food, rent, and expenses would be added to it, and that she must work as a prostitute. She lived in total confinement in poor conditions, with no heating and no warm water. She was regularly beaten and suffered extreme sexual violence. She reveals that if women and girls were disobedient, they would be sent out to "known sadistic clients ... and girls became very traumatized. Some behaved as if they were raving mad."[8] Most of the women took drugs or drank alcohol before working, and Nu said she could only do her work "when she was high." The drugs and alcohol were supplied by the brothel owner and added to her debt. She witnessed forced abortions and a number of other symptoms as a result of the work they were forced to do, including:

Stomach aches, fevers, injuries, nervousness, hysteria, emotional disturbances, mental breakdowns, including suicides. Some girls got drunk and urinated and vomited all over, and the mama-san increased their debts as a penalty. Others

---

[7] See for example Kevin Bales and Zoe Trodd, *To Plead Our Own Cause*, Sanije at 56, and Joy at 171–72: "The first time I was pregnant was in 2000. Johnson asked me to abort. I didn't know how to do it, but he gave me something to drink. And when I drank it, I miscarried then in February 2001, I was pregnant again. He said I had to do what I did before, but I said 'no, I don't want to do that anymore.' It was very painful. He said that if I didn't take the drink he would use a knife to cut my stomach. He was very serious. He said if I didn't want to drink what he gave me before, he would force me to do it." Inez also recounts forced abortions at 183.
[8] Kevin Bales and Zoe Trodd, *To Plead Our Own Cause*, 94

who took drugs got aggressive. We were under constant pressure and we often fought, screamed, and punched one another. There was also a lot of peer bonding as we only had one another to depend on.

[She explains] I feel ashamed about being in prostitution, but I can't change my past. I haven't told my present boyfriend about Japan. I feel embarrassed when people look at me. I think they do so because they know I was a prostitute. I talk loud and rudely. I must take drugs even now, after being so long in prostitution. It makes me feel strong. Society does not accept us. Only women in prostitution won't look down on me and can understand me.[9]

Nu mentions the difficulty of living in a world in which she feels isolated. She is open about her ongoing addiction, and that she talks loudly and rudely – a particularly strong violation of Thai social norms.

Jill ran away as a teenager to escape sexual and physical abuse. Homeless and scared, she was lured into "rape and snuff" circles by a charismatic man named Bruce. She was forced to do "disgusting, humiliating things that have had a devastating effect on my mind, my body, and my soul."[10] When she was finally rescued, she found herself trying to adjust to a life where she was suffering severe emotional trauma and was "free but with no place to go and no one to turn to."[11] Explaining in recovery the consequences of her abuse, she says:

Emotionally, I was still stunned, lost in my own world, trying to readjust to a life that suddenly left me free but with no place to go and no one to turn to. Sleep was filled with nightmares, daytime flashbacks and raging paranoia of being located by Bruce. After three years of eating dog food and being forced to beg for it, I was unaccustomed to eating anything normal and struggled with anorexia. In essence, I still didn't exist as anything more than a slave, except I was an escaped slave.

It has been more than a decade since then. In many ways, I've recovered, having eventually regained enough sanity to get a job and hold it. The physical injuries either healed or scarred, and I learned to compensate. But having survived this experience doesn't mean I've become safe from it.

Depression is still part of my life, as is shame, fear, and a strong drive for self-destruction. I still feel like I'm crazy and fear that I'm a burden to my friends, a failure as an employee, and that I'm destined to again be homeless, vulnerable, and alone …

I escaped without having any sexually transmitted diseases, but there were other serious consequences. My ability to have children was destroyed; my voice is a raspy shell of its former self from being choked with ropes, belts, hands. There are extensive and deep scars many places on my body. Emotionally, the effects are worse. Flashbacks, nightmares, and depression have been constant

---

[9] Kevin Bales and Zoe Trodd, *To Plead Our Own Cause*, 95 and 97.
[10] Kevin Bales and Zoe Trodd, *To Plead Our Own Cause*, 179.
[11] Kevin Bales and Zoe Trodd, *To Plead Our Own Cause*, 179.

battles since my escape. It has taken a great deal of therapy and support from friends for me to evolve to a point where I can move on. It has also seriously impacted my ability to have and maintain relationships. Until recently, my relationships were dominated by failure. Many "romantic" relationships turned out to be with abusive men. In the rare instances that I found a quality person who did love me, I usually destroyed the relationship with my actions. It took many years for me to de-program the need to self-destruct. Recently, I've evolved to the point where I am no longer seeking suicide through self-destruction. Instead, I'm working on living ... maintaining the friendships and relationships with the really awesome people who are in my life now. I have some really wonderful, supportive friends who I love and who I believe love me. A great deal of therapy has gone into believing that I'm worth these quality friends and can maintain the relationships. I've hurt too many people in the past through my low self-esteem and self-destruction. But going forward, it's my goal to see beyond the horrors of my past and fatalistic programming and, instead, focus on the future and on being authentic to myself ... and on a commitment to living.[12]

Jill's narrative shows the self-destructive patterns of seeking out those who would emulate her mistreatment, and her retreat from positive influences and experiences demonstrates the desire to avoid even greater hurt from the potential loss of anything good, where the not having is better than the loss. Her view of what she perceives to be sufficient recovery is really no more than just enough to function, to regain "enough" sanity, to hold down a job, to learn to compensate for her trauma. But she still feels unsafe, fearful, shameful, and vulnerable. Rather than being able to assume her freedom fully, she explains she has had to "evolve" within it, so that she no longer seeks out suicide through self-destruction. Instead, she gradually adapted, carrying and learning to live with the burden of her memories and symptoms. Toward the end of her narrative, she assumes a purposeful commitment to truth and living that will likely continue to shift and destabilize, in a constant battle with the self.

## PROCESSING TRAUMA AND RESULTANT CONFUSED STATES OF THINKING

The struggle to live with trauma is compounded by an inability to understand what caused survivors to be targeted for exploitation and abuse, often resulting in self-blame for being duped or persuaded by false promises of love or of legitimate work. Survivors can't understand why misfortune falls on them; although they rationally understand the circumstances

---

[12] Jill in Kevin Bales and Zoe Trodd, *To Plead Our Own Cause*, 179–80.

that led them there, they still struggle to understand or accept that it happened to them. Choti states "what can I tell you? Life was just so traumatic. The night that my houses burned down, not only were my eyes weeping, my very soul was torn, shattered. It was almost like I was ripped apart. Each time I look back, there is something inside me that is unbelievable."[13] Healing from trauma requires survivors to accept what has happened to them. But in order to accept their past, they must try to understand it. The need to identify why they ended up in slavery at some point requires survivors to acknowledge that there was a "why," that there was a justification for their mistreatment. However, the process of trying to empathize or understand their abuser's perspective or motivation, leads to the realization that there can be no acceptable justification for their slaveholders' actions. This creates a vicious cycle of anger and a rejection of acceptance, which inhibits healing.[14]

Survivors also express anger because of a lack of agency and rights that caused them to be disempowered before, during, and after enslavement, and they express anger at what they have lost. For example, Mende Nazer expresses anger at being pulled away from her family and not knowing whether they were alive or dead. Her story and feelings are complex: Having been taken following a raid on her village that killed her mother and brother, she attempted to adapt to her enslavement by formulating a new concept of family in her desire to recreate what she had lost, viewing her owners and their children as a replacement family. On being told she was moving to London she felt upset because she would miss the children in her slaveholder's household, but this led her to the realization that she had purposefully forgotten her own family in order to avoid confronting the pain. She had created a proxy family for herself from people who could not give her the love and loyalty her real family would represent. The realization of that loss led her to feel grief, shame, and anger:

… and I, for my part, began to forget my own family. I'm ashamed to say this now, but after I had been with Rahab four years or so, my memories just began to fade. Rahab had told me when I first arrived that I would stay with her for the rest of my life. I'd started to really believe her. And if I did ever think about my wonderful, living family, it just caused me grief and pain. For all I knew, they had all died in the raid. It was too horrible to think about. So I just blanked it out completely.

---

[13] Choti in Laura T. Murphy, *Survivors of Slavery: Modern-Day Slave Narratives* (New York: Columbia University Press, 2014), 163.
[14] Henry Krystal, "Trauma and Aging," 83.

I had started to tell myself that my future, such as it was, now lay here, in Khartoum. I had a new family now, albeit that I was their slave and they were my masters. There was no one that I could turn to talk about the past – to remember the laughter and the love, to reaffirm my true identity. I had nothing tangible to remind me of my life as a Nuba, as not one single thing had survived the raid.

The news that I was being sent abroad reawakened my love for my family. I had been sleepwalking through a nightmare. I had been clutching onto a false hope – that here in Khartoum was my new home. But now I was simply to be passed on, like a useful household appliance. The only place where I had ever found real love and loyalty was with my real family. Somehow I had to find them. So much time had already gone by. I didn't even know if they had survived the raids. The last thoughts coursing through my mind in the early hours were of anger and escape – and the hope of being reunited with my family.[15]

Mende initially represses her memories of her own family and attempts to recreate some semblance of love and family through the children of her slaveholders. Her identity was stripped away through the burning of her village, the murder of her mother and brother, her mistreatment, and the taking of cultural beads that she wore and which were her only remaining link to her culture, family, and community. Survival required her to adapt and construct ways to fill her emotional needs, and to replace what was lost from any possible source. When she was rejected from this fantasy, discarded like a chattel to be transported to the UK, the realization that this was not family was shattering for her. It is telling that later in her narrative she tries a second time to hope for a recreation of family through her "owners" in the UK, and was confused and conflicted about this. Although she was being treated more kindly, and she felt she was being "taken in like one of the family," she was having to work harder than in Khartoum and part of her "felt like I was still being treated like a slave" despite it being clear that was her position in the household.[16] In her narrative, she continues to shift from security to insecurity, trying to build a sense of normalization and family, while at the same time struggling with the realization that she was enslaved and owned.[17]

The added complexity of survival is that seemingly innocuous events can trigger traumatic memories creating a kind of continuous trauma even in survival. Even happy events can remind survivors of what was lost. Studies in the way the brain is affected by trauma show damage to

---

[15] Mende Nazer and Damien Lewis, *Slave: The True Story of a Girl's Lost Childhood and Her Fight for Survival* (London: Virago, 2010), 181 and 201.
[16] Mende Nazer and Damien Lewis, *Slave*, 255.
[17] See for example Mende Nazer and Damien Lewis, *Slave*, 260.

the function of thalamus, which takes in sensory information and motor signals, and sends them to the cerebral cortex which puts it all together. It is the integrating function of the brain. Where the thalamus breaks down, as with severe trauma, this creates disassociation, meaning survivors continue to have emotions without context. They have no context as to how the terror they feel in the moment of being triggered relates to the past or present. In her narrative, Beatrice describes in the present tense events now 20 years past, and says "If I close my eyes, the memories of pain take me back to a time when I felt alone. It happened two decades ago, but it feels as if it were happening right now."[18] In these moments, survivors lose symbolic capacity; they are able to recognize they feel this way because of traumatic experiences but are unable to dispel their feelings and react as if the trauma we happening at that moment.[19] Each trigger then creates a new trauma, so the original trauma becomes just one part of a continuum of traumas and overwhelming reactions to seemingly innocuous events. Further, repetitive exposure essentially etches those memories more and more powerfully into the brain.[20] Although with help these imprints can be changed, in many cases this continuum of trauma is an everyday reality and many survivors do not have access to the kind of support needed to alter those imprints.

### GENDER AND TRAUMA

There are also potential differences between the experiences of men and women. There is a recognition that women suffer an underlying insidious trauma by dint of the fact that they are women, and through practices that are not overtly violent or threatening to bodily well-being at the given moment, but which do violence to the soul. For example, the persistent expectation that rape or abuse may occur, which manifests as hypervigilance and numbness to friendly overtures.[21] Human experience is often framed as meaning the "male human experience" and what is normal is placed in the context of white, young, able-bodied, middle-class, cis, Christian men.[22] Patriarchal systems are often sustained by force and

---

[18] Kevin Bales and Zoe Trodd, *To Plead Our Own Cause*, 161.
[19] Bessel van der Kolk, "The Body Keeps the Score: An Interview with Bessel van der Kolk," in Cathy Caruth, *Listening to Trauma*, 155–57.
[20] Bessel van der Kolk, *The Body Keeps the Score* (London: Penguin Books, 2015), 318.
[21] Laura S. Brown "Not Outside the Range: One Feminist Perspective on Psychic Trauma" in Cathy Caruth, *Trauma*, 107.
[22] Laura S. Brown "Not Outside the Range," 101.

terror, by custom and shaming, and maintained by economic power, and existing systems of dominance and subordination render women vulnerable to being groomed, trafficked, and sexually exploited.[23] This is reflected in the first Palermo Protocol where the particular vulnerability of women and children is explicitly recognized in the treaty title and in several of its articles.[24]

The unbalanced power relations between men and women continue to affect men and women's sexuality and reinforce the expression of the idea of men's unlimited access to women's bodies and sexuality in accordance with their economic and social power. It also entails the assumption that sexual needs are a kind of right that every (male) individual is entitled to.[25] The historical, generational assumption of ownership over women's bodies means that women's "private" traumatic experiences affect the way trauma is expressed by outsiders. For example, women's traumatic experiences can be devalued compared to others, particularly where sexual abuse has occurred. We also see the perpetuation of the myth of the willing victim in the perception of the "self-defeating woman" who is assumed to have contributed to or chosen her exploitation, whereas the survivor of enslavement in the agriculture sector in pursuance of employment to support their families is viewed as innocent.[26] This means that for women, particularly those subjected to sexual slavery, there is an increased risk of a minimization of their experiences and in the way they are valued. In some cases, survivors start to believe what others project onto them, compounding self-blame and feelings of worthlessness, and having the potential to cause a denial of trauma and inhibit telling.

However, my findings also suggest that male sexual slavery is likely to be more prevalent and more hidden than currently understood. Men are unlikely to be identified as having been sexually enslaved because they are more likely to be engaged in several types of slavery, for example enslaved in the agriculture or construction sectors, or subjected to forced criminality or domestic servitude, while also being forced into sex for commercial purposes. This was the case with Tung, who was arrested

---

[23] Cathy Caruth, *Listening to Trauma*, 146.
[24] See for example the Protocol to Prevent, Suppress and Punish Trafficking in Persons Especially Women and Children, supplementing the United Nations Convention against Transnational Organized Crime 2000.
[25] European Parliament, Directorate General for Internal Policies Policy Department C: Citizens' Rights and Constitutional Affairs: Gender Equality, "Sexual Exploitation and Prostitution and Its Impact on Gender Equality" (2014) PE 493.040 at 19.
[26] Laura S. Brown, "Not Outside the Range," 102.

for forced cannabis farming but who had also experienced domestic servitude as well as sexual slavery – moving between forms of enslavement throughout the latter half of his enslavement. It was only when he was imprisoned and met other men that had experienced the same, and worse, that he felt able to reveal his sexual enslavement. Current Global Slavery Index estimates are that only 1 percent of those in sexual slavery are male, but anecdotal evidence from the narrative corpus, my own interviews, and from NGOs, indicates that this is disproportionately representative of female sexual slavery.[27]

A report by the NGO Hestia notes that 8 percent of males to whom they gave support had been sexually exploited. This gap in our understanding of the prevalence of male sexual slavery has ramifications for the support provided to survivors to enable them to realize full freedom, and for our estimations of organized crime, hidden slavery, and the risks of re-enslavement. The report reveals that feelings of shame and humiliation about sexual slavery meant that male victims had more difficulty than women discussing intimacy. They also struggled to break out of masculine stereotypes, were unlikely to report the crime, and were less likely to receive support services for sexual exploitation compared to female victims.[28] One survivor, Juan, stated, "It is hard – every time I tell my story I feel people do not believe me because I am a man, and should not have fallen into this situation."[29] My findings also reveal that there is a correlative subconscious gender bias in identifying victims of sexual slavery that reinforces gender stereotypes of prostitution, with law enforcement assuming that women will have experienced sexual exploitation, and that men will not have.

## THE PROBLEM OF TELLING

The paradox of the need to be witnessed is that for many survivors their trauma is such that it can establish an inability to tell. The sheer horror of their experiences inhibits their ability to express, and in some cases acknowledge, their experiences. For example, Keith struggled to express

---

[27] www.alliance87.org/2017ge/modernslavery#!section=0
[28] Kevin Bales advises that from experience it is also transgender men in forced sexual exploitation that are woefully undercounted Kevin Bales, in conversation, June 25, 2018. However, this is not revealed by the narratives analyzed and did not arise in my own limited experiences with survivors and so was not examined in the main text.
[29] Hestia, *Underground Lives: The Reality of Modern Slavery in London* (2017), 17. www.hestia.org/Handlers/Download.ashx?IDMF=68f44ab0-fa94-49eb-ac4d-d4ae2b1f8586

emotion, and over 17 pages of narrative Val was only able to explain the detail of her exploitation in the following paragraphs, indicating that her exploitation had occurred over a much longer period:

There's a man abusing me and nobody's talking about it and he thinks he has the right because he's been told I'm his wife." So, I could, you know, I could continue doing whatever he wanted me to do without, you know, asking questions, and if I didn't do what he wanted he was, he was very, he was very violent ... but it was just this man who was constantly in my life and abused me, that I felt there was something *wrong*.

... I remember at some point I had refused to follow him because he had said I had to follow him to the forest where he was looking after some animals. He had given me something like jewellery and he told me never to remove it and he said, "as long as you have that you have to do what I want you to do." And he told me to follow him, and I refused. And he went and came back really drunk and when he came back, he was carrying a big stick, and he hit me on the head.

(Long pause) And then for me that was it. It was, I remember talking to my older sister and I said, because nobody even knew about all this stuff that was going on in the background with him saying I couldn't, you know I had to do everything I wanted him to do. And I remember telling my sister "I think one day this man will kill me."

The problem of telling is made worse by their own astonishment that they have survived, combined with a fear that others won't believe the enormity of their experiences, meaning the opportunity for witnessing has the potential to be lost. Often survivors will anticipate others' disbelief, repeating that they are not lying, asking "why would I lie"?[30] And hiding their trauma because "who would believe what we have to say"?[31]

A refusal to revisit the past is seen in many narratives and is more often a retreat from trauma while at the same time being confronted with its effects on a daily basis. Aida states:

I just want to forget everything because I really feel like dying inside when I remember my experiences in the movement. So, when I just don't want to remember the experiences, I take a breather and go outside. I just want to forget ... or else I'll go crazy. A soldier told me that in the movement I would just die without a future. They made me understand that I am still so young. That's really true. We're still so young to be in this struggle, and we end up not being able to follow the laws outside the movement. I just want to laugh. I am always crying because of my problem.[32]

---

[30] Dwain, as told to Andrea Nicholson, November 3, 2017. With thanks to Atleu.
[31] Kevin Bales and Zoe Trodd, *To Plead Our Own Cause*, 101.
[32] Kevin Bales and Zoe Trodd, *To Plead Our Own Cause*, 193.

This is sometimes seen in forcible attempts to deny or endure the pain "by pushing it deep down inside and trying to forget it ever happened,"[33] as if forgetting were a possibility. Zamira says "I don't want to talk anymore about that time. It was the worst period of my life. It is now past, and I have closed that door behind me ... my mother and I are now living together and trying to support ourselves."[34] However, they also may not want to be exposed in this way. Dwain explains it as follows:

I never used the word master but that's a whole different angle of slavery in itself isn't it? I was just referred to as "that boy" or they rang a bell, and that was my ... that's why I don't like school bells or any bells. Now you know why I don't like bells. And of course, most people would never ever believe that from me because I don't show it, I don't want to show it, and I simply don't want the pity for it. I'd rather if I told you, you were like "oh, that's a big shame, anyway, let's move on." You know, and that would be that. If I needed something from you to help me move on and that "oh here let's move on," and that would be that. I've slept since and I've slept for a reason, to try and forget what happened the day before, I can't get any of this out of my head as such, I've put them under a different sort of lock and keys and convincing myself that they've gone forever.

In telling, Dwain reveals seemingly innocuous things that are meaningful to him but which he would normally have kept to himself because of what they represent and the memories they conjure up (the bell). He wants to forget and self-anaesthetize through sleep and tries to place his memories under "lock and key" in his mind, but he recognizes that this is not possible and that he is "convincing" himself those memories are gone. The reality is that these events continue to play out in his mind. Fundamentally, he does not want to be pitied, his desire to move on is reflected in a rejection of his vulnerability and the vulnerability that others see in him. The numbing or retreat that we see in Dwain's narrative, and in many survivor narratives, is a type of defense mechanism that is a conscious or subconscious repression of trauma, and leading to isolation, denial, and a cessation of feeling. It reveals the centrality of the threat of death in slavery, the loss of future, and of the self, all of which are at the heart of the traumatic experience. Rather than a passive shutdown of memory, the numbing defense mechanism is an "active, persistent, violent refusal; an erasure,"[35] a psychic closing off akin to anesthesia.

---

[33] Kevin Bales and Zoe Trodd, *To Plead Our Own Cause*, 242.
[34] Kevin Bales and Zoe Trodd, *To Plead Our Own Cause*, 66.
[35] Dori Laub, "Truth and Testimony: The Process and the Struggle," *American Imago* 48, no. 1 (1991): 59.

Dissociation has been seen in other survivor groups, particularly in combat veterans with C-Ptsd. Studies with those other groups suggest trauma may produce long-lasting alterations in the regulation of natural substances having the effect of opiates within the central nervous system (endorphins, endogenous opioids). This self-numbing has been likened to the effects of morphine.[36] However, in survival, individuals nevertheless continue to be confronted with the life process, their purpose, and prospective future. While self-anesthesia cocoons the survivor from the world in an attempt to "forget the past and move on,"[37] and "start life afresh,"[38] or in the hope of rediscovering their pre-enslavement self,[39] it is also tragically impossible, and this numbing creates an isolating feeling, making survivors feel that they are outsiders; strangers to their own families or communities. It is paradoxically the very strategy that prevents growth from occurring.

Phrases like "you cannot imagine ..." are common. For example, Christine can tell us "some of the things they did to me and other girls and women, but there is still much that I cannot speak of,"[40] and Tamada states that "the situation of a slave is more than I can say."[41] Where there is a repression of trauma, survivors are unable to express their feelings and experiences and we can observe a lack of emotional detail in their narratives. Survivors may describe in detail their daily routine, but not their feelings. Jennifer was placed in a labor camp in China and made to carry out heavy and other labor. At one point, one of the items she had to make was a toy rabbit. Her narrative runs for two pages, but she dedicates only six lines to discussing the hardships of her life in the camp. Instead, the remainder of her narrative is an extremely detailed step-by-step description of how the rabbits were made, what they looked like, and the hours she was required to work. The need she eventually identifies is for sleep. There is no expression of emotion in her narrative other than that of exhaustion.[42] This avoidance of revisiting feelings is also

---

[36] Judith Herman, *Trauma and Recovery*, 44.
[37] Kevin Bales and Zoe Trodd, *To Plead Our Own Cause*, 139.
[38] Kevin Bales and Zoe Trodd, *To Plead Our Own Cause*, 139.
[39] See Inez who states: "It has been more than a year since all this occurred, I cannot seem to get past the ordeal ... but I lack confidence and never felt secure. Once in a while, I still have anxiety attacks. I still remember the horrible beatings, the constant threats, and the drunk and pushy customers. I am trying to be the person I was before I came to the United States." Kevin Bales and Zoe Trodd, *To Plead Our Own Cause*, 184.
[40] Kevin Bales and Zoe Trodd, *To Plead Our Own Cause*, 100.
[41] Kevin Bales and Zoe Trodd, *To Plead Our Own Cause*, 159.
[42] Kevin Bales and Zoe Trodd, *To Plead Our Own Cause*, 26–28.

found in narratives where the majority of the telling is the description of capture, journey, and escape, but which reveals little of the consequences and emotions of enslavement and freedom.

It is likely that this inability to tell is in part an inability to identify and describe emotions in the self, a known effect of significant trauma.[43] However, some detail will have been left unsaid as the majority of the narratives available were also gathered in relatively short semi-structured interviews where expression will have been hindered by the interview method and questions, the relationship with the interviewer, the location, the individual's age, and time constraints. For example, Patience states "I went through some rituals,"[44] either unable or unwilling to express what rituals these were and what she was put through in those rituals. However, it is not clear whether this is due to trauma or whether the environment in which she gave her testimony restricted her expression. Further, while Murphy notes a lack of detail as a pattern across narratives,[45] and while it is certainly evident in a number of narratives (either in small part, or throughout the narrative) there are many survivors that are able to express themselves more fully and relate explicit emotional and graphic detail that belies the generalization that survivors are unable to tell.

There are marked contrasts in narratives by survivors who do not retreat, or who are unable to employ this strategy for keeping trauma at bay. Instead, they are overwhelmed with their memories, expressing their raw emotions and explaining the things they were put through in graphic detail.[46] Sina Vann's narrative is a good example of this. Despite an extensive and detailed emotional narrative, she states: "everyone has four compartments in their heart. And two we can open up and share to others, and another one we can share with our families. And the other compartment is a secret place that I myself don't know how to get into to share out of that compartment."[47] Although she is able to express her emotions in detail, there are aspects of her trauma that are so repressed that she cannot express, nor access herself. Of course, we have no way of

---

[43] See Henry Krystal, "Trauma and Aging," 79.
[44] Kevin Bales and Zoe Trodd, *To Plead Our Own Cause*, 68.
[45] Laura T. Murphy, *The New Slave Narrative: The Battle Over Representations of Contemporary Slavery* (New York: Columbia University Press, 2019), 382–405.
[46] See for example, Kevin Bales and Zoe Trodd, *To Plead Our Own Cause*, Christine Stark at 100–3, and Nu at 94.
[47] Laura T. Murphy, *Survivors of Slavery*, 244.

knowing what survivors are holding back and while some survivors seem particularly able to express themselves, it is clear that an inability to tell affects even those most able.[48]

### DISSOCIATION AND ALIENATION

As part of my interview with Dwain, I asked him to draw a picture of something that was important to him in his journey and then explain his drawing. Figure 4.1 was mainly drawn in orange pen, except for the word green which is written in a green color.

He said:

This box here, as you can see there's the 1, 2, 3, 4, and is it 4 sides? 1, 2, 3, 4 5. 5 sides but I think the one that you can't see underneath is the side that I hide. So, this box here represents me, and that side that you can't see is on its, well it's on its arse basically, and that's why I won't let it be shown. This is where I want to be, this spinning top; spin, spin, spin, and it's sharp not flat and rotund, it's a straight line and spinning fast, and if I spin so fast, I'll probably fly.

This one here is this cloud, it's scaring the birds away who want to settle down and peck and do all the other stuff that's not nice. So, this good cloud here is saying go away.

This one in particular, this is one of the first ones I drew.

Interviewer: This, the box?

Yeah. It's specifically this way because I wanted to show you that bit; that bottom bit there isn't really shown because that's like me, I've got all this, but the other side that you now know of, it doesn't like to be shown. And what I'd always wanted to be is a spinning top. I mean you could just spin to oblivion let's say ... this one is where I'd like to be. This is getting those people away who just like to sit on you and crap on you basically.

I'm a lot simpler than you could possibly imagine, but my only issue is that I'm so complex because I'm so hurt by the fact that I can't change things. I'm so hurt that those years have gone, and I can never get them back. Never. And as I've now opened my eyes again to think "God have those many years passed me where nothing has happened in my favour"? Apart from my blessings, and I can't simplify them, but my three children, apart from that, a lot has come and washed past me without even me getting on the bandwagon or trying to say "oh well hold up for me, I'm coming," you know. It's just left me behind, continuously.

In his drawing, Dwain found ways to visually articulate his situation, and these images (box and spinning top) helped him to orientate himself in his situation in a way that allowed some sense of dignity and agency.

---

[48] See for example, Christine Stark in Kevin Bales and Zoe Trodd, *To Plead Our Own Cause*, 100–3; and Sina Vann in Laura T. Murphy, *Survivors of Slavery*, 231–46.

## Bearing Witness: Trauma in Contemporary Slave Narratives 111

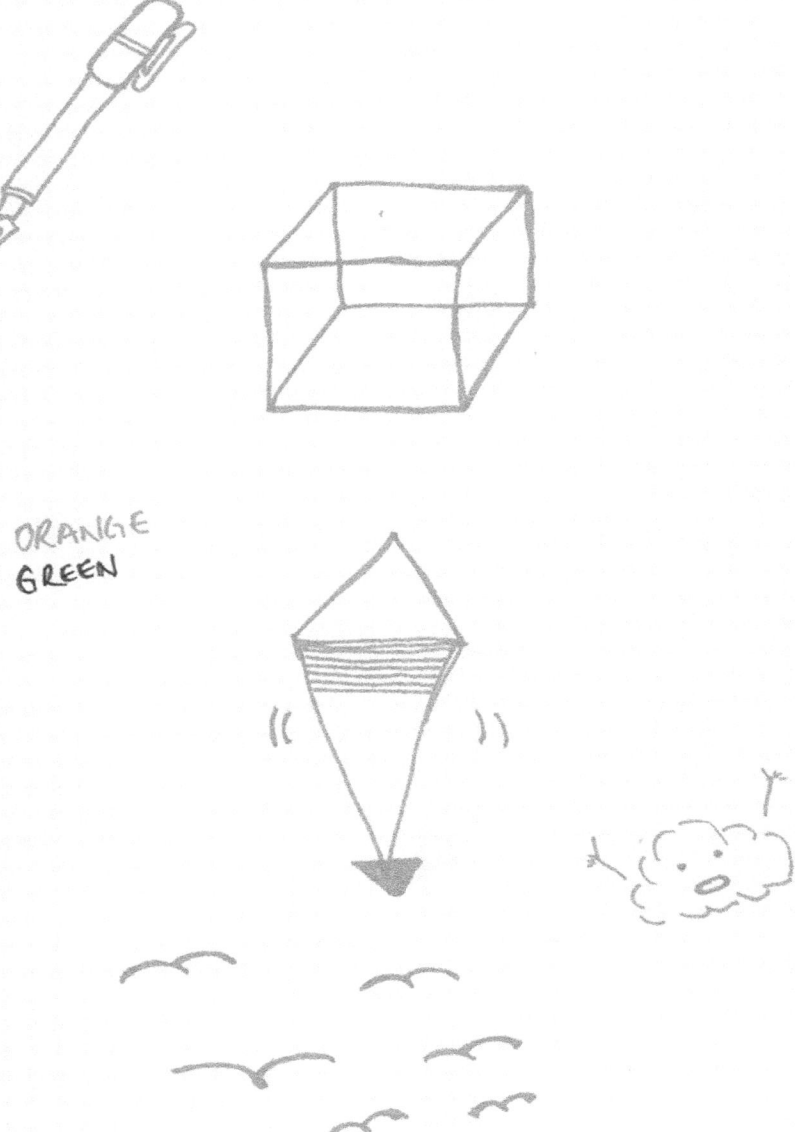

FIGURE 4.1 Drawing by Dwain on matters meaningful to him, including abstract representations of himself.

The box is a metaphor about presenting personas that are necessary for survival, whilst keeping his sense of "real" self (as opposed to his projected self) hidden from his tormentors. The box is something that he has control over. Similarly, the spinning top metaphor represents an idea of freedom that is intrinsically linked to the ability to travel, revealed earlier in the interview. The fact that the side of him connected to his trauma is "on its arse" and he chooses a spinning top that wants to fly as representative of where he wants to be provided a strong contrasting image of freedom, where the weight of the box is finally gone.

In describing the box as representative of himself, Dwain suddenly depersonifies that aspect of his internal landscape relating to his trauma by saying he won't let "it" be shown and doesn't like "it" to be shown. He also explicitly states this is a side he hides, that he "won't let it be shown" and that "it doesn't like to be shown." So, while all the sides of the box represent all aspects of him, he abstracts the side of him that he has consciously chosen to conceal. He acknowledges it but tries to contain and hide it from others. This attempt to disassociate or divorce from his trauma while paradoxically acknowledging it is now an irremovable part of his structure. The box raises the impossibility of wanting to reveal and have his pain witnessed, but also of wanting to conceal it from others to project a "normal" self to both us and to himself. This complexity is emulated in his statement that he is "a lot simpler than you could possibly imagine, but my only issue is that I'm so complex."

There is also a hint of dissociation in the final paragraph where he talks of the large part of his past life that was essentially stolen. He is dissociating himself from his past, as he used to do from the present. The box and spinning top are a kind of lifebuoy, and there is a persistent sense that he is not really participating in his own life since he became free. As can be seen in this extract of Dwain's narrative, the survivor, in the act of bearing witness, is therefore confronted with a dilemma. The process of testimony holds out the promise of truth and a return to the sane, normal, connected world. But the commitment to this truth forces the realization that the restoration of what has been lost cannot be regained, causing additional grief and loss.[49]

Keith also visualized the trauma he has tried to suppress, describing:

... a six-foot safe. Old fashioned with a turning lock on it; almost like a like a door on a ship or a submarine or something. It's really old-fashioned and there

---

[49] On this see Dori Laub, "Truth and Testimony," 79.

would be things like the door started to open and like all the hinges had rusted and the door has started to open, and there were hands on the inside trying to push this door open. And I would be on the outside trying to keep the door closed. But I wouldn't see myself, it would be as if my mind is trying to keep this door closed, I'm looking at the safe thinking that "no I can't open this I can't open this." And as time went on, through therapy I realise that the safe represented what has happened to me. The people that hurt me were inside that safe, and to move on, it was me that opened that door and let the demons out of the safe, so I could exorcise the demons if you like. Because I don't see them as people. I don't see them as people anymore, the oppressors or whatever you want to call them, the defendants, do you know what I mean? ... but it was my way of dealing with things like seeing them, as almost the undead and demons, demonised people, evil, do you know what I mean? But I have to open that door fully to let them out of the safe, to get rid of the demons. And I envisage myself.

In liberation, Keith continues to struggle with the difficulty of his trauma. In person, he was particularly anguished by the above image, relating the first half as if it were a horror story with hands grasping to open the safe and cause harm. He only envisages himself once he envisages destroying his trauma.

### SPECTRALITY AND OTHERNESS

Feelings of spectrality and otherness are another feature of enslavement and its resulting trauma. During enslavement, individuals' identities are stripped away. Victims are kidnapped from their communities, their villages burned, and their families and cultures lost. Perpetrators of slavery will often control victims by trafficking them to other countries, denying them their beliefs, and attempting to force a different religion on them, and many victims are renamed, often with a name that is derogatory, or which denies their heritage.[50] They are objectified and treated as lesser, at times as if animals or chattels, making them question their part in the world as a purposeful human being. After a whole night of gang rape in a cell, Dina heard the screams of pigs being pushed into their pens. She says "I knew what that feeling was like – I was no better than the pigs to these men; they could have killed me. Something inside me did die, and I will never be the same again."[51] Often their loss is less tangible but relates to a loss of a part of themselves that cannot be recovered. They are closed off; lost to the world and to themselves.

[50] Kevin Bales and Zoe Trodd, *To Plead Our Own Cause*, Ravi at 74, and Tamada at 159.
[51] Kevin Bales and Zoe Trodd, *To Plead Our Own Cause*, 105.

Jean Robert was a restavec, an unwanted illegitimate slave child whose physical and emotional abuse was sanctioned by Haitian society. He says the "daily exclusion from any community or family often leaves no visible scars, but the trauma lasts a lifetime .... Since their most basic rights – to family's love and protection, health care, and education – are denied, restavecs are invisible children, observers instead of participants in their own society."[52] He repeats the statement that children are observers later in his narrative.[53] Many survivors are left destitute, feel ruined and dirty, and in some cases despised members of society. They are the invisible people, viewed by outsiders as damaged, worthless, and in some cultures deserving of their enslavement, rather than the unseen victims they are. Slowly, the perspective that they are "a nothing"[54] invades their thinking so that survival requires a difficult and significant reconstruction of the self in order to continue.

Even witnessing the more favorable treatment of others can give rise to feelings of alienation where we might assume it would instead bring revelation. When Mende had the opportunity to speak with other servants and realized they had freedoms she was not granted, and were appropriately paid and well treated, this didn't cause her to question her own mistreatment, but rather her otherness:

I wondered why. I concluded that I must be different from them in some way. But how? Was it because I was black and they were Arab-looking? Was it because I was a Nuba? Who had decided that they would be servants and I would be a slave? Who? Was it Rahab [her slaveholder]? Was it fate? Was it God? As the days wore on I became more and more aware of the difference between us and I became more and more depressed. They had new clothes, mine were old rags. They were treated well, I was cursed and beaten ....[55]

... I was a non-person. I didn't really exist. I had no doctor, no dentist, no school, no friends, no family, no money, no bank account, no taxes to pay.[56]

The contrast in her treatment compared to others, giving rise to feelings of otherness, combined with her spectrality, caused Mende to retreat to the past in misery. Depressed, seeking comfort, wallowing, she stopped eating and her hair fell out. She became even further isolated and alone.[57] Being moved from Khartoum to the UK also meant she lost the

[52] Jean-Robert Cadet, *Restavec*, 202.
[53] Jean-Robert Cadet, *Restavec*, 203.
[54] Laura T. Murphy, *Survivors of Slavery*, 109.
[55] Mende Nazer and Damien Lewis, *Slave*, 186.
[56] Mende Nazer and Damien Lewis, *Slave*, 293.
[57] Mende Nazer and Damien Lewis, *Slave*, 262–63.

relationship she had built with the family in Khartoum, the slaveholding family that she had imagined in her desperation as a replacement for her own. She started to feel suicidal, reflecting on what could have been and allowing loss and grief to overtake her.[58]

It is not only the fear and horror of what happened that causes spectrality, displacement, and numbing, but the shame of the things survivors have been made to do and the person they were made to become. Survivors forced into sexual slavery in particular recount feeling dirty and in freedom suffer discrimination and ostracism from their communities.[59] Rosa was trafficked from Mexico to the USA at the age of 14 with the promise of better pay for cleaning in a hotel, but on arrival was forced into sexual slavery. She states "I cannot forget this happened. I can't put it behind me. I find it nearly impossible to trust people. I still feel shame. I was a decent girl in Mexico. I used to go to church with my family. I only wish none of this ever happened."[60] Survivors can also then become ashamed of being ashamed, which can also cause self-silencing.[61] Even in freedom, survivors talk as if they are sitting slightly outside of society, looking in, rendering them ghostly, and further isolating them at a time when their freedom should enable them to build community. We see this very clearly with Christine Stark, and with Shamere McKenzie who expresses the desire to leave a "legacy" in this world, implying her life before now has had no imprint.

## "WILLING" VICTIMS AND CRIMINALS: SUPPORT SERVICES AND LAW ENFORCEMENT PERCEPTIONS OF SURVIVORS

Survivors often manage to escape when they move into a state of action and determination as a result of a particularly violent episode. After being handed over to a shrine at the age of ten, left hungry, repeatedly raped, and bearing three children at a young age Patience decided then "when life became tough for me, I decided to run away .…"[62] The same occurred with Pranus, a Lithuanian man I interviewed who was trafficked to the

---

[58] Mende Nazer and Damien Lewis, *Slave*, 264.
[59] See for example, Kevin Bales and Zoe Trodd, *To Plead Our Own Cause*, Maria at 49, Adelina at 53, and Dina at 104.
[60] Kevin Bales and Zoe Trodd, *To Plead Our Own Cause*, 187.
[61] Judith Herman, "The Politics of Trauma: An Interview with Judith Herman," in *Listening to Trauma: Conversations with Leaders in the Theory & Treatment of Catastrophic Experience*, ed. Cathy Caruth (Baltimore: John Hopkins University Press, 2014), 147.
[62] Kevin Bales and Zoe Trodd, *To Plead Our Own Cause*, 68.

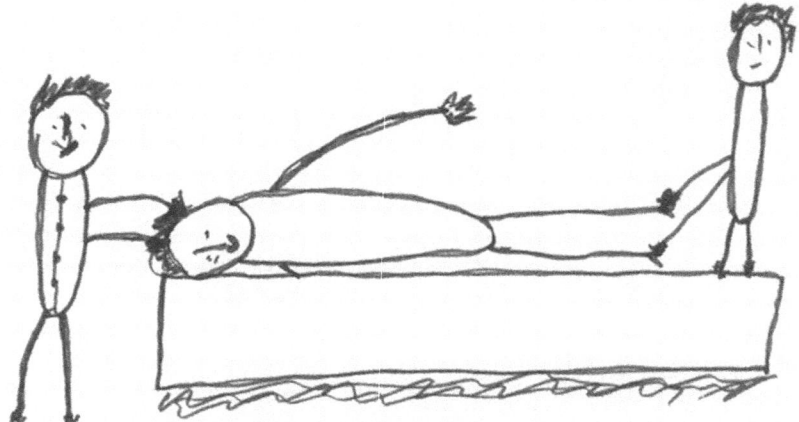

FIGURE 4.2 Drawing by Pranus on an important moment for him, visualizing the incident that prompted his escape.

UK and subjected to severe labor exploitation. He explained that it was the most violent moment in his experience that caused him to look to escape. In his drawing Pranus chose to visualize the moment that represented both the height of his abuse, but which also served as the catalyst for his escape (Figure 4.2). Despite a choice of 35 colors, he used one dark grey pen; a color typically associated with darkness and fear but which for him also became the catalyst for freedom.

Pranus was fortunate in that once free he was very well supported by the police and being a Lithuanian national had no issues remaining in the country. However, the treatment of survivors following discovery by the authorities can be problematic, in the UK and globally. In the wake of freedom from slavery, many survivors are left to deal with the consequences of criminal activity, imprisonment, and issues with repatriation. The way in which they are treated on rescue, combined for many with the insecurity of their status in the country in which they were discovered (and a fear of being repatriated) can unsettle their freedom and impact their recovery. Many survivors are only discovered following arrest or imprisonment, having been forced into one or more illegal activities, such as drug trafficking, prostitution, cannabis farming, and/or bank fraud. Often individuals are discovered following arrest, not as part of a recovery mission. Even where the authorities are alert to the characteristics of enslavement, there are instances where an investigation of a person's vulnerability is not pursued. Thus, arrest is not always the discovery expect, but can instead leave survivors being viewed and treated first and foremost as criminals, with the implication that they are not a valuable member of society.

An example is Irina, who travelled abroad to work in waitressing for an employment agency in order to supplement her income. She travelled to Russia on the promise of a job, only to be met by two men who beat her and took her to work in a brothel managed by the Russian mafia. Eventually, she was helped to escape and found herself in the Netherlands where she went directly to the police and told them everything she knew. However, she was immediately charged for using a false passport for which she was fined. She wasn't able to pay the fine and was subsequently imprisoned for three months. She states:

> I did not commit any crime in those countries and I was put in prison for absolutely nothing. The people who involved me in that situation are still free and continue traffic women under government cover. My rights were violated – who will pay me back for all of my suffering? In those countries, the rights of immigrants in difficult situations are violated and their governments do not want to take responsibility for what is happening in their territory.[63]

Treating survivors as criminals can then affect their self-perception. Where self-identity impacts our perceptions of how others see us, the converse also applies. Perceiving survivors as criminals and not as victims alienates, redefines, and shames them, and being viewed and treated as a criminal can give rise to a simmering anger that is typically linked to a sense of injustice. Survivors also become angry at being subjected to prosecution and incarceration (often leading to deportation) where there was no legitimate consent or autonomy on their part to the criminal act, and particularly where their traffickers remain free. As we have seen with Irina, this anger is then projected onto all authority and can result in displacement, an unconscious defense mechanism where emotions, ideas, or wishes are transferred to another "target" to allay anxiety in the face of aggressive impulses.[64]

Shamere McKenzie was similarly cast as a criminal for crimes she was forced to commit during her enslavement. Shamere was trafficked into sexual slavery and was liberated from her trafficker's control when they were both arrested. Despite clearly being a victim, she was charged with prostitution-related offences.[65] She explains,

---

[63] Kevin Bales and Zoe Trodd, *To Plead Our Own Cause*, 215, see also Christine and Dina at 105.
[64] Laura T. Murphy, *Survivors of Slavery*, 170.
[65] https://survivorsofslavery.org/survivorsspeakers/shamere-mckenzie/

I spent three weeks in prison and was sent to a programme for victims of sex trafficking. At this programme, I received services such as counselling, housing and other basic needs. Then I was offered a plea to the Mann Act – knowingly and willingly transporting minors across state lines for illegal purposes. MINORS!!! Yes, one of the girls was twelve years old, and because I drove, I had to take responsibility for my actions. I didn't willingly drive; neither did I know she was twelve years old.

I felt so stupid. How could I not know she was twelve? I did her make-up even if I knew, what could I have done? I took the plea and felt like my life was over. Here I was being charged for something I was forced to do. My sentence was five years' probation and two hundred hours of community service. In addition, I had to register as a sex offender. I thought my life was over, and there was no reason to live. I dropped out of school and was about to attempt suicide when my best friend talked me out of it.[66]

Despite her being forced to carry out the offences for which she was charged, Shamere was still placed in a position where she had to bear responsibility for her actions, even though essentially those actions were not willingly hers. Her detention caused her to seriously consider suicide, and her criminal record would have had ramifications long after her imprisonment and subsequent community service. Experiences like Shamere's will have repercussions for survivors' mental health. Further, they are often confronted with having to disclose their criminal status affecting access to accommodation, educational establishments, and employment, creating a lifetime income gap. The stigma not only associated with their acts during enslavement, but now also as a convicted criminal continues to other them in liberation, rendering them outsiders in the society in which they are trying to position themselves.

In 2017 I interviewed Tung. Tung is a young Vietnamese man who was trafficked, exploited, and enslaved in the UK. He was excited and happy to travel, not knowing that his parents had incurred considerable debt. Brought to the UK via Russia and the French migrant camps, he was trafficked on arrival in the UK to work in a Chinese takeaway. Required to work up to 19 hours a day without breaks, he slept on the floor of a small storage room behind the kitchen with several others. He was only allowed out once a week, accompanied, to buy basic provisions. Over a period of six years he was then trafficked within the UK and forced to manage cannabis farms. Eventually, the increasing debt meant he was forced into sexual slavery, suffering genital mutilation and severe physical and psychological impacts on his health. He was eventually arrested

---

[66] Shamere, Laura T. Murphy, *Survivors of Slavery*, 52.

and imprisoned and it was only during his interview with the Home Office during that time that the authorities identified him as having been a victim of "modern" slavery. Unfortunately, Tung was then a victim of the notorious historical National Referral Mechanism (NRM) decisions: as he was no longer enslaved, he was not entitled to enter the NRM.

Tung was particularly hurt by the inability of services on multiple occasions to identify him as a victim of slavery who needed support, but he was almost dismissive about the fact that his traffickers had not been caught and prosecuted. Throughout the interview, this was not his concern or an expressed need in terms of his view of justice. Instead, Tung's perception of justice revolved around the post-enslavement support available to him (housing, food, dignity, asylum, and legal representation). He also spoke of the shame and fear that he experienced until he was able to compare his experiences with others held in a detention center. Those feelings diminished when he told his story, he explained. This perception of justice as rooted outside of the legal system – in support that involves a context for telling one's story – recurs across several contemporary narratives. These stories are a call for therapeutic justice: a justice model where legal processes act as social agents geared to enhancing psychological wellbeing.[67] He was repeatedly arrested and although the police asked him questions about his circumstances and how he came to be working in the UK on cannabis farms, it is not clear why he was not identified immediately as a victim of trafficking and placed in the NRM. He stated that he felt respected by the police, but when asked what made him feel that way, he said it was because they fed him. In contrast to his treatment during slavery, the smallest gesture seemed respectful to him, when in fact there is little in his testimony to indicate he was treated as a victim rather than a criminal.

In Figure 4.3, Tung (not the survivors' real name) chose to express his emotions in survival and at that moment in time, drawing a landscape in naturalistic colors with expressive lines. At the time of the interview, Tung was desperate to hear whether he would be granted asylum, but was frustrated at the lack of legal support, home office delays, and knew that the fact he had been imprisoned and involved in criminal activity would militate against him. If he was returned to Vietnam, he feared he would be at risk of being trafficked again. Despite his exploitation occurring in the UK, Vietnam held bad memories for him, and he did not want to return.

---

[67] See generally David B. Wexler and Bruce J. Winick, *Law in a Therapeutic Key: Developments in Therapeutic Jurisprudence* (Durham: Carolina Academic Press, 1996).

FIGURE 4.3 Drawing by Tung, depicting his feelings about his place and future.

Tung explained that the landscape he drew was any landscape; it was not Vietnam. The river represented his journey and the boat represented him. He did not know where he was going, and he did not know where he would land. Interestingly, Tung had said he had finished drawing, but when I came to discuss what this meant to him, he picked up a pen and carefully colored in the inside of the boat with red pen, checking I was watching. Given that the boat represented him, it was clear that he wanted a witness to the tightly contained, hot center that represented his internal feelings in what comes across as an overwhelming landscape. The asylum process essentially destabilized his freedom, once again subjecting him to an unknown future and filling him with anxiety and insecurity, while already in a fragile state of being.

### LOSS AND THE INABILITY TO MOVE FORWARD IN LIBERATION

Following escape, the loss from having to leave children and other survivors behind, the death of family and friends, the risk of re-exploitation, feelings of shame, isolation, and vulnerability all serve to destabilize freedom. The impact on relatives is also significant, with survivors believed to be dead and families having to reconnect and support someone living with C-Ptsd, often resulting in strained relationships and a lack of trust for both the survivor and their family.⁶⁸ For William, hearing of his family's suffering over the years he was enslaved left him with feelings of insecurity and the awkwardness of connecting with a brother who had assumed him dead.⁶⁹ Despite this, or perhaps because of this, many post-emancipation narratives seek to reconnect with those lost to slavery. Kavita is suicidal upon gaining freedom. Her feelings change when she becomes involved with helping children at the shelter and she views it as "starting her life afresh."⁷⁰ This is perhaps an attempt to remove herself from her past, whilst engaging with it constructively as a means of self-healing. Survivors' pain continues even once free, because freedom is not merely freedom from the condition of slavery. Where loved ones have been lost and the effects of trauma, isolation, and alienation continue to play out, survivors will never feel freedom from the concern of slavery. Eventually Kavita became "happy, very, very happy ..." but unable to let go of her experiences and forget the circumstances in which her sister remained: "each time I think about my sister and what she has to go through in her daily life, I am just so hurt, so resentful, and so angry."⁷¹

Another significant challenge of living through enslavement and emerging into freedom is the sudden need to take responsibility for the self. Survivors struggle to capture the concept of freedom and what this means. When Azad was asked "Did you ever even dream of a day that it would be different?" he replied "no, there was just no dream. It was like a vision I couldn't begin to think of; it was an impossibility."⁷² Suddenly there is an unexpected future that is unknown, and which comes at a time when they are struggling to adapt to the notion that they are truly free. Mende Nazer captures this when she states "all I can think about right now is how to convince myself that I am really, truly free. Until then, I can't even think about the future. I just want to experience this feeling of freedom for a while. Then later, I might think about what my life might bring."⁷³ She suddenly found herself in a situation where after years of

---

⁶⁸ See for example, Kevin Bales and Zoe Trodd, *To Plead Our Own Cause*, Vi at 44, Maria at 52, William at 249, Patience and Maria at 186.
⁶⁹ Kevin Bales and Zoe Trodd, *To Plead Our Own Cause*, 300.
⁷⁰ Kevin Bales and Zoe Trodd, *To Plead Our Own Cause*, 139.
⁷¹ Kevin Bales and Zoe Trodd, *To Plead Our Own Cause*, 139.
⁷² Laura T. Murphy, *Survivors of Slavery*, 149.
⁷³ Mende Nazer and Damien Lewis, *Slave: The True Story of a Girl's Lost Childhood and Her Fight for Survival* (London: Virago, 2010), 311.

being controlled and having nothing, she had to decide everything. Seemingly innocuous matters like what to wear, when to eat, and when to sleep were overwhelming. Far from the euphoria, we might expect, freedom can be frightening and full of responsibility for the self that hasn't grown naturally over time as it does for most. Not only do these smaller day-to-day decisions bring challenges, but survivors also have to learn how to not be afraid anymore. In other words, there is a need to adjust to freedom first, before survivors can start to cope with their trauma. They need time to convince themselves they are truly free. Once the feeling of freedom is experienced for a while, then they can think about the future and what that might bring. This may be more acute for adults, who typically receive less post-discovery care than children.

### RESILIENCE IN SURVIVAL

What is most striking across the body of narratives is survivors' resilience and persistence. In this respect, the nineteenth-century survivor Scott Bond recounts the story of an elderly slave who:

> After telling me many other stories of the hardships of the slave, he said that after all, the things that looked hardest to him, were really blessings in disguise. These hardships had developed his self-reliance and resourcefulness, and now that he was a free man and a citizen, he could see a benefit, even in the hardships he had undergone. He said that he knew he was a Christian and that he was respected by all his neighbors, black and white .... This instance is but one of ten thousand, showing that the Negro in his long apprenticeship, has gained in adverse circumstances, that he has wrung victory from oppression.[74]

These characteristics of self-reliance, resourcefulness, empathy, resilience, and persistence are necessary tactics for survival and employed as a coping mechanism. And here we once again connect to the survivor as warrior, who finds formidable strength and inner resources to get them through their lives. In so doing, they achieve something incredible, worthy of so much pride and self-regard; they achieve resistance in survival, although the evidence suggests that survivors will very rarely see themselves in this way.

The theme of the survivor as warrior (in psychiatry referred to as the hero), where the survivor assumes a role as the defender of others, or as a

---

[74] Scott Bond, *From Slavery to Wealth. The Life of Scott Bond. The Rewards of Honesty, Industry, Economy and Perseverance* (n.p.: The Journal Printing Company, 1917), 3–31. http://docsouth.unc.edu/neh/rudd/summary.html

leader or advocate, is often present as a result of survival guilt. The experience of freedom from slavery, from the anticipation of death that slavery can bring, and the contrast between slavery and freedom can deliver a new profound knowledge of life that also connects to the survivor as warrior.[75] In this new comprehension, living out the mythology of the warrior is a way of gaining mastery over their trauma, but requires survivors to both directly and indirectly, and consistently, confront their experiences, which can lead to a form of continual trauma. This pattern has also been seen in other survivor groups. In survivors of slavery, the warrior typically manifests as a propensity in survivors to move into caring and activist professions.

Shame and guilt go hand in hand, and these two emotions apply where survivors feel they could have saved or done more for others with whom they were enslaved, or from a perceived failure to be resistant to their enslavement. Many survivors are therefore faced with acute feelings of guilt for survival where others remained enslaved, were murdered or disappeared, or took their own lives, and survivors can also feel shame for their perceived impotence (transmuting into feelings of cowardice) in not saving those individuals. Where the deaths or disappearance of others is described, they rarely experienced an opportunity for mourning, which reinforced the perception that they were disposable. As a witness to the enslavement, abuse, and murder of others, many survivors carry a sense of responsibility to give voice and corporality to those unable to bear witness for themselves. Bearing witness becomes an "act of solidarity"[76] that enables a transformation of guilt to responsibility, which has enormous therapeutic value to survivors and can be an important means of reintegrating the fractured self in survival.[77]

Seeyawati explains why she feels the need to fight for others who are experiencing similar exploitation as hers:

Look at me, I don't belong here, I'm not a bonded labourer. Why should I care? But that's not the right thought. The thought that comes from inside, a thought that says "Look, I've reached a level of progress. And I'm here; they're not." The only thought that should be is "How is it possible for me from that position to get to the people from here to join me?" And that thought should be the running thought in every individual who's moved beyond this. If you don't care, how would things ever change?[78]

[75] Sometimes equated with Freud's concept of a death drive, and adaptations of it by, for example, Cathy Caruth and Robert Jay Lifton, but refuted by Judith Herman.
[76] Cathy Caruth, *Listening to Trauma*, 142.
[77] Cathy Caruth, *Listening to Trauma*, 13.
[78] Laura T. Murphy, *Survivors of Slavery*, 172.

Where survivors are driven to some kind of social action, regardless of what kind, it has been seen in other survivor groups that this does lead to "particularly good recovery."[79] The ability to achieve meaning out of life and so assert presence by leaving a legacy supports growth, giving meaning to a "new" and unexpected life. However, this drive to action also means that survivors are repeatedly confronted with reminders of the past, and others can fail to see the degree of trauma playing through them. As outsiders, our experience of the myth of the warrior is to place him or her in the context of the powerful savior, a celebrated figure, but rarely are the experiences that lead to the creation of the warrior exposed.[80]

The survivor Shamere Makenzie also acknowledges the need to bear witness for others, writing:

> It took me five years to start speaking about my experience. As I travel throughout the country and speak to various people on this issue, I now realise that I went through the trauma not for myself, but for someone else .... I believe I am the voice for those still enslaved, the voice for those who perished while enslaved, and the voice for those who are free but have not the courage to speak up .... I am determined to use my story to make a difference in the life of someone else, leaving a legacy in this world.[81]

Leaving a legacy in the world is a way of creating meaning out of life, a means of imprinting and asserting her presence and becoming less ghostly. Nevertheless, living gives rise to a number of challenges that survivors are often unequipped to manage, or they are confronted with policies, structures, and attitudes that cause further harm. Survivors are left in a permanent state of survival and have to draw on unknown reserves to adjust and deal with day-to-day living.

To conclude, Christine's narrative summarizes a great deal of the effects of slavery discussed in this chapter, which acutely demonstrates the simultaneous presence of knowing and not knowing, of intrusive and constrictive symptoms that are at the heart of the challenge of recovering from trauma:

> It is no small achievement to survive sexual slavery. Survivors are split into pieces, fragmented, broken, filled with despair, pain, rage and sorrow. We have been hurt beyond belief. We are silent; we are numb. Our eyes see, our ears hear,

---

[79] Judith Herman, "The Politics of Trauma," 142.
[80] On this further, see Judith Herman, "The Politics of Trauma," 138, and Judith Herman, *Trauma and Recovery: The Aftermath of Violence – From Domestic Abuse to Political Terror* (New York: Basic Books, 2015).
[81] Laura T. Murphy, *Survivors of Slavery*, 53.

but we do not tell. Our voices are non-existent, but even if they did exist, who would believe what we had to say? Who would listen? Who would care? We are dirty, ruined, despised, the whores of the earth. The men who use us throw us away. We are garbage to piss on, to pile up in the corner. We are their property, they own us. The rest of you turn your backs, avert your eyes, pretend not to see, go your own way. You leave us to predators.

But we endure. We survive. It should be asked, "why do these women stay alive?" sometimes, maybe much of the time, we don't even know. Sometimes we do wish we were dead; we wish they would kill us; we can't take it anymore. So why do we stay alive? We stay alive because we do not want them, the masters, to win. We stay alive because there is something we want, something we seek. We may not know exactly what it is; we may not even have ever experienced it. Or we may have known it only for a moment when something deep inside, deeper even that they can penetrate, stirred, and we felt alive, joyous, loved, at peace. We stay alive because we are women in search of our lives, we are women in search of freedom.

I stayed alive because my belief in something better than what they offered was greater than their hatred or destruction. I stayed alive because I wanted to be free – more than anything. I wanted to be free ...

... it is only recently that I have been free from their sexual and physical abuse, and to be honest I don't always know what to do with myself. I was beaten and raped, or at least verbally assaulted, virtually every day of my life. The intensity of my emotions doesn't match up to normal life. Other survivors talk about this too. Even though we have escaped, we live in the pimp's world. We have flashbacks and night tremors. The pimps harass us, so we spend much of our time waiting, wondering when they're going to hurt us again. Our worldview is one of war, constant rapes, and beatings, we may escape, but we will always be isolated, we will never be part of society. We know too much, we have seen too much. The world does not want to acknowledge the truth of women's lives ...

I escaped the pimps. It took me more than twenty years to do it, but I did it .... I want to be free. And I will be free, and I want my sisters to be free. And I will be free, and help women and girls escape, or I will die trying. I have been in a sort of exile myself, on the run, surviving, remembering, waiting for them to kill me, gathering my strength. I have been outsmarting them, outfighting them, and speaking out to help other women and girls ...

... it is difficult to know what to do with yourself when all you have known is chaos and destruction and the streets. You're not good company, you're not polite of talking or thinking about socially acceptable things. You're talking about your life. You're talking about the lives of other women and girls who are still held captive, who are still being hurt, who may not survive. You feel an urgency, a bond deeper than blood to the very women and girls they tried to make you hate ...

There are many women, strong women, brave women all across the world who are rising up to meet and to end the tidal wave of male violence against women. We escape and we organize and we educate and we go back down into the trenches to pull out our sisters. This is war, a battle of life and death. A battle that women must win ... the pimps do not know state or national boundaries;

women in battle must not know them either. We must be on the lookout for each other. The brothels of the world house all the women of the world. We must go into those brothels, search one another out. We must break down the doors, beat back the pimps, and get out the women and girls held in cages as I go back, back into brothels and porn houses, I will be on the lookout for you. I hope I will never find you there, but if I do, you have my word that I will lend you my hand.[82]

The effects of a fundamental and seemingly permanent loss of liberty, and of the exercise of powers of "ownership" over individuals, leaves survivors struggling to assume full lives in freedom. This struggle results in their need to do and be more, to find meaning in liberation, and to fight for the liberation of others still enslaved. Survivors therefore carry a burden of responsibility not only for their own growth, but for the growth of others. However, they are at the same time trying to deal with their own trauma and the ways in which that trauma manifests. Narratives reveal the difficulties survivors experience in managing their behavior or dealing with the effects of substance abuse inherited from their enslavement (or assumed in liberation as a coping mechanism). The effects of slavery on the person in liberation renders them vulnerable to further exploitation, and survivors can experience homelessness, anorexia, depression, self-harm, and a range of physical and psychological symptoms associated with C-Ptsd. Their behavior can violate social norms, alienating them further and bringing another source of shame and anger in survival. Self-destructive behavior patterns can also extend to their personal relationships and leave them open to further abuse. Such challenges are exacerbated by patchy and often hard to access mental health care, which is often not appropriate to the survivor of slavery, either culturally, or because of the complexity of the trauma they have experienced. Women and men may experience their trauma differently in the light of their particular vulnerabilities, and children in particular are robbed of parental support at critical points in their development. Powerless in terms of their age, physical ability, and legal capacity, children are forced to become adults before they are cognitively ready to do so.

Growth requires survivors to confront and make sense of their past, bringing up feelings of anger for lost childhoods, opportunities to build their own families, and to have lived a "normal" life. While telling is understood to be fundamental to growth, trauma also inhibits the ability to recall and to reveal. Keith continues to experience emotional detachment making it difficult for him to access and confront his trauma, and

---

[82] Kevin Bales and Zoe Trodd, *To Plead Our Own Cause*, 101–2.

Aida reveals her forceful attempts to forget what cannot be forgotten, and which she needs to make in order to function. Trauma is also often hidden to the person traumatized, and even in longer unstructured interviews and autobiographies, survivors struggle to put into words what they feel. In this respect, visual representations have added valuable capacity for expression, but the analysis of trauma in this group as evidenced by the corpus echoes an ongoing theme – one addressed in the next chapter on recovery – that freedom is not the happy moment of liberation so often perceived by non-survivors, but instead a long, complex, and challenging state of existence.

# 5

## Assuming "Full" Freedom

### *Challenges in Recovery*

"Something inside me did die, and I will never be the same."[1]

If the previous chapters reveal anything, it is the complicated and contradictory states of existence in slavery and liberation, the desire for growth and normalcy, the blurred boundaries, and the mountainous psychological challenges survivors face. In this final chapter, I bring these findings together and look at survivors' actions and feelings as they strive to achieve meaningful freedom. I argue that survival exposes the interplay between agency and responsibility; where survival brings the potential for agency, it also brings a corresponding responsibility for the self and for others. The paradox of this potential for growth is that at the same time these things – agency and responsibility – confront survivors with challenges *to* growth. There are no rights without responsibility, but the assumption of responsibility is complicated and impeded by misunderstanding and by fragmented and incohesive support systems. The chapter explores the needs that survivors express, looking in particular at the attitudes and practices of the authorities, the limitations of central processes, and the psychological and physical challenges of survivors' "new lives," identifying the value survivors place on recognition, community, family, education, and rights.

The interplay between agency and responsibility becomes very apparent when reading across the corpus. Survival brings with it, finally, the potential for agency, but survival and agency also bring responsibility for

---

[1] Dina, in Kevin Bales and Zoe Trodd, eds., *To Plead Our Own Cause Personal Stories by Today's Slaves* (New York: Cornell University Press, 2008), 105.

the self and for others. The paradox of this potential for growth is that at the same time these things, agency and responsibility, confront survivors with challenges *to* growth. Without support to assume responsibility for the self, survivors are unable to exercise or exert their rights. This is further inhibited by the lack of specific and cohesive survivor support services. Without structures that assist with capabilities, survivors will always be left behind.

### THE MISCONCEPTION OF LIBERATION AND RECOVERY AS CONCOMITANT STATES OF BEING

Discovery and liberation are often fearful events for survivors, not the exciting happy moments envisaged. It is rare that survivors express joy about that moment. Rather, many don't understand what is happening at the moment of liberation, particularly when their discovery or escape is the consequence of a raid by the authorities. For some, they seize an opportunity for escape but have no idea who to turn to or where to go. Fearing recapture and punishment, they are thrown into a situation of confusion and may have an inability to communicate in the language of the country in which they were enslaved. At this early stage of liberation, faith organizations and NGOs are fundamental to enabling survivors to hold on to new-found liberty, meeting survivors' primary need for a place of safety, and then providing the services required in the immediate aftermath of enslavement (such as medical care, food, clothing, and safe accommodation). However, survivors are confronted with having to adapt to a new environment, with the combined effects of destitution and isolation, and subjected to rules, systems, and processes they are unused to while also continuing to suffer the effects of complex trauma. Kavita recalls that when she entered the ashram that supported her through the process of liberation and recovery "I would just weep inconsolably for days on end" but "... slowly and steadily I got out of the vacuum or the shell."[2]

The shifts in recovery emerge over time, when liberation can be processed, circumstances understood, fears allayed, support put in place, and safety and security not only provided, but felt. However, these initial needs are merely the start of the journey to recovery. The trauma of

---

[2] Kavita, in Laura T. Murphy, *Survivors of Slavery: Modern-Day Slave Narratives* (New York: Columbia University Press, 2014), 60.

slavery, the realities of freedom, and the risk of re-enslavement (whether actual or perceived) pose significant challenges for survivors, destabilize recovery, and can create a vicious cycle of exploitation. Rachel Lloyd explains that the long-term recovery needs of survivors include being "able to move past a sense of being perpetual victims and having no control over what happens to them. They need to feel empowered, utilise safe strategies, recognise unhealthy and manipulative relationships before they even begin, understand what might make them vulnerable, and take steps to mitigate that, whether it's cutting certain people out of their lives or becoming economically independent. Most of all, they need to finally understand what makes for a healthy, intimate relationship, an understanding that has been distorted over the years and which, if not corrected, puts them at risk for victimisation over and over again."[3] But this process can take years, and the absence of appropriate services, and the incohesiveness of services where they do exist, leaves survivors shouldering the responsibility for their survival at an acutely vulnerable point in their lives.

Survivors live in constant fear of recapture and struggle to attain feelings of security and liberation. They have lost family members or find themselves separated from the communities they constructed with others with whom they were enslaved. They suffer acute feelings of guilt and shame, and experience discrimination as a result of their enslavement, with many excluded from liberation and continuing to be treated as "other," and find they do not enjoy the same rights or entitlements as others. For example, in Niger, slave status is still inherited and those born from historical slave lines are still essentially born into slavery, with their "masters" having *de facto* ownership of their bodies, labor, produce, and progeny. Critically, even where manumitted, masters can still exercise "rights" to, *inter alia*, approve marriages, and decide how free men and women can vote.[4] Those previously enslaved may also find themselves ostracized from their communities where public opinion is law, experiencing cultural and social restrictions on their liberties, or may even be murdered for offending community values. Many survivors are forced back into exploitation because of the combined effects of poverty and discrimination, and this is particularly true for those who suffered sexual exploitation. For those that are trafficked into sexual slavery, the shame and stigma attached to such practices can and does deeply affect

---

[3] Rachel Lloyd, *Girls Like Us: A Memoir* (New York: Harper Collins Publishers, 2011), 194.
[4] www.antislavery.org/english/english/niger_schools_appeal/slavery_in_niger.aspx

survivors' ability to achieve the shift from being enslaved for sexual purposes, to being seen (and seeing themselves) as independent individuals free of discrimination and stigma. Studies that have shown some service providers believe survivors have "chosen" their situation, and that survivors feel isolated and humiliated believing others see them as "prostitutes or willing participants" in their enslavement.[5]

Escaping or reaching support services is also not necessarily the start of their journey in recovery and liberation. Survivors can easily be drawn back in and where partners are abusive a form of Stockholm syndrome can occur. Survivors can normalize the abuse they suffered: "all that bad shit, and it's just normal to me. I don't feel shocked or anything. All that stuff, getting raped, pimps, that's ... you know, the life. That's just what it is"[6] and their abusers can provide an understanding that few outside of "the life" can. Even three years after her escape, Rachel Lloyd was tempted to return to her trafficker because no one knew what she had been through other than him. She states, "very few relationships are *all* bad ... Girls relapse because the pain is no longer tangible. Human beings have a remarkable ability to forget pain."[7] When her trauma is triggered, he is still the only one she wants to talk to, despite her recognizing the abusive and exploitative relationship she had with him. Nevertheless, he remains "the only one who'll understand."[8] After years of abuse, indoctrination, and control, the temptation to return to their exploiters is also fueled by the belief that sex for commercial purposes is all they are good at, or for. This is demonstrated in those survivors that "choose" to remain in prostitution because "life has become this way now."[9] In some cases, they will have little alternative due to destitution, an inequality in rights, and societal perceptions of women's perceived roles.

Finally liberated, survivors suddenly find themselves without income, secure permanent accommodation, and without the support of their trafficked community, leaving them questioning their liberation. By contrast to the uncertainties of liberation, their state of existence during their exploitation was a known. They received food, accommodation, and

---

[5] Heather J. Clawson et al., *Study of HSS Programs Serving Human Trafficking Victims: Final Report* (US Department of Health and Human Services, Office of the Assistant Secretary for Planning and Evaluation, December 2009).
[6] Isabel, describing to Rachel Lloyd, *Girls Like Us*, 206.
[7] Rachel Lloyd, *Girls Like Us*, 187, 188.
[8] Rachel Lloyd, *Girls Like Us*, 185.
[9] Dina, *To Plead Our Own Cause*, 106.

some form of community. The conditions of their exploitation became their "normal," whereas liberation is an unknown. It is fraught with risk, confronting them with the reality of the long road to recovery and the difficulties of fitting into society. The potential for a future that has been hereto unseen and so long denied is frightening. Their trauma is exposed to them in this new liberation, and collectively these things can leave them reconnecting with a world that is abusive, but which is known.

### THE LACK OF SUITABLE PROVISION TO SUPPORT SURVIVORS IN FREEDOM

Effective monitoring and evaluation by NGOs of their own progress and outcomes, service providers' ability to bring about interventions (such as safe housing, lawful extraction, and health care), legal support frameworks, and the provision of crisis management services are therefore key to supporting survivors' transitions to freedom.[10] The ability to provide intensive support services when risks arise is essential to prevent destructive behaviors and survivors returning to exploitative situations. But meeting these needs is challenging where support typically involves multiple services, not all of which are available in the survivor's country of exploitation (or origin where repatriated). These services can include caseworkers, outreach street workers, counsellors, shelters, drop-in centers, various health services, emergency accommodation, and law enforcement. As a result of the various organizations and individuals involved, where systems are in place they are often fragmented. Many have developed reactively and in response to the growing awareness of slavery and consequent increases in victim identification. The variance in the availability and coordination of care creates complications for both survivors and service providers, particularly where there are no standard protocols and where survivors are resistant to help.[11] In some instances survivors are not recognized as victims of slavery at all, leaving them

---

[10] For more on this see Freedom Fund's monitoring & evaluation techniques: https://freedomfund.org/impact/monitoring-and-evaluation/.

[11] Heather J. Clawson, and Lisa Goldblatt Grace. *Finding a Path to Recovery: Residential Facilities for Minor Victims of Domestic Sex Trafficking* (US Department of Health and Human Services, Office of the Assistant Secretary for Planning and Evaluation, January 2007). Although not used as standard across the industry or globally, it should be noted that the Human Trafficking Foundation Slavery and Trafficking Survivor Care Standards do aim to provide a blueprint for UK-wide service providers offering care to survivors of slavery.

trying to adjust to a life where they are "free but with no place to go and no one to turn to,"[12] having to "find [their] new normal."[13]

While NGOs specific to the issue of modern slavery are now more widespread, many have had to adapt existing provision for refugees, sex workers, domestic abuse, and migrants. There remains a lack of knowledge and understanding of human trafficking and modern slavery affecting the treatment of survivors on discovery, the services that are provided to them, and the suitability of responses and support. A systematic review of exit and post-exit interventions showed a wide variance in participants' length of stay, ranging from 4 to 72 months, creating a lottery of support,[14] with short periods of support undermining already fragile feelings of security. Combined with a lack of income and the uncertainty over the availability of support, survivors are placed in a situation that seems no better or worse than the situation they were in prior to seeking help. Further, detention plans and treatment can coincide with criminal charges, complicating recovery and forming a questionable association between survivors' willingness to aid prosecution and the length of time support is made available.

Limitations on support agencies can also lead to survivors being placed in inappropriate accommodation that can compound their trauma. Typically shelters have little experience of, and are not set up to deal with, the complexity of trauma experienced by survivors of slavery, and some crisis shelters are fundamentally inappropriate given the survivor's experiences, needs, age, or gender. In one example, the only available safe house accommodation for Dwain, a survivor of domestic slavery, was 97 miles away from his partner and three children. Other examples include survivors with children placed in one-bedroom rooms in shared houses, survivors being placed in mixed accommodation, or in domestic abuse safe houses. The latter is common for survivors of sexual slavery but can cause conflict with existing residents who express concern that their location will be revealed by the presence of survivors who might be traced by their traffickers.[15] Those concerns are borne out by studies evidencing that traffickers often know the location of their victims and

---

[12] Kevin Bales and Zoe Trodd, *To Plead Our Own Cause*, 179.
[13] Leah (2016). www.antislavery.ac.uk/items/show/140
[14] Nathaniel A. Dell et al., "Helping Survivors of Human Trafficking: A Systematic Review of Exit and Postexit Interventions," *Trauma, Violence and Abuse* (2017): 6.
[15] See the interview with Nancy Hormachae, Attorney, in Rachel Shigekane, "Rehabilitation and Community Integration of Trafficking Survivors in the United States." *Human Rights Quarterly* 29, no. 1 (2007): 129.

have been known to recruit outside facilities and in some cases send girls into shelters to recruit or retrieve.[16]

Survivors also face additional barriers to support as a result of the eligibility criteria maintained by residential facilities, which would typically exclude many survivors of slavery. These criteria usually concern an inability to shelter minors, those with severe mental disorders such as psychosis or suicidal thoughts, and where there is evidence of active and severe substance abuse, addiction, or violent behavior.[17] In the UK, 26 per cent of survivors weren't able to enter safehouses because they didn't meet the eligibility criteria, declined support, or because contact was lost.[18] The imposition of eligibility criteria is understandable and in many cases necessary, but it makes it difficult to support survivors of slavery effectively and to extract them permanently from exploitation. Where length of stay is often variable and limited, this also makes it impossible to build survivors' trust and begin meaningful support. Until appropriate accommodation and extended stays are assured, and one-to-one case management can be provided at risk points in their liberation journeys (such as at the point of discovery and extraction, where they are a flight risk, and when prosecution occurs), survivors will continue to be at risk.[19]

However, despite these issues, and whether centralized support systems exist or not, time and time again NGOs have proven vital to survivor support and recovery. The support of NGOs has a central importance in narratives, with survivors detailing the safety and security they offer, and the inception of recovery as a result. NGOs are crucial to the transition from exploitation to safety, the first stage in recovery, providing survivors with a nurturing environment that can ensure their continued liberation. Ravi states his time in an ashram was "beautiful":

The first day I came to the ashram, the other kids showed me around the place, where the bathing area was, where the bathroom was. They showed me where the cocks and rabbits lived. I was fed a good meal and I went to sleep. It was just beautiful the first time I knew that I was not going to be beaten or tortured. What

---

[16] Heather J. Clawson, and Lisa Goldblatt Grace, *Finding a Path to Recovery*, 3.
[17] Heather J. Clawson, and Lisa Goldblatt Grace, *Finding a Path to Recovery*, 4.
[18] Christine Beddoe, Lara Bundock, and Tatiana Jardan, *Life beyond the Safehouse for Survivors of Modern Slavery in London: Gaps and Options Review* (Human Trafficking Foundation, July 2015).
[19] See Heather Clawson and Lisa Goldblatt Grace, *Finding a Path to* Recovery; and Samantha Ferrell-Schweppenstedde, *Day 46: Is There Life After the Safehouse for Survivors of Modern Slavery?* (The Human Trafficking Foundation, October 2016).

I like best here are the studies, the playing, the food, the interactions. I love it. I don't think I'll like my home anymore.[20]

Sumara identifies the support the NGO Sankalp gave her and her villagers, not in terms of accommodation, but in terms of providing them with a perspective of a life in freedom that eventually galvanized the community to rebel.[21]

NGOs are ideally placed to meet survivors' fundamental and immediate needs, either by experience, or location. This indicates that centralizing survivor support will not necessarily provide the most effective change to survivors, particularly where there will be financial and political limits to provision (given the conflict with immigration policy). Instead, and additionally, we should be looking to identify the consistency of available services to provide culturally appropriate wrap around support within each area thereby removing some of the responsibility for the self that is borne by survivors at this time. Providing better financial support to communities and NGOs to expand existing support structures, capacity, and services, is likely to have a greater impact within current frameworks than relying on a central (government) support system. Central systems are typically only able to provide minimum levels of support and would be comparatively more expensive, meaning governments would continue to rely on NGOs to fill gaps in services while diverting critical funds to central systems that fail to address survivors' needs. Further, a central system is unlikely to be able to provide mid- to long-term support, such as helping survivors build life skills, independence, and resilience, and helping them to integrate with society, build healthy relationships, and ensure their readiness for employment.[22] The complexity of the trauma suffered by survivors is not always understood or is underestimated, and their ability or desire to engage with these measures will be accompanied by suspicion of "counterfeit nurturance,"[23] any support provided requires strong relationships of trust to be built with those not perceived to be part of competing systems that are at the same time trying to criminalize or deport them.

---

[20] Ravi in Kevin Bales and Zoe Trodd, *To Plead Our Own Cause*, 77.
[21] http://antislavery.ac.uk/items/show/119
[22] Examples include the CAST "empowerment model." Another is the City Hearts "Fresh Start" programme.
[23] Robert Jay Lifton, "The Concept of the Survivor," in *Survivors, Victims, and Perpetrators: Essays on the Nazi Holocaust*. Edited by Joel E. Dimsdale (Baskerville, VA: Hemisphere Publishing Corporation, 1980), 122.

## THE BURDEN OF RESPONSIBILITY
## FOR THE SELF PLACED ON SURVIVORS

Some survivors are not provided with any support at all and have to find their own way in liberation. For example, Jill recounts the way her situation and condition was dismissed in the moment of discovery:

> In 1984 my captivity came to an abrupt end. Bruce was arrested on unrelated charges, and I was able to escape after he'd been handcuffed and taken away. The police who arrested Bruce offered me no support, despite finding a young girl locked in a closet, bound, gagged, and blindfolded. Even my request for a female officer to speak to was denied. The police told me that they were there to execute a warrant and that I'd better shut up or I was going to be arrested too. I wasn't even eighteen yet.
> 
> Taking whatever money I could find in the house, I left immediately, taking a taxi to the airport and flying to the first destination available with the amount of money I had. After arriving in a new city, I found a cheap hotel and literally slept for days. The face I saw in the mirror when I awoke was hardly like the one I'd seen at age fourteen.[24]

Despite the clear exploitation and abuse that was demonstrated in the way she was found and in her physical condition, she was instead treated as a potential accomplice and not a victim of slavery. She was essentially abandoned to find her own solutions. After years of control and abuse, suffering severe physical and psychological trauma, she was left entirely to take responsibility for herself.

Even within existing support frameworks, survivors still have to take responsibility for themselves in the day-to-day task of living. Muhsen explains "freedom can be a frightening thing when you are not used to it, when you are used to having other people make all your decisions for you, when you have no choices to make. I couldn't think straight ... I felt so helpless."[25] Mende Nazer recounts how she "suddenly" found herself in a situation where after years of being controlled she had to decide everything. Seemingly innocuous matters like what to wear, when to eat, and when to sleep were overwhelming. Far from the euphoria we might expect at liberation, it was instead frightening and full of a responsibility for the self that hadn't been learned naturally over time.[26]

---

[24] Jill, in Kevin Bales and Zoe Trodd, *To Plead Our Own Cause*, 180.
[25] Zana Muhsen and Andrew Crofts, *Sold: One Woman's True Account of Modern Slavery* (London: Sphere Publishing, 2010), 260.
[26] Mende Nazer and Damien Lewis, *Slave: The True Story of a Girl's Lost Childhood and Her Fight for Survival* (London: Virago, 2010), 294.

The effect of these combined problems ultimately places the burden of responsibility for survival on the survivor at a highly vulnerable point in their journey. How then do survivors assume more agency in liberation? How do survivors move from the limited agency exercised in slavery to becoming someone "who acts and brings about change, and whose achievements can be judged in terms of her own values and objectives, whether or not we assess them in terms of some external criteria as well?"[27] The ability to achieve self-ownership, and with that the capability to assume and exert rights is an expression of individual power. This means the survivor ultimately bears the responsibility for their own physiological and safety needs, while dealing with trauma crises, while at the same time navigating the various systems they have entered. When survivors do feel that they finally have more agency, they are unable to exercise it as they are at the mercy of external processes (such as immigration and asylum processes) over which they have no control. This destabilization of agency is compounded by fragmented services and the lack of legal assistance and interpreters. Further, central support mechanisms can present barriers to agency where the availability of ongoing support is typically linked to prosecution:

We talk about these protections for women and also women being able to stay in our country, but that is if they cooperate with the prosecution, but some women may not be able to do that because literally their loved ones could be murdered back in the countries they come from.[28]

With the availability of central support mechanisms often premised on cooperation in prosecutions, the responsibility falls to the survivor to seek out support from fragmented provision and where they often have little understanding of what they are entitled to.

The identification of victims and support for survivors is also often secondary to law enforcement and immigration objectives and policy and is "prosecution oriented" rather than "victim-centred."[29] Where survivors are liberated by law enforcement, they are not always able to understand whether they are being rescued or arrested. Despite the existence of legislative provisions protecting them from prosecution in some states, there continue to be reports that survivors are treated as criminals

---

[27] Amartya Sen, *Development as Freedom* (Oxford: Oxford University Press, 1999), 19.
[28] Inez, in Laura T. Murphy, *Survivors of Slavery*, 106.
[29] Rachel Shigekane, "Rehabilitation," 114.

and/or illegal immigrants first, and victims second.[30] The narratives below identify examples of some of the problems that are encountered globally, and which are more problematic in some states than others. However, while there are several explicit references to concerns about the way the authorities approach and process survivors (data), the majority do not talk about their experience with the authorities. This may be because survivors feel unable to criticize the authorities or that survivors didn't have much encounter with the authorities. It may also imply that the greater experience of arrest on discovery is not significantly negative and/or that the authorities instead supported them. However, in some cases, survivors' treatment at the hands of the authorities has been traumatic. With corruption rife in many countries survivors can be fearful and distrustful of the authorities, and their mistreatment "breeds distrust of law enforcement, confirms stereotypes used by traffickers to enforce control, and results in a lifetime of challenges that cannot be overcome by victims ... [therefore] arresting victims does not reduce the vicious cycle [of trafficking]; it perpetuates it."[31]

Several narratives expose examples of the police "rescuing" women and re-trafficking them between brothels, and themselves engaging the services of those sexually enslaved:[32]

The police, yes the police, sell us for another cycle of slavery. Do you think it is in their interests to see my occupation de-criminalised? Of course not – then they lose their share of the money. In one day we pay almost 15,000 riel ($3) in bribes to the district police, to the municipal authorities and the local authorities. Then another group of police come and arrest us. If we do not run and hide we are resold into slavery. Your solution is to ask these people to protect us. Think again. They live off our blood.[33]

---

[30] See for example, Heather Clawson and Lisa Goldblatt Grace, *Finding a Path to Recovery*; Rachel Shigekane, "Rehabilitation"; Dell et al., "Helping Survivors"; Cathy Zimmerman, Mazeda Hossain and Charlotte Watts, "Human Trafficking and Health: A Conceptual Model to Inform Policy, Intervention and Research." *Social Science & Medicine*, 73 (June 2011); Micah Bump et al., "Second Conference on Identifying and Serving Child Victims of Trafficking," *International Migration* 43, no. 1/2 (2005); and Samantha Ferrell-Schweppenstedde, *Day 46: Is There Life After the Safehouse for Survivors of Modern Slavery?* (The Human Trafficking Foundation, October 2016).
[31] Richard, Stephanie. *Victims of Human Trafficking Should Not Be Arrested for Crimes Their Traffickers Force Them to Commit: A Study of Data from the Coalition to Abolish Slavery & Trafficking (CAST)* (The Coalition to Abolish Slavery & Trafficking, January 2016), 1.
[32] See for example, Bahar, in Kevin Bales and Zoe Trodd, *To Plead Our Own Cause*, 135.
[33] Dina, *To Plead Our Own Cause*, 104.

Another survivor, Rita, was working in a hotel in Nepal where a friend convinced her she would earn more as a dancer and introduced her to two "brothers" who asked her to carry diamonds to India. Travelling to Manakamana before heading to India, they gave her food and soda which was drugged, and she woke to find she had been sold into sexual slavery. Rita recounts the times the police would raid the brothel, noting that the owner was often tipped off by the police and was therefore able to hide the girls inside cupboards and walls, or shift them to another location:

They don't call the police "police" but call them "uncle" I think the police of the lower ranks provide information. That's how it was with them. We would be hidden inside, and the police would go back with nothing.

…we were harassed by lawyers and police after we came back to Nepal. The way they questions – it is like scratching a wound. They question us if we went knowingly. "they have done this willingly," that's what they think. We have come back from that sort of place with all the pain and suffering, and even then we have to file a complaint with the police. The men there question us and ask, "how many did you sleep with?" after a man was writing down the complaint, there were many boys and other men present. Those policemen should have thought about how awkward it would be for this girl, being questioned like that in the presence of everyone, but they don't. Forget about giving us justice – instead, in front of everyone, they ask us questions. They shame us in public. It's more painful because of this.

I had suffered as much as I could take. But thanks to the support of Maiti Nepal we were able to come here to Kathmandu. I work as a counsellor. Those who have been sold and have returned are suffering lots of pain and grief. They aren't able to tell others or share this with anybody. We go to them and talk to them, hoping to lessen their grief, and we give them advice. People may detest me, but I always wished to return to Nepal. That wish of mine was fulfilled. When I arrived at Maiti Nepal the brothers and sisters here gave me encouragement.[34]

This raises questions about the value of introducing alternative state mechanisms, improved scrutiny and processes, and of the value of community in assisting survivors and tackling slavery. Further, it explains the reluctance some survivors have in cooperating with the authorities in countries into which they have been trafficked.

### THE IMPORTANCE OF SURVIVOR ENGAGEMENT

An understanding of the corruption that occurs in law enforcement in different origin countries could be utilized to adopt informed strategies for assisting survivors and engaging them in prosecutions. The way Rita

[34] Rita, in Kevin Bales and Zoe Trodd, *To Plead Our Own Cause*, 117–18.

was questioned implied they felt she was to blame for her enslavement. She was not viewed as a victim as she was perceived to have "done this willingly," adding to her shame and indicating the bias and prejudice that underlay their treatment of her. Having finally reached a potential place of safety, she was questioned intrusively and insensitively, like if "scratching a wound," and in an inappropriate setting without thought for her needs, further exacerbating or creating a new trauma. Over half of her narrative recounts her treatment at the hands of the authorities, indicating how much impact the process had on her.

The concept of the willing victim, and its correlation with "iconic" victim constructs, is a damaging misconception that misunderstands the nature of consent and the degree to which survivors are conditioned, threatened, and controlled. That the notion of the "willing victim" continues to be adopted is supported by studies that evidence some providers believed survivors have "chosen" their situation. Such attitudes are then projected in a way that further isolates and humiliates survivors and leaves them believing others see them only as "prostitutes or willing participants."[35] Forms of discrimination and misconception, and the extremes of survivors' experiences in slavery often also contribute to a culture of disbelief that is highly damaging.

That survivors are heard and believed is central to their perception of justice, "justice is being heard, support is people hearing."[36] The way some survivors are questioned carries overtones or direct statements placing the responsibility for their circumstances on them rather than acknowledging their exploitation was something done *to* them by others. They are undermined, disbelieved, stigmatized, or treated as criminals where they should be treated with sensitivity and unbiased inquiry. It is telling when Amasya states she "had no other choice" than to go to the police, implying this was a last resort, and when she did go to the authorities, she says her experience was brief but "unimaginable." She states:

We were unable to make ourselves understood, nor did we have any documents, so they kept us one night at the police station. The next day we were taken to the immigration police for deportation. Thank God our stay was not long; we had to stay there for one night, as the bus to Armenia was leaving in the morning

---

[35] Heather J. Clawson, Nicole M. Dutch, Amy Salomon, and Lisa Goldblatt Grace, *Study of HSS Programs Serving Human Trafficking Victims: Final Report* (US Department of Health and Human Services, Office of the Assistant Secretary for Planning and Evaluation, December 2009).

[36] Maria, in Kevin Bales and Zoe Trodd, *To Plead Our Own Cause*, 169.

and the drivers agreed to take us to Armenia on the condition that we would pay them in Yerevan. I do not want to remember again the night that we spent in the immigration police. Even though I have seen the horrors of war, that night was unimaginable.[37]

The distrust that is created in such circumstances is exacerbated when survivors are in a strange country and unable to speak the language and these issues with language and identification are common. The need for and lack of legal representation, and the use of legal vernacular create barriers for survivors who also often don't understand the processes they are going through and what their rights are. Their fears and frustrations are therefore worsened where there is little or no access to interpreters, and where interpreters adopt a dismissive attitude toward them and fail to translate accurately.

In 2017, I interviewed Tung who, having been enslaved in the UK for six years, had learned sufficient English to realize his interpreter was not translating accurately during an interview with the Home Office. He was aware that the interview was very important for the purposes of a finding of modern slavery (which would provide him with additional support and would potentially allow a defense for his crimes under S.45 of the Modern Slavery Act 2015), but which would also have serious ramifications for his claim for asylum. He became aware that the interpreter was from a different region of Vietnam and was not interpreting his dialect accurately. The interview turned into an argument where he ultimately refused to continue after he was informed a different interpreter could not be provided, and he was left feeling an acute injustice had been allowed to occur.

Arrest is an intimidating process, particularly where there is little understanding of what is being said and what is happening. Many survivors that are being rescued by law enforcement are not able to understand they are not instead being arrested. With survivors carrying negative and fearful perceptions of the authorities and of detention, either from experience, or as a result of their slaveholder's dogma, they are at risk of reengaging with their traffickers rather than reaching out to the authorities for help.

Identification is also problematic. Many survivors are discovered following arrest, but in Tung's case, this only occurred on his third arrest. Prior to that, despite his being a child by law, and unable to speak adequate English, he was not identified as a potential victim of trafficking and was instead placed in care pending trial (from which he absconded and was

---

[37] Amasya, in Kevin Bales and Zoe Trodd, *To Plead Our Own Cause*, 123.

caught again by his traffickers). A US study of sixty-one victims of human trafficking, forty-two had arrest records and, of those, twenty-eight had at least one arrest that was directly related to their trafficking. Of those arrested *only* for crimes relating to their trafficking (15 per cent), they were arrested between one and forty-two times, with an average of nearly fifteen arrests each. Others not related to trafficking were arrested on average over eleven times.[38] Carla, one of the survivor participants, was forced into sexual slavery as a teenager and held for thirteen years. Over that time, she was arrested thirty-two times and convicted of fifty-two offences, mostly relating to prostitution. She received fines, was put in prison, and held on probation. Susan, another woman in the survivor group, was arrested thirty-eight times over eight years for burglary, prostitution, and drugs.[39]

Irina's narrative demonstrates the problems with forced criminality, the betrayal felt when the authorities treated her like a criminal, and the discord between the aims of immigration and prosecution. Irina had lived in Russia with her two children but despite working as a senior accountant and later a physiotherapist, her income was insufficient, and she struggled with debt. Looking for work abroad for a temporary period to boost her income, she was offered waitressing work in Germany by what seemed to be a legitimate employment agency. However, on arrival, her passport was taken from her and she was informed she owed them 1,000 Euros and would be working as a prostitute, not a waitress. She refused but was beaten and threatened and warned that the police had been bought off and without her passport she would be viewed as a criminal. Fearing for her life, she cooperated. Trafficked between various brothels, she eventually escaped after she was helped by the women in the club to retrieve her documents and get away, and then by a man who owned a nightclub. She says:

Many good Dutch people tried to help me, but I was always followed by the Russian gangsters. I needed to get to the police, but it was dangerous. The Dutch people I was staying with brought my twenty-one-year-old daughter to the Netherlands to help me. With my daughter, who speaks English, I went directly to the police. But at the police station, I was immediately separated from my daughter and detained for five days by the Dutch national police.

So began a long, terrible process of multiple questionings and misunderstandings by the authorities.

The authorities wanted to charge me for using the false passport that I was provided with by the criminals. I gave the Dutch police all of the information about what had happened, including information about the traffickers, the Russian

---

[38] Stephanie Richard, *Victims of Human Trafficking*, 6.
[39] Stephanie Richard, *Victims of Human Trafficking*, 7.

mafia. I told them everything I knew, and I thought they would help me. I was not provided with a lawyer and I was suddenly told that I had to work out the fine levied by the judicial system of the Netherlands for the use of a false passport. I hadn't even used that passport and did not agree with the decision of the court. But who listened to me? After all the assistance that I provided the investigators, I was placed in humiliating conditions and remained in serious danger without protection form the Russian gangsters.

After determining the crime had taken place in Germany, the Dutch national police turned me over to the immigration police and they placed me in a shelter. I provided the authorities with of the information again while the police investigated and verified every part of my story. After two weeks, I was released from the shelter and I returned to my daughter.

But, eventually, my daughter had to go home to work. I stayed in the Netherlands for two years, living only on the small benefits I received with the help of the kind Dutch people. Finally, I grew tired of this situation. I could not wait any longer for my appointment in court living in such circumstances. I told the Dutch authorities that I wanted to go home. I said that I would return if they needed me to testify, but I was very, very tired. My health was poor. I missed my daughters, I was constantly depressed and often thinking about suicide.

But instead of helping me go home, the Dutch government decided I had not suffered enough and placed me in prison of three months because I didn't pay the fine for using the false passport – a fine that I didn't know about. There was a contradiction between the Dutch national police who wanted the fine paid and the immigration police who acknowledged that I was a victim of trafficking.

For one month I was not allowed to get in contact with lawyers or with my relatives. I started a hunger strike to defend my innocence, but as a result I was put into solitary confinement with only a mattress on the floor.[40]

Having finally escaped and sought assistance, demonstrating a willingness to assist with intelligence gathering and the prosecution of her traffickers, she was instead separated from daughter, charged, imprisoned, and given no access to legal advice. She felt "punished" by a system that should have recognized her as a victim. Her narrative exposes the challenges for survivors in asserting their rights, with conflicting policy aims and systems taking the decisions and autonomy out of survivors' hands.

### THE EFFECTS OF CONFLICTING STATE POLICIES

Often prosecution and repatriation processes go hand in hand. For some the prospect of repatriation is a relief, providing an opportunity to divorce from the country in which they were exploited and escape the people that trafficked them. However, for others re-trafficking is a risk

---

[40] Irina, in Kevin Bales and Zoe Trodd, *To Plead Our Own Cause*, 214–15.

precisely because they are being returned to their country of origin and their vulnerability in the aftermath of slavery can leave them open to exploitation if they are returned too soon.[41] Their fragile new world can be shattered by news of repatriation; it wrenches them from any community they have built, from the support systems available to them, and destroys their emergent futures. Katya explains that,

> Going back to the Ukraine would be like going back to my own grave. Vladimir is still there with all of his clubs and associates. I am scared he would hurt me if I returned. The police there would never protect us, as they are corrupt ... I have fallen in love with this country. The laws work here, the police are good, and there are people here who will help people like me. The government attorneys and FBI agents I work with really care about me and my case. I am trusting people for the first time. I feel safe and protected...this country can protect me and provide me a future.[42]

Moving on can also mean survivors revisiting what they are moving away from, triggering the trauma of their enslavement in myriad ways. Before they are returned survivors need a degree of personal and emotional growth to enable integration and independence and reduce the risk of homelessness or re-exploitation. Regularization of immigration status, rather than repatriation, often provides a continued sense of security where survivors are able to trust in the legitimacy of systems, exercise rights, trust the police, and continue to integrate with communities. Where immigration status is settled, this has been seen to improve mental health outcomes and bring improvements in employment and education.[43] Once their immigration status is settled, survivors enjoy accompanying rights that grants political freedom, with the opportunity "to discuss and debate – and to participate in the selection of – values in the choice of priorities."[44] However, uncertainty and delays in the decision-making process are common and can be debilitating, preventing survivor growth and integration. After two years, Vera was still waiting to hear about a conclusive grounds decision and had to leave her safe house before she received a decision. She said:

---

[41] The Anti-Trafficking Monitoring Group, *Hidden in Plain Sight: Three Years On: Updated Analysis of UK Measures to Protect Trafficked Persons* (London: Anti-Slavery International, 2013), 47.
[42] Katya, Laura T. Murphy, *Survivors of Slavery*, 35–36.
[43] Mirian Potocky, "The Effectiveness of Services for Victims of International Human Trafficking: An Exploratory Evaluation," *Journal of Immigrant and Refugee Studies*, 8 (2010), 376.
[44] Amartya Sen, *Development as Freedom*, 5.

I have been here [the UK] for two years ... I feel like nobody cares about me ... if you wanted someone to be safe and you say you want to help someone, try to finish everything in a short time, help her get everything she needs, but not keep her safe [just] to live again on the streets ... Why do you [Government] makes us wait for two years to make us ready for our life? Always I am trying to forget my past and move on, but I cannot.[45]

To Dwain, the lack of security in repeated temporary extensions to his entitlement to stay is equal to abandonment. He explained that a failure to take responsibility for him has travelled with him all his life, from the reason for his enslavement as a child, to the reason for his continued unsettled immigration status as a liberated adult. His uncertain immigration status means he is unable to find permanent and decent work. Since his liberation, he has been homeless and regularly destitute. He continues to carry his trauma with him, but he connects the potential for growth with the regularization of his immigration status:

It's 20 years ago. It shouldn't mould my life, but it has. It has to a point where it's got flippin' chains on me that won't release and there's no human that can release it. Even I can't release it as much as I think. I'll try and forget about it and move on, but you've seen I can't. So, the system has to release it for me, but it won't.

Dwain also equates the granting of permanent residence as symbolic of freedom and social acceptance. Describing the effects permanent residence would have for him, he says it would provide him with:

A passport; recognition; acceptance. And I can make a decent woman of my partner, and I can take my kids on holiday. That's all ... I've not wanted to be in the shadow for this long. I've asked for, what's the word? Acceptance, you know, I've filled in the application form more times than there's human beings on the planet. And still no, no, no. Why?
...just to be able to travel you know. If you go to that travel agency and say, "can I get a flight to Tenerife please?" And the following week I'm there. That would be freedom to me. I've been stuck in your country for this long... [Dwain then discusses his struggles with regularisation of his immigration status and gaining a passport, as his birth was not registered, nor does he have his parents' birth certificates].
 Interviewer: So, really you're identifying the ability to travel, which is linked to them giving you a passport, as symbolic of a lot more.
 Oh yes, it is ... You've read it. It really is. It's so symbolic that I would probably keel over and cry in front of anybody because what that's shown me is finally what I've strived for forever, which is acceptance. I didn't choose to be this way,

---

[45] Christine Beddoe, Lara Bundock, and Tatiana Jardan, *Life Beyond the Safehouse for Survivors of Modern Slavery in London: Gaps and Options Review* (Human Trafficking Foundation, July 2015), 22.

it's just what happened. What I've tried to do is live with the Achilles heel that I have, if it is that. But because I'm living with it, why can't anybody just respect that and work with me on it rather than against me? Or like ... you know, people like me are treated like criminals.

How can I be a criminal? I didn't choose this. I didn't choose to come into a country I didn't even know I was coming into illegally. So, because of that, why am I still being punished?

So, it [freedom] would take a lot, it would wind me probably, it would take all the wind out of me, but positively. Because then the new wind that would come would be a positive energy, a more vibrant, optimistic, looking forward to the future, you know, because I feel like I can make a difference in my future now rather than sleeping on it ... But I'm now limited to what I can do, if I don't sleep on it what do you want me to do? Scream on it? Because if I scream on it, I'll get put inside some prison or mental institution. I'm trying to keep my sanity so that when the good times do come, I can actually recognise it as good times.[46]

Ultimately, for Dwain, freedom is not just the ability to travel, with the choice that travel implies. The things that would *enable* travel, namely permanent residency and a passport, mean something more profound to him: acceptance as a "legitimate" person. To be acknowledged by society and to integrate with it fully is to have his existence acknowledged and an opportunity to gain official confirmation he is a free human being. Permanent residency would indicate a system designed to support rather than obstruct, which can in his words stop "coding" him as an "anomaly." Were Dwain to realize "full freedom," he would move beyond his current situation of stasis – "only being," "sleeping on it" – and have the capacity to envisage and enact multiple futures.[47]

### THE FUNDAMENTAL IMPORTANCE OF SOCIAL BELONGING TO "FULL" FREEDOM

Dwain's narrative demonstrates the fragility of hope following survival, and Ramphal doesn't want to discuss his hopes for a future at length because it feels so "big a dream" to hope for.[48] However, in trying to envisage and construct their futures, four key themes emerge from the body of survivor narratives. These are education, family, purpose, and community. Survivors want to start life "afresh"[49] and "forget the

---

[46] Dwain, interview by Andrea Nicholson, November 3, 2017. With thanks to Atleu.
[47] Andrea Nicholson, Minh Dang and Zoe Trodd, "A Full Freedom: Contemporary Survivors' Definitions of Slavery." *Human Rights Law Review* 18, no. 4 (2018).
[48] Laura T. Murphy, *Survivors of Slavery*, 155.
[49] Kevin Bales and Zoe Trodd, *To Plead Our Own Cause*, 139.

past and move on."⁵⁰ Typically this means having a home, building a family, learning, working and earning their own money, with work in particular described as "satisfying" and giving rise to feelings of pride.⁵¹ For children, moving on often means a return to safety and "play," encouraging them to engage and interact with the world around them and claim a part of their lost childhood, allowing for a freedom and innocence that was denied in slavery. Adults returning home engage with and help their community as a way of educating and empowering others.⁵² Narratives contain references to returning to communities, being useful in communities, working toward societal and familial acceptance. They detail a drive to help others, to re-establish connections with lost relatives, and to build their own families. Re-establishing a sense of family and community is therefore vital to survivors' mid- and long-term needs, and community integration is a fundamental aspect of this.

The pain of loved ones who were lost or left behind continues in freedom, because freedom is not merely freedom from the condition of slavery, but also involves the opportunity to regain what was lost. Tamada states she is happy now that she has built a family and Dia explains that she wants to find a husband and details the dreams she has not for herself, but for her children.⁵³ The drive to start afresh therefore often concerns a return to community, or the building of a new community. By creating a family, returning to the safety and security of their pre-enslavement community, or building a new community, survivors create for themselves the opportunity to give and receive nurture, build potential for shared responsibility, and engage with an environment of their construction where they can be accepted and supported. For many survivors, community is about reconnecting with family, for example, Miguel states "what I really hope for is to see my family and to be with my family. And you know, it's been four years since I've seen them, and I'm still here. But, you know, America is beautiful, but it's not with my family."⁵⁴

Reflecting Maslow's hierarchy of needs, after the more immediate physiological and safety needs are met, social belonging becomes an

---

⁵⁰ Kevin Bales and Zoe Trodd, *To Plead Our Own Cause*, 139.
⁵¹ See Miguel and Christine, in Kevin Bales and Zoe Trodd, *To Plead Our Own Cause*, 144–45 and 157, respectively.
⁵² Marsha, in Kevin Bales and Zoe Trodd, *To Plead Our Own Cause*, 211; Minh Dang, in Laura T. Murphy, *Survivors of Slavery*, xvii.
⁵³ See also Bales and Trodd, *To Plead Our Own Cause:* Choti at 236, Shylealie at 237, and Sumara at 239.
⁵⁴ Miguel, in Laura T. Murphy, *Survivors of Slavery*, 127.

important part of survivor growth and enables the continuity of those earlier needs. Social belonging not only relates to support networks and the creation of a new and positive environment (or a reconstruction of a familiar environment), it decreases feelings of isolation and otherness by enabling social connection; "people need to connect to people, not programs (sic)."[55] Reconnecting with, or building community, is therefore something to live for. It is integral to growth and is an opportunity to bear witness; an opportunity for existence: "I feel as if I have nothing left to be alive for. I have no family; it is just me. No one will be able to tell stories about my childhood."[56]

However, many survivors experience difficulty in reconnecting. If survivors have been removed from their communities by their enslavement, family members and survivors don't know each other anymore and survivors' experiences have altered who they are and how they behave, with family's having to learn the facets of a different person than the one remembered, and where in many cases they believed them to have died. Survivors feel broken and foreign: "when I went back in June, I was very happy to see my parents. But then I felt like I was disconnected; I felt like an alien in my own country because I don't feel any connection to my family, my friends, my nieces – they're all grown and married."[57] And many survivors never knew their surviving relatives: "What if he is just some man pretending to be my uncle?"[58] So the fear of exploitation resurfaces.

Reconnecting also causes an unexpected confrontation with aspects of their trauma. Beah discusses his uncle calling him "son" and is slightly bemused – "no one had called me son in a long time. I didn't know what to say."[59] Reconnecting with family can be such a shift from their prior existence that it can be very difficult to acclimatize to "normal" family life: "I had to adjust to people being happy all the time."[60] Beah states "I was worried about living with a family, I had been on my own for years and had taken care of myself without any guidance from anyone. I was afraid I might look ungrateful to my uncle, who didn't have to take me in, if I distanced myself from my family unit. I was worried about what to do when nightmares and migraines took hold of me. How was I going

---

[55] Rachel Lloyd, *Girls Like Us*, 230.
[56] Ishmael Beah, *A Long Way Gone*, 167.
[57] Beatrice Fernando, in Laura T. Murphy, *Survivors of Slavery*, 202.
[58] Ishmael Beah, *A Long Way Gone*, 172.
[59] Ishmael Beah, *A Long Way Gone*, 172.
[60] Ishmael Beah, *A Long Way Gone*, 182.

to explain my sadness, which I am unable to hide as it takes over my face, to my new family…?"[61]

For others, community is a way of choosing a family of their creation, either replacing families lost, or building families anew where families were the abusers or traffickers. Again, the responsibility for creating a constructive and nurturing environment is on the survivor, but at the same time provides the conditions for greater agency. Survivor groups are one way of achieving this and can be very important to survival.[62] If those previously enslaved are able to build a community of survivors, this environment is an effective means of positioning the self in an accepting community. It is invaluable to recovery: "one of the most critical things for me was being around other girls and women who'd experienced the life … that became the place where I felt most 'normal'. We shared a common understanding, remembered similar feelings, and could talk frankly about our experiences without judgment. Those Friday nights with seven or eight women each week made me feel a little less one-of-these-things-is-not-like-the-other. Less of a round peg in a 'square' world."[63]

Survivor communities can act as a form of "insulation" from the hard realities of survival, particularly the judgment, blame and othering that can continue in liberation, whether felt or actual. People who have been isolated and shamed into keeping secrets can come together as a group and share those secrets without them being public knowledge. To identify with a body of individuals who have also emerged from enslavement diminishes survivors' feelings of isolation. The ability to share and locate their experiences with other survivors reduces feelings of shame, deconstructs the conditioning levied on them during their enslavement, and grows a realization that they are not to blame. Their experiences, choices, and actions are placed in the context of other survivors' experiences and they start to see themselves as more than damaged, despised, and alienated.

However, we rarely offer a treatment that would allow survivors to become therapists for one another[64] and again this responsibility is left to

---

[61] Ishmael Beah, *A Long Way Gone*, 179.
[62] See for example, Dori Laub, "Truth and Testimony: The Process and the Struggle," *American Imago* 48, no. 1 (1991): 69.
[63] Rachel Lloyd, *Girls Like Us*, 208.
[64] Judith Herman discussing Lifton's "Death in Life" in Judith Herman, "The Politics of Trauma: An Interview with Judith Herman," in *Listening to Trauma: Conversations with Leaders in the Theory & Treatment of Catastrophic Experience*, ed. Cathy Caruth (Baltimore: John Hopkins University Press, 2014), 139.

survivors. Art Blank speaks of the difficulty of finding someone who could truly recognize the importance of his experience in the Vietnam War[65] and survivors need to listen to trauma survivors on their own terms and in their current frameworks. In hearing other stories, their own stories "come out through others."[66] Therefore a survivor community, one where only those who have experienced similar abuse can truly understand, is important. Communities provide the environment for self-actualization, slowly revealing to survivors the capability to reach their potential and satisfying the need for purpose and activism. They enable survivors to start to assert their rights and to access the capabilities denied to them in slavery.

### EDUCATION FOR AGENCY

To many, education is a natural step in this journey. Education is liberty, a respite from the internal trauma and the struggles of survival and offers a future that could not previously be envisaged. It is a means of realizing rights and is employed to enable survivors to bear witness. Literacy is as important to survival and liberation in "modern" slavery as it was historically, and can be employed to assume agency in freedom, as a step toward "being," and as a means of providing permanent testimony: "When we have education, paper keeps the story." In many narratives, survivors express that they are driven toward education in the hope of preventing their re-enslavement, of providing the basis for a different future, and of educating others at risk. Education is also therefore a means of resistance and activism, a rejection of the circumstances that led them into slavery, and a means of recording and making known what was done to them.

The denial of an education during enslavement has the effect of ensuring survivors remain ignorant of their rights and makes building a different life in survival a struggle. Education is widely accepted as coexisting with the rights of communities and of unlocking the ability to enjoy all other human rights. Access to education therefore not only reveals the power survivors can claim for themselves, but also the lack of natural right for their traffickers to exercise that denial over him. This realization is expressed and implied in many narratives and supported by the repeated accounts of survivors' motivation post enslavement to gain an education for themselves or for their children. In seeking out an education,

---

[65] Cathy Caruth, *Listening to Trauma: Conversations with Leaders in the Theory & Treatment of Catastrophic Experience* (Baltimore: John Hopkins University Press, 2014), 71.
[66] Dori Laub, "Truth and Testimony," 72.

survivors recover their autonomy and build agency. Education can also be a consolation,[67] providing a respite from their memories, and giving them future perspectives. Many express the joy of learning and the value of education to understanding and realizing rights, to bearing witness ("paper keeps the story"), and to secure meaningful employment. Not only does education provide an avenue for participation in the antislavery agenda, education is a "joy" and a "liberty."[68] It essentially affords a stronger sense, and form of freedom. It is a rejection of the slaveholder's control, an act of ownership for the things denied or withheld from them, and a form of rebellion in liberation.

Access to education can be problematic where many survivors continue to experience poverty and discrimination, or where systems exclude them from what is considered a privilege and not a need. Dwain expresses his desire to go to university, but his ability to access higher education is hampered by his unsettled immigration status. Many survivors state a desire to move into caring professions as teachers, nurses, and support workers, but it is also common for survivors to state their frustration at not being able to afford the schooling that enables this (or where their immigration status prevents them from accessing financial support). Following her liberation, Mariana returned to her community but could not stay for fear her traffickers would find her, and because her community was told she had been working as a prostitute she was essentially ostracized from it. She was left with no home to go to and no income. She explains: "I don't have any place to live. Two months I have lived with my uncle, another two months with my friend. I would like to enter a hairdresser school, but it costs money. I don't have any."[69]

In other scenarios, there is little possibility for survivors to gain the benefits to growth, income, and a more meaningful existence that education can bring. The combination of poverty, discrimination, a lack of services, and trauma means it can take survivors years to realize their dreams, leaving those previously enslaved in stasis and living as if a "perpetual survivor." The psychological effects of trauma mean survivors are rarely in a position to achieve a meaningful existence early on. Theresa Flores recounts the disassociation she experienced which meant that it took two years for the full impact of her experiences to be felt. It

---

[67] Theodore Dwight Weld, *American Slavery as It Is*, 136.
[68] Maria, *To Plead Our Own Cause*, 168.
[69] Mariana, in Kevin Bales and Zoe Trodd, *To Plead Our Own Cause*, 209. See also Iliona at 127, and Katya: http://antislavery.ac.uk/items/show/491

took Zana Muhsen over a year to "find her feet" in the UK, and it took Shamere McKenzie five years to start speaking about her experience.[70] Marsha was only able to move forward after two years when she found an NGO that provided psychological and moral support:

> ...in two months I was back home. But even two years later, I was depressed and had many troubles. Then I found an ad in the newspaper for the St Petersburg Crisis Centre of women, which provides psychological assistance to the victims of human trafficking. I contacted them and they invited me to come in. That is how I came across the Angel Coalition. From them, I received psychological, moral and material assistance. I went back to my town and started an NGO that is a member of the Angel Coalition. It seems like we Russian women are placed in impossible economic conditions ad are not needed by our own country. In other countries, we are spit on as prostitutes when we are really victims. Ten years have passed since I was trafficked, but the situation has not changed. Is the German government really not aware of what is happening in their country? Or are they happy to profit from our suffering?[71]

However, once survivors start to move through the recovery process, they can weaponize their experiences to realize an activist purpose, which can also augment important feelings of genuine self-ownership. In the first instance, this is through a rejection of the survivor as victim. Having known hostility, exclusion, and "personal impotence,"[72] survivors endeavor to reformulate our perceptions of them as human beings first and foremost, rejecting negative labels that have been attached to them and the powerlessness associated with the term "victim."[73] Societal perceptions over time portray victims as blameworthy, blameless, or pathetic, and these portraits link to real-world consequences, dominating the ways in which people think about intimate violence and individual responsibility.

### VICTIMS AND SURVIVORS? LABELS AND IDENTITY

The term survivor is therefore more empowering than the label of victim. The status of the "victim" attracts stigmatization and defines their experience with standards that dismiss agency and deny survivors are "living, changing, growing, interactive person[s]."[74] In other words, it situates

---

[70] Shamere, in Laura T. Murphy, *Survivors of Slavery*, 53.
[71] Masha, Kevin Bales and Zoe Trodd, *To Plead Our Own Cause*, 211–12.
[72] Frances Smith Foster, *Witnessing* Slavery, 11.
[73] See for example, the narrative of Dina Chan in Kevin Bales and Zoe Trodd, *To Plead Our Own Cause*, 103–6.
[74] Kathleen Barry, *Female Sexual Slavery*, 38.

them in their past. It defines them by what is "done" to them and represents them variously as complicit, helpless, or "damaged, passive and powerless."[75] It fails to acknowledge the survivor as active and courageous both during their enslavement and in liberation. Victim discourse therefore disregards resistance strategies employed during enslavement, rather than recognizing survivors were not devoid of agency during their enslavement, rather they were unable to exercise it fully. While the victim is cast to receive pity, the survivor is allowed to retain some measure of dignity and integrity. Victim's actions are questioned, where survivors are celebrated. The image of the victim can violate the normative expectations of our image of the survivor and situate survivor and victim at "opposite poles of an agency continuum."[76] Lloyd explains "I am in a field that values the fact that I am a 'survivor' – it gives me, I've been told, a level of credibility that few other people in the field possess."[77] Assuming the survivor title enables survivors to re-landscape the self and implies *futurity*. Lloyd is "more than a story, more than just my past. Often I'm proving it to myself as much as others."[78] It attracts respect from others and builds self-respect; it implies strength, competence, mastery, self-confidence, independence, and freedom.

However, identifying as a survivor also attracts its own problems. Rachel Lloyd recounts a situation where she was invited to attend the White House for a ceremonial signing of the reauthorized trafficking legislation. While there, a well-known conservative lobbyist whispered to her "Long way from the street, eh?" Lloyd recounts her immediate feelings in the present tense, saying:

I feel like I have been slapped. Hard. The last thing on my mind was the streets, the life, or my past – it has been fifteen years. Yet apparently it was the first thing on his...despite all my accomplishments, despite the momentous nature of the event, all this person saw was my past. Nothing I did, no one I met, would erase the fact that in his eyes, I was still a former prostitute.[79]

The field she works in values her for the fact she is a survivor, because her lived experience gives her authority and brings a much needed perspective, but as a result she is defined by her past. Labelling as a survivor also

---

[75] Joel Best, "Victimization and the Victim Industry," *Society* 34, no. 9 (1997):13.
[76] Jennifer Dunn, "'Victims' and 'Survivors': Emerging Vocabularies of Motive for 'Battered Women Who Stay'," *Sociological Inquiry* 75, no. 1 (2005): 2.
[77] Rachel Lloyd, *Girls Like Us*, 211–12.
[78] Rachel Lloyd, *Girls Like Us*, 242.
[79] Rachel Lloyd, *Girls Like Us*, 210, 211.

therefore brings its own challenges. Spry argues that the classification of survivor "conceals the bodily experience of slavery" and is reductive of survivors' experiences.[80] By using the label survivor we homogenize slavery and conceal the reality of their lived experiences. The agency survivors' employ as "meaning maker of their experience" is denied in having to choose between labels of survivor and victim.[81] This polarity becomes problematic and invades recovery discourse. While "there can be no survivors without victims, masters without slaves,"[82] survivors are both victim and survivor, but, importantly, also more. Rachel Lloyd recognizes the complicated relationship between both acknowledging and moving on from her past, and the difficulty of defining herself:

> Had I worked so hard to be "more than just a survivor" that I'd lost track of what being a survivor really was? Was I so caught up in how far I'd come that I'd forgotten exactly where it was that I'd started? I'd let the media frenzy over "hookers" and "whores" make me want to hide that part of myself, that part I shared not just with these women but with my girls ... I realised that it was owning what I had been through, not hiding it, that had opened the door to real healing for me.[83]

Lloyd recognizes in this extract that her survivorship is precisely what places her in a position to facilitate change and support other survivors, but throughout her narrative struggles with being restricted to the survivor label. While she eventually takes ownership of that part of her, she also later coins a separate term to encompass who she is, adopting the phrase "victorious thriver" over "survivor."[84] Shamere McKenzie shows a similar preference by describing herself as "once a victim, once a survivor, now a liberator."[85] By describing themselves as survivors, *as well as* thrivers, liberators, educators, academics and/or activists, survivors at once identify both with a particular group of those previously enslaved and at the same time with humanity as whole. They recognize the transition between states of existence and employ their experiences for a positive end while at the same time placing those experiences in the past

---

[80] Tami Spry, "In the Absence of Word and Body: Hegemonic Implications of 'Victim' and 'Survivor' in Women's Narratives of Sexual Violence," *Women and Language* 13, no. 2 (1995): 27.
[81] Tami Spry, "In the Absence of Word and Body," 27.
[82] Tami Spry, "In the Absence of Word and Body," 28.
[83] Rachel Lloyd, *Girls Like Us* at 220, 221.
[84] Theresa Flores, *The Slave Across the Street*, 261.
[85] www.sun-gate.org/shameres-story/

and recognizing their growth and contribution to freedom. By associating with and asserting themselves as survivors, thrivers, or liberators rather than victims, individuals at once assume a dominant and purposive role. It is a means of claiming agency and a form of resistance and activism. Identifying in this way, survivors are no longer isolated and hidden, and indicate that they start to see themselves as powerful individuals that can influence the progress of abolition.

Where language is used to marginalize and deconstruct identity, it can be taken up as a tool to reconstruct. Adopting language that claims the titles of, for example, survivor, thriver, activist, teacher, academic, and colleague, rather than victim, is a means of demonstrating to the others and to themselves what their purpose is and presents their wider person to the world. Similarly, the adoption of new names is employed by some survivors as a means of assuming self-ownership and is a resistance to being defined by their experiences, rejecting the exercise of powers of ownership exercised over them. Through this articulation, survivors control how they are seen, how they are represented, and utilize their writing and stories as a call to activism. In her narrative, Christine conceptualizes a community of survivor girls and women, while at the same time drawing on women worldwide as an activist community.[86] In so doing she associates with and creates for herself multiple communities and explains: "now I feel I am free because I am doing things I never used to do before. For me the reason for talking out is to help make another slave free – not just a slave from Sudan, but from anywhere in the world. By talking out, people will be more aware and more able to help people become free."[87] And Ruth explains:

I'm not ashamed to tell them: "I was there, but God brought me out for a special purpose." And this is the purpose, to tell my testimony, and tell people that this thing is happening. Now I talk in villages and schools, telling them about my past experience. After giving then the definition of human trafficking. I always back it up with my story. So people will know that this thing is a real thing. It is happening. I am hoping this thing will come to a stop. We are ready to fight what is going on now.[88]

The preceding chapters have demonstrated that the support survivors need in the short-, mid-, and long-term are still fundamentally lacking. Even where support mechanisms exist, the evidence shows that these are

---

[86] Christine, in Kevin Bales and Zoe Trodd, *To Plead Our Own Cause*, 102.
[87] Mende Nazer and Damien Lewis, *Slave*, 227.
[88] Ruth, in Kevin Bales and Zoe Trodd, *To Plead Our Own Cause*, 244–45.

often fragmented and uncoordinated. The effects of trauma also mean that discovery and its associated processes can be all the more overwhelming and here NGOs and faith organizations are key, supporting survivors through unknown systems and providing crisis management and a consistency of care that is generally lacking. However, little is also known of the trauma of activism. The nature of survivors' role in the antislavery movement means survivors constantly revisiting the past and being placed in situations where the field of expertise is likely to trigger their trauma.

It can be years before survivors are ready to fully integrate with communities, to assume leadership roles, and maintain healthy personal relationships. With the general lack of state services available, the survivor once again bears the responsibility for their recovery and grassroots organizations bear the brunt of formal support. But even in the immediate aftermath of liberation, the mechanisms that exist and the survivor support available are not sufficient for this group. Existing services have been adapted to a group that, while better than none, remain unsuitable for the needs of survivors of slavery. The lack of sustained support leaves survivors feeling powerless and abandoned in the wake of discovery. The problems with structural support are further exacerbated by conflicting state priorities, such as prosecution targets, immigration policies, principles of state responsibility, and the ability of existing state politics and infrastructure to meet "new" problems. In some states, those structures, observance of the rule of law, and the value placed on human rights are lacking and there is little opportunity for the survivor to find justice or to engage with and inform process and policy.

Where the state is unable or unwilling to address the problem of slavery within its borders (or as a result of its practices), this raises an important question about the role of communities in abolition and survivor support. Nearly every chapter of this book has recognized the importance of social belonging. It is key also to recovery, with survivors wanting to find place and acceptance, to reconnect with families and communities lost, or to start anew with families and communities (even communities of survivors) of their own creation. These communities have much to bring to survivors in terms of their perceptions of justice, of futurity, inclusion, and support.

# 6

# Antislavery Strategies and the Survivor as Activist

> People with lived experience of any oppression need to have their own spaces to interact in alternative modalities from the oppressive dominant norm.[1]

Building on the preceding chapters, I examine here the survivor as activist in the context of prevention, state mechanisms, and antislavery participation. The narrative corpus exposes the antislavery strategies that survivors themselves suggest and reveals the challenges that survivors face in engaging with the public and government sector to inform antislavery policy. In a movement dominated by governments, NGOs, and academics, it is survivors who are uniquely placed to lead enslaved individuals to freedom through their actions and their voices. Joining grassroots organizations, educating, training, and informing members of the antislavery movement, they can broadcast the complexity of enslavement and of recovery to inform approaches to identifying and caring for survivors' post-enslavement. The current narrow employment of survivor voice (by which I include survivor participation)[2] presents a missed opportunity for survivors to lead the antislavery agenda and to become an intrinsic part of the process of freedom and recovery for others. Survivors are therefore essential to contemporary

---

[1] Minh Dang, "Paradox of Survivor Leadership," in *Wicked Problems: The Ethics of Action for Peace, Rights, and Justice*, ed. Douglass Irvin-Erickson, Austin Choi-Fitzpatrick, and Ernesto Verdeja (Oxford: Oxford University Press, In Press), 10.
[2] While a distinction could be made between participation and voice, with voice indicating the ability and platforms for speaking out and participation as meaningful involvement in processes, organisations, and research, participation is itself a form of voice and is constructed here as such.

abolition, working with other survivors, services, governments, and NGOs, building alliances, providing consultancy to the antislavery community, and participating in anti-slavery developments. While inclusion is more firmly established in other fields, such as the health sciences, and we are starting to see this movement populated and developed by survivors, they do not yet lead it, nor is it clear how involved survivors are in legislative and policy-making processes.[3] Instead, the corpus reveals that it is mainly survivors that assume responsibility for activism, rather than the antislavery community engaging in proactive and meaningful inclusion.

### SURVIVOR ACTIVISM AND MOTIVATIONS

Survivors express that their activist drive derives from rage felt at their enslavement, the compassion they have for other survivors and those still enslaved, and the guilt they hold for surviving where others were lost or left behind. This survivor guilt, or "death guilt,"[4] also arises from the way survivors felt helpless to save others, or their inability to feel certain emotions. Their sense of debt to the dead and the lost results in their assuming a responsibility toward others;[5] it is an animation of guilt.[6] Nadia explains:

It was not only me that suffered, it was a collective suffering. The Islamic state gave us two choices, convert or die. For those who accepted to convert fearing their lives, their men were killed, women were enslaved, and children were recruited. To date, 16 mass graves have been found, including a mass grave of 80 women they didn't desire, therefore they decided to kill.[7]

---

[3] Sue Lockyer, "Beyond Inclusion: Survivor-Leader Voice in Anti-Human Trafficking Organizations," *Journal of Human Trafficking* (online, 2020): 2; Sisay Abayneh, Heidi Lempp, Jill Manthorpe, and Charlotte Hanlon, "Development of Programme Theory for Integration of Service User and Caregiver Involvement in Mental Health System Strengthening: Protocol for Realist Systematic Review," *International Journal of Mental Health Systems* 12, no. 1 (2018); Mary E. Gilfus, "The Price of the Ticket: A Survivor-Centred Appraisal of Trauma Theory," *Violence against Women* 5, no. 11 (1999): 1248; Susan Mockus, Laura Cinq Mars, Dorothy Guazzo Ovard, Ruta Mazelis, Paula Bjelajac, Janice Grady, Christine LaClair, Cardenia Livingston, Sharon Slavin, Susan Williams, and Jacki McKinney, "Developing Consumer/Survivor/Recovering Voice and Its Impact on Services and Research: Our Experience with the SAMHSA Women, Co-occurring Disorders and Violence Study," *Journal of Community Psychology* 33, no. 4 (2005): 513–25.

[4] The second of Laub's five psychological themes in Robert Jay Lifton, "The Concept of the Survivor," in *Survivors, Victims, and perpetrators: Essays on the Nazi Holocaust*, ed. Joel E. Dimsdale (Baskerville, VA: Hemisphere Publishing Corporation, 1980), 118

[5] Robert Jay Lifton, "The Concept of the Survivor," 118.

[6] Robert Jay Lifton, "The Concept of the Survivor," 120.

[7] http://antislavery.ac.uk/items/show/144.

The impulse to bear witness to their own and others' experiences, the "survivor mission" to speak, act, and seek justice, is part of survivors' struggle for meaning and a means of establishing for themselves some measure of a moral universe.[8] As Christine expresses:[9]

> You're talking about your life. You're talking about the lives of other women and girls who are still held captive, who are still being hurt, who may not survive. You feel an urgency, a bond deeper than blood to the very women and girls they tried to make you hate.[10]

Representing others and themselves, survivors look to find meaning in their lives. Anywar Ricky Richard explains "I feel more satisfied when I serve people...what drives me most is seeing former child soldiers getting rehabilitated. I feel very happy; I feel very satisfied."[11] And Shamere states:

> I now realise that I went through the trauma not for myself, but for someone else. I have had several opportunities because of being enslaved, some of which are mind blowing...I believe I am a voice for those still enslaved, the voice for those who perished while enslaved, and the voice for those who are free but have not the courage to speak up. We all have a story...I am determined to use my story to make a difference in the life of someone else, leaving a legacy in this world.[12]

The corpus reveals that activism re-sculpts survivors' internal monologue enabling them to establish futurity, and challenge societal perceptions. Lloyd explains her embarrassment and shyness "melt away in the presence of other powerful young survivors. I see glimpses of who I might become...and for the first time I am comfortable with the reflection."[13]

Of the five interviews I carried out, it was Val's narrative that was predominantly concerned with her activist drive. Val is the founder and director of the Mojatu Foundation, an NGO that aims to transform communities by developing the capacity and skills of socially and economically disadvantaged and "hard-to-reach" groups. In particular, but not

---

[8] Robert Jay Lifton, "The Concept of the Survivor," 123.
[9] For one of many examples, see the narrative of Chanta, who states "My life has had no significance, no value ... I hope that by sharing my story, my life will finally have meaning and prevent others from the deep sadness in my life." Chanta, in Kevin Bales and Zoe Trodd (eds.), *To Plead Our Own Cause Personal Stories by Today's Slaves* (New York: Cornell University Press, 2008), 207.
[10] Christine, in Kevin Bales and Zoe Trodd, *To Plead Our Own Cause*, 102.
[11] Anywar Ricky Richard in Laura T. Murphy, *Survivors of Slavery: Modern-Day Slave Narratives* (New York: Columbia University Press, 2014), 225.
[12] Shamere, in Laura T. Murphy, *Survivors of Slavery*, 53.
[13] Rachel Lloyd, *Girls Like Us: A Memoir* (New York: Harper Collins Publishers, 2011), 241.

exclusively, Mojatu supports women, girls, and young people of African and Caribbean communities in such a way that they are better able to identify, help, and meet their needs and to participate more fully in society. Explaining her motivation to found Mojatu, Val stated:

It became very powerful in me that I had this call. There was something in me that kept saying "you need to do something, you need to do something," not only for me, but for my family, for my community, for women. It's still there...

It was harder in the earlier years, but I think I've moved on in a very significant way thanks to things I've got involved in, like being involved in setting up the Mojatu foundation,[14] having to work with survivors of female genital mutilation and other abuse. It's when even if it's one person you supported through just sitting down, for example, and listening to them, it's made a huge difference to their life. Or just advising them on the simplest things in life on how to cope. For me it's been a great joy. I'm hoping there is more to do, there is more to do on a much bigger scale...

...but I rebuilt my life and I'm much happier. I've moved on. I've found a way of coping and at least I didn't dwell on those things that affected me. I've used them in a positive way to have a positive impact on the lives of other people and my family, and it's something I want to do more and more.

Val's involvement with the Mojatu Foundation was a way for her to build something positive from her own experiences; it was not only a means of her helping those that may need it, but a means of helping herself. She is "happier" and has "found a way of coping." As a survivor, she is able to listen to others within their shared framework of experience, and as a result of her experiences, she brings a valuable expertise to the Foundation's research and activist mission. Figure 6.1 that Val drew is also dominated by words that she relates to her activism and to the value she sees in education and negotiation.

Describing her drawing she said:

In the middle I have a heart shaped thing I have done there, and in there, there are things that personally I believe in and things that I know probably have helped me in my life - and I've got so many of them, so I'll just read them. So, there is love, responsibility (I have that in abundance), and empowerment and that's really important because it's not only about my own empowerment, it's about empowerment of girls and women. There's also confidence, resilience, and inspiration, which is more drawing from other people and building relationships.

---

[14] Mojatu Foundation is a leading organisation in the global campaign to end female genital mutilation (FGM). They offer training programs and awareness raising campaigns, undertake research and are active participants in local, national and international end FGM campaigns: www.mojatufoundation.org/

## Antislavery Strategies and the Survivor as Activist 161

FIGURE 6.1 Drawing by Val, depicting the things most important to her and related to her activism.

Caring: It's one of the things that if I didn't have caring people in my life I wouldn't be where I am today. Respect, and respecting people for who they are. Caring about humanity and human rights; that's really important. I put down sharing. I'm very open about things that I believe in and I would always share them with people I think or feel matter and people who I think are in a position to influence things. And then there is also equality. Obviously, I care so much about girls and women's rights, but I also care about issues affecting the boy child, I know that's a big issue back home where the over-emphasis on the girl child kind of eliminates the boy child, so I really care about equality and other things. Then openness. I wrote journey because I believe it's good to be reflecting on the life we've gone through, where I mean as human beings, because the things we've gone through are important in terms of shaping the decisions we make about life.

And then focus is a big one for me, because all the time I have to keep thinking "why do I have to do what I do?" and sometimes I have to keep re-checking my focus towards where I want to be, and I think it's really important.

But the biggest one in this heart shaped thing is education. For me that is absolutely key. If I didn't pursue education I think I would have been in, er, probably my life would have taken a completely different path. I know so many of my friends that I went to primary school with were married off at a young age. They remained in those marriages and I still meet them and… (sighs) some of them are in really difficult situations where sometimes I feel like I can't really influence much in terms of them escaping the situations they are in. But education in every social issue, personally, I feel like education is really key.

Right, and then on this side I've just put like little quads which I really like and they all link to the circle there. The first quad is "people's experiences don't define who they are, and they shouldn't anyway," and then the other one is "some negative experiences can be the source of energy we use to change the world." Obviously, it depends on how we see the situation, you know, how people see the situation they are in. They can either give up, or they can decide to do something with it and move on. And then up here we have "survivor's voice is key to bringing about change" and personally I believe if we didn't have survivors of whatever it is in the world, we wouldn't be doing the work we are doing. If people aren't impacted, for example, by modern slavery, would we be talking about it today? Or if we didn't have women who are forced to go through female genital mutilation, would we be talking about it today? So that voice is really key. My last little message there is "time to change!". I think they are all interconnected, to me, probably if someone looked at it they would think "what kind of rubbish is this?" I think for me it sums up maybe where the things that this key, this heart shaped thing, the things that are in there are really key for me, so to speak.

Val's explanation touches on a number of themes discussed in this book but is focused on her moving forward and making a difference. The colors she used are bright, with writing and shapes in pink, blue, red, purple, aqua, and yellow. The heart, encompassing equality, respect, humanity, education, responsibility, empowerment, resilience, focus, caring, love, sharing, openness, confidence, and inspiration are all core to her belief systems and to her unerring activism.

A number of other survivor activists have joined or built NGOs, for example, Minh Dang has formed the Survivor Alliance, a nonprofit organization that unites and empowers survivors of slavery and human trafficking around the world to build a global network of survivor leaders who are engaged in antislavery work.[15] Shamere KcKenzie is CEO of the Sun Gate Foundation, a nonprofit, survivor-led organization based in Alexandria, Virginia, which addresses a critical gap in the human trafficking aftercare community by making a substantial commitment to survivors by funding educational opportunities.[16] However, many other survivors carry out activism through different means, through poetry, research, art, education, teaching, and through Twitter, blogs, and journalism. Thus, survivors work for survivors and in so doing give voice to collective suffering, filling gaps in services, providing support *by* those with lived experience *for* those with lived experience and in so doing bring survivors into a community that understands their experiences and needs from the inside.

Through formal and informal platforms, survivors make valuable contributions to legislation, global understandings of the risks, indicators and causes of slavery, and make detailed and strategic suggestions for abolition. Concrete suggestions and strategies suggested by survivors reframe nonsurvivors' understanding of what will make difference on the ground or provide the evidence for proposed strategies that meet with disagreement. For example, survivors have argued for the decriminalization of prostitution,[17] for equal property rights and equal access to education for women, and for the education of men to prevent harmful cultural practices.[18] Charlotte argues that "mechanisms should be put in place to track and trace missing people and the means put in place to identify the trafficked persons"[19] and Beatrice argues:

We need more public awareness campaigns about the dangers of trafficking, as much to educate those at risk, as to employ communities in identifying and eradicating slavery (intel). We can reduce the power of traffickers by educating at-risk populations.

We need to monitor – and make sure other governments are monitoring – the job agencies that send so many people abroad. Place responsibility on these agencies, make them liable for violations. One idea is to insist that agencies have registration programs, so relatives of workers can always track them down.

---

[15] https://survivoralliance.org/about/
[16] www.sun-gate.org/
[17] See for example, Dina, in Kevin Bales and Zoe Trodd, *To Plead Our Own Cause*, 105–6.
[18] See Hannah Rose Murray, "Voices: Ideas for Using Survivor Testimony in Antislavery Work," October 2019, *Rights Lab, Nottingham*, 14; and the narrative of Dara. http://antislavery.ac.uk/items/show/1303
[19] Hannah Rose Murray, "Voices," 15.

Guarantee rights for non-national workers. So that they are (a) aware of their rights and (b) can enforce them.

Tougher monitoring of tougher monitoring of foreign countries. Every year the State department's annual report on trafficking should list the amount of money each country spends on anti-trafficking efforts. The report should also document the repression of antislavery groups. For instance, in Mauritania the Government still bans the abolitionist group SOS slaves [SOS Esclaves]. States should do more to support antislavery activists in repressive countries where the Government doesn't allow free discussion on the issue of slavery.

We need to give survivors of slavery a platform to speak out and help other survivors to recover… I didn't speak much about what happened to me. I was ashamed, and I quietly prayed to God for strength. Only a few years ago I began to feel I was ready to discuss what had happened to me. We need to remove the shame from slavery. To do that, survivors need to talk openly about their experience in order to help victims of trafficking recover. Our message is that there is no reason to be ashamed, even if people will treat you like an animal. There is a spiritual and psychological side to the recovery process that should not be neglected.

We need to help survivors overcome the shame after they escape.[20]

Asia Graves works as the Maryland Program Coordinator and Survivor Advocate at FAIR Girls, a nonprofit group that fights sexual exploitation and also makes a number of concrete suggestions:

We need critical funding to open specialized homes where girls and boys sold into trafficking can truly receive the compassionate care they deserve. Often, we have nowhere for these young girls to go. Many are hiding in hotels while looking for safe house. This is not how a victim of slavery who has just been freed should spend her first night. Many social service agencies nationwide have the staff and vision to create specialized safe houses, but we need the resources to launch and sustain them.

Educate those likely to come into contact with victims: Every social worker, teacher, nurse, policeman, air steward needs to be educated how to identify and assist victims. This is not expensive training, but it's lifesaving.[21]

Nadia calls for formal recognition of the mass killing, enslavement, and human trafficking committed as a genocide against the Yazidi people in Iraq in order to find a way to open a case before the International Criminal Court. She also appeals to governments to open their borders to survivors, and to take proactive action against ISIL.[22] Withelma argues for an overhaul of child protection systems, suggesting better background checks, increased monitoring, improved cohesiveness and consistency of care, collaboration with local programs to reduce the risk of vulnerability

---

[20] Beatrice, in Kevin Bales and Zoe Trodd, *To Plead Our Own Cause*, 162–63.
[21] http://antislavery.ac.uk/items/show/151
[22] http://antislavery.ac.uk/items/show/144

and trafficking, and the establishment of a telephone hotline.[23] While Dorothy notes that it is hard to offer good alternatives, particularly where seemingly intractable causes such as poverty make solutions difficult, she advocates for education as one means of prevention. For Dorothy, education is not only a human right; it is a shield to protect against exploitation.[24] Dara also identifies education as key, noting in particular how the education of men is important to combatting sexual slavery. She says: "I think we should educate men and I think that we should ask the woman to educate their children too. We can ask a woman to teach their sons. We should start when they are young, because after it's too late. We all matter. Women matter. Please educate your son."

## BARRIERS TO PARTICIPATION

Despite these examples, the corpus reveals that the majority of survivors are not able to infiltrate the structures needed to effect broader change, in part because those structures are not organized in a way that facilitates meaningful participation. While the subjective "outsider within"[25] perspective is generally (perhaps tokenistically) valued, systems and organizations are not always structured to address issues of inequity. Survivors are often aware of their outsider status and mechanisms are rarely structured to reframe power relations and provide the conditions needed to facilitate inclusion and participation. Existing structures and organizations are dominated by nonsurvivors who come from a different standpoint than survivors: a key reason for the absence of survivor engagement.[26] The risk of participation for survivors is exacerbated by unspoken hierarchies, where nonsurvivors hold power, and can struggle to take on board criticism in the way they have approached participation.[27] The consequence of this absence of survivor voice is a tendency

---

[23] http://antislavery.ac.uk/items/show/152
[24] Hannah Rose Murray, "Voices," 14.
[25] Kendra Doychak and Chitra Raghavan, "No Voice or Vote:" Trauma-Coerced Attachment in Victims of Sex Trafficking, *Journal of Human Trafficking* 6, no. 3 (2020).
[26] Minh Dang, "Epistemology of Survival: A Working Paper" (2021), 2. www.minh-dang.com/publications; Sandra Harding, "Rethinking Standpoint Epistemology: What is 'Strong Objectivity?'" *The Centennial Review* 36, no. 3 (Fall 1992): 437–70.
[27] See Karen Countryman-Roswurm and Bailey Patton Brackin, "Awareness without Re-exploitation: Empowering Approaches to Sharing the Message About Human Trafficking," *Journal of Human Trafficking* 3, no. 4 (2017); Navid Pourmokhtari, "Global Human Trafficking Unmasked: A Feminist Rights-Based Approach," *Journal of Human Trafficking* 1, no. 2 (2015).

to homogenize survivor groups, meaning anti-trafficking interventions inadvertently minimize or ignore intersecting vulnerabilities and the creation of policies that fail to be tailored to survivors' particular needs.[28]

While survivors have penetrated the antislavery movement, built organizations, and led initiatives, it is clear that there is a long way to go. Wider cultural and systemic factors will continue to inhibit participation: Gender, disability, ethnicity, and social standing all impact perceptions of "legitimacy," survivors' political visibility, and access to dominant structures. While higher levels of democracy have been shown to be significantly related to lower levels of slavery,[29] and are more likely to provide the conditions for survivor voice and inclusion in state processes, but the corpus shows that even in strongly democratic States, survivors struggle to access and inform the necessary platforms for widespread change.

Where survivors do manage to break through into the relevant hierarchies, problems with tokenization, power imbalance, and a failure to learn and adopt trauma-informed approaches not only inhibit the likelihood of effective survivor engagement but also risk secondary victimization. By way of example, the survivor and researcher Mary Gilfus notes the price survivors are asked to pay for "entry into the academy and professions," noting that:

> They [survivors] are expected not to say who they are and what they see. They are expected not to expose the ordinariness, yet the outrageous severity, of the daily violence or residual pain in their lives…survivors are supposed to be silent about their own identities as outsiders, survivors and as it relates to oppressive practices that determine the unequal social distribution of traumatic inquiry.[30]

While survivors are expected to understand the unspoken rules of participation, they also continue to be asked to "tell the facts," to expose the detail of their enslavement, rather than being asked to participate on the same terms as nonsurvivors. As we have seen in Rachel Gilfus' comments, survivors are expected to come to the table and set aside their trauma in their practice, but can often also be asked, at the same event, to detail their trauma for those in attendance. However, the participation of survivors in a professional setting "does not signal agreement to share

---

[28] Sue Lockyer, "Beyond Inclusion," 7.
[29] Todd Landman and Bernard W. Silverman, "Globalization and Modern Slavery," *Politics and Governance* 7, no. 4 (2019).
[30] Mary E. Gilfus, "The Price of the Ticket," 1248.

past experiences of human trafficking."[31] The problematic demands on survivors, the conflation of their survivorship, and their professional lives are demonstrated clearly in Rachel Lloyd's account of the many issues she and other survivor activists have faced. She writes:

Today I was humiliated. Publicly. It happened at an anti-trafficking event where I was presenting to over 100 law enforcement and I'd just finished a solid, engaging presentation that acknowledged the fact that I was survivor but that didn't go into details about my "story," concentrating instead on the issue itself, how far we've come and how far we still need to go.

Grasping me by my hand and framing it with, "what Rachel didn't tell you was" the host inexplicably felt the need to fairly graphically describe my past including my "multiple rapes by multiple men."

The organization GEMS that I'd built from scratch into the largest service provider to commercially sexually exploited and domestically trafficked girls in the country. I'd spent two hours as a professional, as the Chief Executive Officer of GEMS, as an expert, and within a couple of minutes he reduced me to a rape victim.

In my own life, just a few examples include: a funder who without warning chose to read aloud an excerpt from my book that described my experiences with johns at a non-trafficking related event and then asked other people in the room to discuss it; flyers for a speaking event put on by an anti-trafficking coalition that read "Rachel Lloyd – Sex, Drugs and Violence"; staff at a large organization that works on trafficking and gender-based violence tell me laughingly that they were going to be my "new pimps"; organizers of a conference quizzing me not about my work but about my time in the life to decide whether I should speak at the conference. I could go on with numerous examples of the challenges that I experience doing this work but what's more worrying to me is if these are just a few of the experiences that I, as a nationally recognized expert, as a CEO of a leading organization, as someone who hasn't been in the life for almost 20 years, who should be on some level inoculated from this by years of professional experience and education, am experiencing and am often hurt and shocked by, how is the movement treating emerging leaders? What are newer leaders, younger leaders experiencing? Unfortunately working with a variety of survivor leaders, both at GEMS and across the country, I'm seeing passionate, committed individuals who are willing to use their voices to make a difference but are overwhelmingly being hurt by the very people claiming to want to "help" them.

Flyers for an awareness event advertising "Buy a Sex Slave"; an advocate at an event claiming that babies who were in the womb while their mother was in the life were trafficking survivors and that anyone in their life in the future (a broad

---

[31] US Department of Health and Human Services, National Human Trafficking Training and Technical Assistance Center. "Toolkit for Building Survivor-Informed Organizations: Trauma-Informed Resources and Survivor-Informed Practices to Support and Collaborate with Survivors of Human Trafficking as Professionals" (2018), 5. www.acf.hhs.gov/otip/resource/nhtta corgtoolkit.

span that seemed to include everyone from their friends, adopted family, and the mailman) were all also trafficking survivors; a TV show that has filmed victim/survivors without their knowledge; t-shirts directing people to pray for pimps and johns; an incredibly graphic video clip shown at an event where there were many survivors present; a reporter known for anti-trafficking work who chooses to include the most salacious details in every story about survivors. And over and over again, survivor leaders showing up for events, agreeing to interviews, engaging with organizations only to discover that the only interest people have in them is for their 'story' and ideally the more sensational, the more graphic the better.

She adds:

We're often shamed by those same people for somehow not being grateful, that are responses are only because we're still struggling with our own trauma, or laughably as if our commitment to raising awareness or fighting the issue is somehow far less valid than the organization that's "just trying to help." Our concerns are frequently dismissed with comments about how "serious" this issue is, as if hurting survivors isn't serious, or that we're wasting energy when we should be focusing on the "real" problems. All of these responses simply minimize the damage that's done and survivors are left feeling guilty, "over-sensitive" or questioning their own healing and recovery.[32]

While there are excellent examples of the emerging movement to address these problems, progress is slow and for the most part survivor participation is typically led by select individuals who have gained political visibility through extensive self-directed positioning and who are iconified as "survivor-leaders" to the exclusion of the many survivor activists working in different ways. In other words, the responsibility continues to rest on a few survivors' shoulders to represent what is often problematically seen as a homogenous group and where the weight of responsibility for training and access to such roles also typically rests with those survivors, rather than a responsibility adopted by those needing to employ their expertise.

Survivor participation is further inhibited by the concept of the iconic victim, the preconceptions of victims of different genders and of the different forms of enslavement and human trafficking. The iconic victim has emerged as one who is perceived as innocent or blameless in their enslavement, is "documented," characteristic, confident, literate, and diplomatic. They are fully formed, recovered, and professional advocates able to handle the challenges of participating in a system that often does

---

[32] Rachel Lloyd, "At What Cost? The Road to Anti-Trafficking Is Paved with Good Intentions," *Canadian Women's Foundation* (2014). https://canadianwomen.org/blog/what-cost-trafficking/

not reflect their gender, ethnicity, or even their views. The iconic victim is also paradoxically conceived as passive, but who also has agency, even where that agency is limited by the very processes they are trying to engage with. An example is criminal prosecution processes in which survivors' voices are valuable (and their agency recognized) only in relation to the testimony they provide.[33] This is particularly the case where support is predicated on engaging in prosecution processes.[34]

As Minh Dang has observed, those who fit the stereotypical victim narrative, who are educated and articulate, are elevated, and others compared against them. Survivors who don't meet that standard are often labelled as "too emotional," "unprofessional," or "not captivating."[35] There is no room for those who are viewed as blameworthy, typically those who experienced forced sexual exploitation for commercial purposes, those who experienced forced criminality, or those who accessed countries via illicit routes. Survivors in these categories are reframed as other. They are criminals, and undeserving, reflecting the growing security narrative that reconfigures human trafficking as crime-related illegal immigration.[36] The migration-crime-security nexus, or crime master narrative, views survivors as criminals first, and victims second.[37] Not only has this been shown in preceding chapters to affect survivor identification and recovery, here we see the same affect their participation in antislavery systems even where identification and growth has been experienced.

There is depressingly little evidence in the corpus of survivor participation in state processes, and in particular, meaningful survivor participation, and only a small number of narratives relate survivors' roles

---

[33] Jonathan Todres, "Widening Our Lens: Incorporating Essential Perspectives in the Fight against Human Trafficking," *Michigan Journal of International Law* 33, no. 1, 59; Jayashri Srikantiah, "Perfect Victims and Real Survivors: The Iconic Victim in Domestic Human Trafficking Law," *Immigration and Nationality Law Review* 28 (2007): 783.

[34] See, for example, Linda G. Mills, "Killing Her Softly: Intimate Abuse and the Violence of State Intervention," *Harvard Law Review* 113 (1999): 570–71; G. Kristian Miccio, "A House Divided: Mandatory Arrest, Domestic Violence, and the Conservatization of the Battered Women's Movement," *Houston Law Review* 42 (2005): 243–44; Cheryl Hanna, "No Right to Choose: Mandated Victim Participation in Domestic Violence Prosecutions," *Harvard Law Review* 109 (1996).

[35] Minh Dang, "Paradox of Survivor Leadership," 6

[36] Maria De Angelis, "Narratives of Human Trafficking: Ways of Seeing and Not Seeing the Real Survivors and Stories." *Narrative Works* 7, no. 1 (2017): 45 and 49–50.

[37] Human Trafficking Foundation Online Forum, "The Voice of British Survivors of Human Trafficking" (January 25, 2021). https://static1.squarespace.com/static/599ab-fb4e6f2e19ff048494f/t/601be6342f537f095a0763a3/1612441143314/British+survivors+online+forum_25+January_minutes.pdf

in informing policymaking and legislation. The major exception is the United States, which has for decades regularly heard Congressional testimony from survivors, and which established a US Advisory Council on Human Trafficking in 2015 that has engaged survivor consultants to inform its strategies. Further, the US Office for Victims of Crime and the US Bureau of Justice Administration have funded forty-two anti-trafficking task forces since 2004. The National Institute of Justice also provided three years of funding to conduct a peer-based (survivor-led) process and outcome evaluation of one of these task forces: The San Francisco Mayor's Task Force on Anti-Human Trafficking and the Task Force. The researchers identified a range of factors that inhibited participation, including a lack of formal consideration for the group to become part of the task force, differing philosophies and orientations that created tension and a reluctance to adopt alternative views, a desire to look for more complex narratives than existed, challenges in sharing space, and the impact of bureaucratic processes on the publication of vital outputs, such as safety policies.[38] More widely, they also discovered that of the Federal, State and local law enforcement and social service providers, less than half had accumulated high quality data, few had conducted evaluations, and none included sex worker rights organizations.[39]

While the findings reveal some of the problems with existing antislavery architecture, which typically created absent survivors' perspectives, the funding and participation of survivor consultants also helped to reveal the gaps and shortcomings, and the organizational practices that inhibited survivor participation and antislavery progress. They represent a learning opportunity, and a welcome initiative to engage survivors in their professional capacity. However, in order to achieve systematic change, Minh Dang suggests that the antislavery community should not ask how to incorporate the voices of people with lived experience while preventing and mitigating additional injustices and suffering. Instead, it should be asked: "How do social movements develop and conceive by, of, and for the people who have suffered most? If movements have already begun,

---

[38] Minh Dang and Alexandra Lutnick, "Forging Partnerships Between Researchers and the Researched: A Community Based Anti-Trafficking Response" (2017), 5. https://sftaskforce-eval.files.wordpress.com/2018/02/danglutnick_sswr2018_forgingpartnerships_final.pdf

[39] Alexandra Lutnick and Minh Dang, "Forging Communities of Sex Worker and Anti-Trafficking Activists," The American Society of Criminology Annual Meeting, November 2, 2017. Philadelphia, PA: https://sftaskforceeval.files.wordpress.com/2018/02/forgingcommunities_asc.pdf

how do we uproot the foundation of exclusion from the core infrastructure of movement leadership?"[40]

POSITIVE DEVELOPMENTS

Despite protracted progress towards survivor participation, toolkits are starting to emerge. For example, the National Human Trafficking Training and Technical Assistance Center has developed a toolkit for building survivor-informed organizations. The toolkit, which provides trauma-informed resources and survivor-informed practices to support and collaborate with survivors of human trafficking as professionals, is premised on four guiding principles. Those principles are concerned with: (1) empowerment-based engagement; (2) culturally relevant, sensitive, and inclusive engagement; (3) ethical engagement; and (4) trauma-informed engagement (which itself has a further six sub-principles: Safety; trustworthiness and transparency; peer support; collaboration and mutuality; empowerment, voice, and choice; cultural, historical, and gender considerations).[41] Hart et al. have also produced "Tips for Anti-Trafficking Professionals When Working with Survivor Leaders,"[42] and the Anti-Trafficking Monitoring Group (a coalition established in 2009 to monitor the UK's implementation of European anti-trafficking legislation) has collaborated with the Survivor Alliance to train peer researchers and has published the group's reflections and learning on that training as a way of informing and encouraging others to bring survivors on as co-researchers, rather than solely the subjects of antislavery research.[43]

Minh Dang has also recommended a range of actions that would accelerate meaningful participation, including: adding a line item to budgets for survivor participation and develop a fundraising plan to support it; working with allied organizations to recruit survivors; requesting

---

[40] Minh Dang, "Paradox of Survivor Leadership," 6; Anton Törnberg, "Combining Transition Studies and Social Movement Theory: Towards a New Research Agenda," *Theory and Society* 47, no. 3 (2018): 381–408.
[41] Minh Dang, "Survivors Are Speaking: Are We Listening?" (2018). www.minh-dang.com/publications
[42] Catie Hart, Celia Roberts, Geneviève T. Tiangco, Kae Kae Baybie, Monica Anderson, Ummra Hang, alix lutnick, Minh Dang, "Tips for Anti-Trafficking Professionals When Working with Survivor Leaders" (n.d.): www.survivoralliance.org/survivor-engagement-resources
[43] Kimberley Hutchinson, KJ, and Nancy Esiovwa, with additional support and editing by Anna Sereni, "Agents for change: Survivor peer researchers bridge the evidence and inclusion gap," Anti-Trafficking Monitoring Group (2020).

anonymous survivor input through surveys of program participants; offering gift cards or financial compensation in exchange for participation; inviting survivors to join the Board of Directors or an Advisory Board, to review and provide input on program plans, training curricula, and media campaigns; involving survivors in the identification of research questions and measurement variables; developing employment opportunities for survivors within organizations and providing support for their success, such as discussing confidentiality, making workplace and cultural norms explicit, and if necessary, training other staff members on how to engage; and investing in survivor leadership programs such as the National Survivor Network in the United States, Utthan in India, and the Survivor Alliance.[44]

In order for survivors to take center stage in the antislavery movement, there is a need for them to receive training and leadership support.[45] The training and mentoring of survivor participants is also slowly being adopted by organizations, mitigating the pedestal effect and a recognition that training is also a responsibility to be assumed by nonsurvivors wishing to enable survivor inclusion. Prior to making a presentation, Ishmael Beah describes how valuable it was to attend a workshop aimed at teaching survivors how to speak in more compelling ways.[46] Shamere McKenzie reports that she was shown how to start a career in public speaking and was given the tools to move forward in her professional life. She states: "The staff at Shared Hope treated me equal and transformed me into being more than a survivor. They empowered me while teaching me the diplomatic approach to being part of the anti-trafficking movement."[47] The need for training is emulated by Dang and Lutnick in their work with The San Francisco Mayor's Task Force on Anti-Human Trafficking. They noted that due to limited previous exposure to research, it wasn't until the end of the project that members began to grasp the research question and processes. Their suggestion is that projects which seek to involve survivors will want to build in time for general education on research by providing "research 101" type training. They also noted that external support

---

[44] Minh Dang, "Survivors Are Speaking."
[45] Minh Dang, in Laura Murphy, *Survivors of Slavery*, xvii.
[46] Ishmael Beah, *A Long Way Gone: The True Story of a Child Soldier* (London: Harper Collins Publishers, 2007), 196.
[47] Shamere, in Laura T. Murphy, *Survivors of Slavery: Modern-Day Slave Narratives* (New York: Columbia University Press, 2014), 52–53.

structures would have been beneficial to deal with the way in which the work triggered past trauma.[48]

Members also wanted to take on additional project work but could only do so if unpaid and/or they were unable to step away from childcare duties. At a minimum, stipends that account for childcare costs and meeting preparation time are crucial.[49] Similarly, there is a growing recognition that survivors should be employed on equal terms, that they should receive equivalent stipends for their work, something particularly important where their exploitation has often been founded on a denial of agency and income. Essentially, where there exists an inequity between survivors and nonsurvivors, the assumption that survivors would provide professional services pro bono can be considered another form of exploitation.

Lastly, future studies are needed that examine peer-researchers' participation on well-being. Future work is needed to explore in more detail the benefits and challenges of peer involvement as it relates to trafficking research. Where meaningful and effective survivor inclusion and participation is facilitated, it can help to reframe power relations, challenge generalized truths and encourage shifts in organizational communication.[50]

---

[48] Alexandra Lutnick and Minh Dang, "Researcher-Survivor-Ally Evaluation of the Mayor's Task Force on Anti-Human Trafficking Draft Final Summary Report" (2018), Prepared for the National Institute of Justice, Washington, DC, 11–12.
[49] Alexandra Lutnick and Minh Dang, "Researcher-Survivor-Ally Evaluation," 9.
[50] Kendra Doychak and Chitra Raghavan, "No Voice or Vote."

# Conclusion

Through survivors' narratives, we are granted privileged access to survivors' internal and external worlds. These important representations have enabled a close analysis of their meanings, emotions, experiences, needs, and strategies. The analysis of survivors' narratives in this book has revealed some key points that have arisen in nearly all, or all of the chapters, and which fundamentally start to unravel the complexity of what it means to be "owned" by another, and reveal the effects of enslavement in liberation. That the binary of free and unfree is illusory is one of the most prominent. Instead, slavery and freedom are complex and fluctuating states of existence, neither entirely cheerless nor joyous. Adjusting to a life of slavery brings as many challenges for those enslaved, as does the adjustment to liberation and the struggle for "full" freedom. The liberated slave may still feel like a slave, but an "illegitimate" slave, and while they may carry an inherent desire for freedom, the slave faced with an opportunity for liberation may retreat to what is known than risk facing the unknown.

An analysis of the corpus reviewed in this book also revealed the ways in which survivors employ resistance strategies, from the smaller subversive acts of practicing their faith or attending small schools in secret, the hiding of cultural mementos, and the remembrance of alternative names for themselves and their children, to the denial of their bodies as a commodity through self-destructive acts, and in liberation through their activism.

Another prominent theme has been of responsibility. The responsibility the survivor carries, whether self-imposed or placed upon them, comes to bear in liberation at a point when survivors are arguably least prepared. They bear the responsibility for accessing and engaging with support processes and systems, with prosecutions, and with the smaller responsibilities of daily living that can seem overwhelming to the newly liberated. In the light of limited mental health care provision, survivors also have to assume responsibility for integrating into society, building community, and for their own growth and futurity. They bear the loss of identity and culture, feeling their way toward sculpting new identities in liberation, ones that they seek to remove from their pats, but which inevitably are molded by that past. And they bear responsibility for others, adopting activist and leadership roles to be a voice for others lost to slavery.

The importance of telling in framing their new reality, and to confronting (or retreating) from the past is fundamental. In each chapter, the central role of narratives has emerged, whether enabling survivors to achieve personhood, to sculpt a new identity, in coping with trauma, or in the ability to represent a whole person to the world, one made of more than their trauma, survivors have found telling an important and valuable part of their journey. Not all survivors will want to make their stories known, and not all will want their stories made public. The disadvantage of narrative giving is in the effect of capturing an individual within the parameters of their words and limiting their story in time.

While I have focused on a few core motifs, only a fraction of the existing narratives and of their value has been explored in this book. If one thing was to be derived from this analysis, it is the importance of narratives to both the antislavery movement and, fundamentally, to survivors. These narratives are not just stories without purpose, they are a form of survivor activism and a unique and unmined resource for the antislavery movement. The corpus lends itself to many disciplines, from the arts to the sciences, and can be explored to understand almost all aspects of antislavery research, from the measurement of global slavery through to perpetrator motivations, trafficking routes, and the effectiveness of central and local support mechanisms to name a few. The giving of narratives is a means by which survivors give voice and are heard, and their reading and analysis a form of bearing witness. Given their potential for understanding the risks, causes, and effects of slavery, attending to survivors' narratives will be crucial to the successful progression of abolition.

In March 2013, Minh Dang penned an open letter to the anti-trafficking movement, which proposes a number of guiding principles. In her letter, she writes:

> I have often described my experience of trafficking as being like that of a caged animal at a zoo—an exotic creature that people could see from afar but could not touch. People who paid my owner were given special privileges to use my body

for their entertainment. My movements were restricted and monitored, and my environment was not native to me. I was isolated from others in my own species. Although this simile fits, I have come to find that I also often felt like an alien. I always knew that I resembled human beings because of my two eyes, two arms, two legs, and same general body shape; however, it appeared as if I were not thinking or living like other human beings I witnessed.

The majority of my healing work thus far has focused on reconnecting with my humanity and the humanity of others. I have had to learn (or relearn) that I am human, that I was always human, and that the people out there—you as well as those who hurt me—are also human. My basic relationship to who I am, what I can expect of others, and what is possible in the world was damaged. As we incorporate survivors into the antitrafficking movement and encourage them to be at its forefront, we need to recognize their humanity.

...I am as worthy as any other being on the planet just because I am. I am a human being, not a human doing...

The first time I shared my story publicly was in April 2006 at a poetry reading in Berkeley. I was taking "Poetry for the People," a course designed and taught by the late June Jordan, a scholar, activist, and writer. It was my last semester of my undergraduate degree, and I was in the midst of emancipating myself from my slave masters. When I finally broke free, I felt liberated, and poem after poem about my years of enslavement began to flow out of me ... I write so that I exist. I write for myself, and I speak for myself. I have learned that in sharing my own journey, I empower others to do the same. From my own experience of doing social justice work, I have come to believe that fighting for others is not enough. I am adamant that any pursuit of social justice must coincide with our own pursuit of personal justice. Individual healing and community healing must go hand in hand. As Dr. Martin Luther King Jr. said, "Injustice anywhere is a threat to justice everywhere." If we tolerate a lack of self-love in our own lives, how can we truly promote self-love in the lives of others? If we enact micro- or macroaggressions on the people nearest to us, how do we also enact these aggressions in the world at large?[1]

In her call to action, Dang expresses several of the elements I have found in the corpus of survivors' narratives. She highlights the need for the antislavery community to consider long-term recovery needs, to support survivors' potential to become more than just "victims and survivors," and for organizations to work in partnership with survivors, rather than simply representing them. Dang's view of healing is intimately associated with reconnecting with her humanity and the humanity of others, and as Keith stated, the feeling of slavery is to be "stripped of every humanitarian feeling ... stripped of everything."[2] Survivor narratives have much to reveal about what is needed in recovery. Dang also relates the impact of

---

[1] Minh Dang, in Laura Murphy, *Survivors of Slavery*, xvii–xx.
[2] Keith, interview by Andrea Nicholson, May 17 and 19, 2018.

slavery on self-identity and the effects of trauma, but in several places in her full letter elaborates on the importance of telling and the responsibility of the listener, arguing that in order to truly understand the listener should share the pain of survivors' experiences, be prepared "to hold the horrors of human trafficking,"[3] and give careful consideration to the way we use and represent survivors' voices.

Dang's words and the outcomes of this narrative analysis expose the degree to which current antislavery structures and policies are inadequately framed for survivors. A survivor-centric model would require a re-focusing of approaches to trafficking and slavery to provide more effective and concerted formalized long-term support. Access to education and training would not only enable survivor growth but would facilitate their integration and bring value to communities and state economies. A re-evaluation of visa and evidence requirements, as well as of the independence of decision-making bodies in central support mechanisms, would meet one of the core needs of survivors: the need for community, acceptance, and belonging. A legislative framework that considers definitions of slavery not by type or categorization, but on lived experiences, and which is devised with more than tokenistic survivor participation would not only support those who had been subjected to the crimes set out but would mean legislation is fit for purpose and recognize survivors' agency and capabilities. Approaches to survivors, to their employment, participation, and giving of narrative, would be reformulated to acknowledge their expertise, AND consider their suggestions for change and their strategies for prevention. My book also argues for a review of the means by which survivors are interviewed and provide evidence. The interview methods I employed can be adapted to facilitate a deeper and more detailed narrative. Where circumstances do not allow for a full free telling of narrative, the community falls on to standard structured and semi-structured interviews. Working in partnership with survivors, there is potential to revisit these approaches to identify more effective ways to gather narratives, to understand what survivors want from the opportunity to tell, while simultaneously managing the interviewers' expectations.

As I progressed through my research, it also became clear that trauma infused every aspect of survivors' stories, a leitmotif that permeated every theme, whether survivors were seeking escape or recovery from trauma, or surrendering to it and understanding its impact. Their trauma is so

---

[3] Minh Dang in Laura T. Murphy, *Survivors of Slavery*, xvi–xvii.

ingrained, so much a part of survivors' experiences in slavery and in their survival, that no chapter was absent its influence. While there exists a wealth of literature on trauma, there have been no studies on the effects on survivor activists of a role that is so intrinsically linked to their past, their grief, and their loss.[4] It is now, when the global community's awareness of, and response to, slavery is materializing that such studies would be immensely valuable. The analysis I have undertaken of contemporary narratives provides insights into both risk factors and recovery needs, enabling the identification of suitable interventions both pre- and post-enslavement, and ultimately reducing the economic cost of organized crime, improving the effectiveness of central antislavery mechanisms, and supporting survivors in successful ways that enable them to assume "full freedom" and participate in society.

However, a question to ask ourselves is how we employ both survivors' narratives *and* their expertise. Do we minimize their role only to that of survivors, repeatedly defining them by their past, or do we recognize their experiences mean they are uniquely placed to offer insights and solutions that does not rely on requiring them to repeatedly revisit their trauma? Interviewers, sponsors, NGOs, and the media continue to tokenize survivors and limit their narratives to the trope of capture, enslavement, and escape. We rarely see survivors explicitly defined first and foremost as activists, leaders, and professionals. It was Douglass that argued:

> The man who has *suffered the wrong* is the man to *demand redress* – the man STRUCK is the man to CRY OUT – and that he who has *endured the cruel pangs of Slavery* is the man to *advocate Liberty*. It is evident that we must be our own representatives and advocates, but peculiarly – not distinct from – but in connection with our white friends. In the grand struggle for liberty and equality now waging, it is meet, right and essential that there should arise in our ranks authors and editors, as well as orators, for it is in these capacities that the most permanent good can be rendered to our cause.[5]

Survivors are more than storytellers. Rather than passive victims re-telling the atrocities of their treatment, survivors can be, and are, experts, leaders, and scholars. Adopting language that claims survivor *and* titles such as thriver, activist, teacher, expert, leader, academic, and colleague is a

---

[4] While Joy Degruy has self-published a study of slave trauma, this concerned generational trauma as a result of ancestors enslaved during the sixteenth to nineteenth centuries. Joy Degruy, *Post Traumatic Slave Syndrome: America's Legacy of Enduring Injury and Healing* (self-published: Joy Degruy Publications Inc, 2017).

[5] Frederick Douglass, "Our Paper and Its Prospects," *The North Star*, December 3, 1847, 2.

way of showing respect for the leadership and voices of those formerly enslaved, demonstrating their purpose to others and to themselves, and of presenting more of their person to the world.

Survivors' narratives also offer a rich resource that holds much more potential for further work in this field. My research has revealed gaps in the extant literature that I was unable to explore due to time, research parameters, and the limits of my own expertise. Most prominently visual narratives are ripe for exploration. The creative process can encourage people to express and understand emotions and provide a valuable alternative narrative for consideration. They are an equally revealing means of testimony by which survivors can be "seen" in the marks, traces, materials, and colors used; the hypervisualization of text used as a representational strategy to accomplish what written and oral language cannot.[6] Pictures enable survivors to express through their marks, colors, and composition what cannot be expressed with language. Where the speaker is defeated, the creator is not. Survivors have used photography to represent their experiences and emotions, using symbolism to represent the violence they suffered, and images to highlight what is valuable to them both in liberation, and to reflect nostalgia for lost childhoods.[7] Art therapists have gathered important representational paintings from whole liberated villages. Survivors have painted murals and self-portraits,[8] created artisan puppetry, and designed tattoos to hide scars and branding.

Art has an immediate emotional effect; it has an impact and accessibility that can get lost in written narratives, and murals have the potential to draw communities into antislavery efforts, while at the same time speaking to survivors in their own frameworks. Survivor art would provide a whole other narrative resource that is particularly suited to emotional and symbolic expression. It also opens the possibility of examining survivors' work as protest art, of evaluating art's capacity to raise public awareness, and, as a form of survivor participation and representation,

---

[6] Indeed, Douglass captured this deftly when he stated: "it is evident that the great cheapness and universality of pictures must exert powerful, though silent, influence upon the ideas and sentiment of present and future generations." See John Stauffer et al., *Picturing Frederick Douglass: An Illustrated Biography of the Nineteenth Century's Most Photographed American* (New York: Liveright, 2015), 130.

[7] https://snowdropproject.co.uk/our-story/blogs-and-media/survivor-voices/; http://hannahrosethomas.com/yezidi-women/

[8] See the self-portraits by former ISIS slaves gathered by the artist Hannah-Rose Thomas and clinical psychologist Sarah-Whittaker Howe. http://hannahrosethomas.com/art-with-former-isis-slaves/

to understand the value of its therapeutic and developmental effects for this group.

However, the analysis of written narratives is also in need of further exploration. Currently, written narratives are in one sense homogenized, with child and adult voices treated as one. What do child voices reveal about resilience to, or the differing effects of the trauma of enslavement and what would this mean for support infrastructures? How does their cognitive ability and expression differ and what does this mean for interpretation? What distinctions are to be found between children rescued in their childhood, compared to adults reflecting on childhood slavery? What are the limits of children's voices and what does this mean for interpretation?

The analysis of narratives as a whole would also be greatly enhanced by the application of other interpretative methods. While the method of analysis employed here was especially revealing, more could be illuminated through corpus linguistic analysis, which would expose collocations and grammar patterns that could reveal unseen meanings. Married to other approaches, combined methods can be used to further analyze and test the findings in this book and the extant literature, and draw out new findings in thousands, rather than hundreds of survivor narratives. Last, but importantly, it must be asked what survivors would see in this corpus that I and other nonsurvivors cannot? Survivor academics would bring a unique expertise to analysis, potentially revealing insights that could not be understood by those who cannot see from within.[9]

This last suggestion for the future of narrative analysis is particularly important to me. In conducting the research for my book, I have been confronted with a strange conflict. I have striven to be respectful and truthful of survivor's telling and have argued throughout for an acknowledgement of survivors' selves as more than their enslavement and for their participation as colleagues. However, in writing this book, I am myself representing, interpreting, and employing their voices. I have reproduced and analyzed what survivors have said, but I am simultaneously acutely aware that I continue to represent from a position of emotional

---

[9] Narratives would also provide a good counterpoint to the claims made by those in critical modern slavery studies. For more on these perspectives see e.g. Joel Quirk and Julia O'Connell Davidson, "Moving Beyond Popular Representations of Trafficking and Slavery," *Open Democracy*, January 11, 2015; Joel Quirk, "The Rhetoric and Reality of 'Ending Slavery in Our Lifetime'," *Open Democracy*, January 30, 2015; Julia O'Connell Davidson, *The Margins of Freedom*; and Angelo Martins Jr. "Interview with Julia O'Connell Davidson on Modern Slavery," *Theory, Culture and Society* 33, no. 7–8 (2016).

and academic safety. I have stated in my first chapter that analysis has necessitated interpretation and that interpretation has come from a very different standpoint, a space and set of experiences that are not shared by survivors. The truth of survivors' meanings has as far as possible been tested across the corpus analyzed, but a survivor is likely to see the flaws, nuances, and potential antislavery strategies that I have missed.

Having started this final chapter with Minh Dang's open letter to the anti-trafficking movement, it seems appropriate to close with an unpublished poem she has given permission to include:

Beautiful Women<br>Minh Dang

beautiful women
you are everything I hoped
my mom would be
my mom was beautiful
once
wasn't she?
but she couldn't see beauty
in me
or in you
beautiful women
you break
my heart
you show what I yearn to be
what I yearn to see
in myself
beautiful women
you show me how
how to what?
how to ... everything
beautiful women
who sing and dance
you remind me to play
you remind me
that freedom comes when we laugh and grin
and our hearts are tickled by rainbows
beautiful women
you don't hold up half of the sky
you *are* the sky
the earth
the first touchstone for all new life
beautiful women
how do you share so freely
and tolerate the fear of loss?

you have lost so much
how
do you hold the immensity of your pain
nestled next to the purity of your joy?
how do you wake up
each morning and
live into the questions?
beautiful women
shine when no one is watching
hug your brokenness and your wholeness
celebrate the growth that comes after a fire
beautiful women
I see you
I hear you
I am you

# Appendix: Table of Narratives Analyzed

| Survivor's Name/ Pseudonym | Country of Origin | Country of Enslavement | Year | Source | Gathered by: NGO/Journalist/Congress/ Not Known |
|---|---|---|---|---|---|
| Shengqi | China | China | 1997 | TPOC | CT |
| Sam | China | China | 2003 | TPOC | Self-authored |
| Ying | China | China | 2004 | TPOC | UN (Commission on Human Rights) |
| Jennifer | China | China | 2005 | TPOC | CT |
| Bin | China | China | 2005 | TPOC | City Council Human Relations Committee, Chicago |
| Abuk A. | Sudan | Sudan | 1999 | TPOC | NGO (Christian Solidarity International) |
| Abuk G. | Sudan | Sudan | 1999 | TPOC | NGO (Christian Solidarity International) |
| Yei | Sudan | Sudan | 1999 | TPOC | NGO (Christian Solidarity International) |
| Achai | Sudan | Sudan | 1999 | TPOC | NGO (Christian Solidarity International) |
| Ajok | Sudan | Sudan | 1999 | TPOC | NGO (Christian Solidarity International) |
| Anyang | Sudan | Sudan | 1999 | TPOC | NGO (Christian Solidarity International) |
| Abuk K. | Sudan | Sudan | 1999 | TPOC | NGO (Christian Solidarity International) |
| Mary | Sudan | Sudan | 1999 | TPOC | NGO (Christian Solidarity International) |
| Marco | Sudan | Sudan | 1999 | TPOC | NGO (Christian Solidarity International) |
| Isra | Thailand | Canada | 1999 | TPOC | NGO (Toronto Network against Trafficking in Women) |
| Vi (Quang Thi Vo) | Vietnam | American Samoa | 2001 | TPOC/SOS (identical) | CT (2001: SN:107–63) |
| Shanti | India | India | 2001 | TPOC | NGO (Free the Slaves) |

| Munni | India | 2004 | TPOC | NGO (Free the Slaves) |
| Munni Devi | India | 2008 | SOS | NGO (Free the Slaves) |
| Maria | Italy/France/Netherlands | 2002 | TPOC | Self-authored |
| Adelina | Albania | 2005 | TPOC | NGO (IOM, with the Association of Albanian Girls and Women, Albania) |
| Sanije | Albania | 2005 | TPOC | NGO (IOM, with the Association of Albanian Girls and Women, Albania) |
| Valdete | Greece | 2005 | TPOC | NGO (IOM, with the Association of Albanian Girls and Women, Albania) |
| Ada | Italy | 2005 | TPOC | NGO (IOM, with the Association of Albanian Girls and Women, Albania) |
| Elira | Italy | 2005 | TPOC | NGO (IOM, with the Association of Albanian Girls and Women, Albania) |
| Flutura | Italy | 2005 | TPOC | NGO (IOM, with the Association of Albanian Girls and Women, Albania) |
| Kimete | Italy | 2005 | TPOC | NGO (IOM, with the Association of Albanian Girls and Women, Albania) |
| Odeta | Italy | 2005 | TPOC | NGO (IOM, with the Association of Albanian Girls and Women, Albania) |
| Miranda | Belgium | 2005 | TPOC | NGO (IOM, with the Association of Albanian Girls and Women, Albania) |
| Zamira | Belgium | 2005 | TPOC | NGO (IOM, with the Association of Albanian Girls and Women, Albania) |

*(continued)*

| Survivor's Name/ Pseudonym | Country of Origin | Country of Enslavement | Year | Source | Gathered by: NGO/Journalist/Congress/ Not Known |
|---|---|---|---|---|---|
| Patience | Togo | Ghana | 2004 | TPOC | NGO (International Needs) |
| Arvind | India | India | 2004 | TPOC | NGO (Free the Slaves) |
| Rambho (Kumar) | India | India | 2004 | TPOC | NGO (Free the Slaves) |
| Rambho Kumar | India | India | 2004 | SOS | NGO (Free the Slaves) |
| Rama | India | India | 2004 | TPOC | NGO (Free the Slaves) |
| Ravi | India | India | 2004 | TPOC | NGO (Free the Slaves) |
| Shanawaz | India | India | 2005 | TPOC | NGO (Free the Slaves) |
| Sandeep | India | India | 2005 | TPOC | NGO (Free the Slaves) |
| Ashok | India | India | 2005 | TPOC | NGO (Free the Slaves) |
| Battis | India | India | 2005 | TPOC | NGO (Free the Slaves) |
| Nuch | Thailand | Japan | 1995 | TPOC | NGO (Human Rights Watch) |
| Pot | Thailand | Japan | 1995 | TPOC | NGO (Human Rights Watch) |
| Kaew | Thailand | Japan | 1997 | TPOC | NGO (Human Rights Watch) |
| Nu | Thailand | Japan | 2000 | TPOC | UN and NGO (United Nations Development Fund for Women & Coalition against Trafficking in Women) |
| Seba | Mali | France | 1996 | TPOC | Told to Kevin Bales |
| Christine | USA | USA | 1997 | TPOC | Self-authored |
| Dina | Cambodia | Cambodia | 1999 | TPOC | Told to the First National Conference on Gender & Development, Cambodia |

| Name | Origin | Destination | Year | Type | Source |
|---|---|---|---|---|---|
| Anita | Nepal | India | 1994 | TPOC | CT |
| Rita | Nepal | India | 2002 | TPOC | NGO (Panos Oral Testimony Programme, Nepal) |
| Olga | Russia | Israel | 2000 | TPOC | UN (IOM) |
| Amasya | Armenia | Turkey | 2000 | TPOC | UN (IOM) |
| Farida | Armenia | Turkey | 2000 | TPOC | UN (IOM) |
| Alina | Armenia | UAE | 2000 | TPOC | UN (IOM) |
| Illiona | Armenia | UAE | 2000 | TPOC | UN (IOM) |
| Shahnara | Armenia | UAE | 2000 | TPOC | UN (IOM) |
| Tamara | Armenia | UAE | 2000 | TPOC | UN (IOM) |
| Alana | Romania | Russia | 2005 | TPOC | Told to Siddharth Kara |
| Milena | Romania | Russia | 2005 | TPOC | Told to Siddharth Kara |
| Bahar | Moldova | Turkey | 2005 | TPOC | Told to Siddharth Kara |
| Maria | Romania | Ukraine | 2005 | TPOC | Told to Siddharth Kara |
| Kavita | India | India | 2004 | TPOC | NGO (Free the Slaves) |
| Kavita | India | India | 2004 | SOS | NGO (Free the Slaves) |
| Miguel | Mexico | USA | 2005 | TPOC | NGO (Free the Slaves) |
| Miguel* | Mexico | USA | 2005 | SOS | NGO (Free the Slaves) |
| Roseline | Cameroon | USA | 2005 | TPOC | NGO (Free the Slaves) |
| Christina | Cameroon | USA | 2005 | TPOC | NGO (Free the Slaves) |
| Tamada | Niger | Niger | 2005 | TPOC | NGO (ASI) |

(*continued*)

| Survivor's Name/ Pseudonym | Country of Origin | Country of Enslavement | Year | Source | Gathered by: NGO/Journalist/Congress/ Not Known |
|---|---|---|---|---|---|
| Beatrice | Sri Lanka | Beirut | 2005 | TPOC | CT |
| Maria | Mexico | USA | 2005 | TPOC | NGO (Free the Slaves) |
| Joy | Nigeria | Netherlands | 2006 | TPOC | Told to E. Benjamin Skinner |
| Selek'ha | Mauritania | Mauritania | 2006 | TPOC | NGO (ASI) |
| Omoulkhér | Mauritania | Mauritania | 2006 | TPOC | NGO (ASI) |
| Jill | USA | USA | 1997 | TPOC | Self-authored with Katherine DePasquale |
| Ragaa | Egypt | Egypt | 1997 | TPOC | NGO (Egyptian Centre of Human Rights for National Unit) |
| Inez | Mexico | USA | 2000 | TPOC | CT (2000: SN.106–705) |
| Inez* | Mexico | USA | 2000 | SOS | CT (2000: SN.106–705) |
| Maria | Mexico | USA | 2000 | TPOC | CT |
| Rosa | Mexico | USA | 2000 | TPOC | CT |
| Aida | Philippines | Philippines | 2001 | TPOC | Quaker United Nations Office |
| Dia | Columbia | Columbia | 2001 | TPOC | Quaker United Nations Office |
| Manju | Sri Lanka | Sri Lanka | 2001 | TPOC | Quaker United Nations Office |
| Jean-Robert Cadet | Haiti | Haiti | 2002 | TPOC | UN (ILO International Institute for Labour Studies) |
| Jean-Robert Cadet | Haiti | Haiti | 1998 | Autobiography | Self-authored |
| Jean-Robert Cadet | Haiti | Haiti | 2011 | Autobiography | Coauthored with Jim Luken |
| Chantha | Cambodia | Cambodia | 2003 | TPOC | NGO (World Hope International) |

| | | | | |
|---|---|---|---|---|
| Chariya | Cambodia | Cambodia | 2003 | TPOC | NGO (World Hope International) |
| Mariana | Ukraine | Germany | 2003 | TPOC | NGO (La Strada Ukraine) |
| Masha | Russia | Germany | 2006 | TPOC | CT |
| Irina | Russia | Germany | 2006 | TPOC | CT |
| Faith | Zimbabwe | Johannesburg | 2005 | TPOC | UN (IOM) |
| Joyce | USA | USA | 2002 | TPOC | Told to John Bowe (journalist) |
| Salma | Mauritania | Mauritania | 2003 | TPOC | Self-authored |
| Salma | Mauritania | Mauritania | 2009 | Antislavery.ac.uk | Told to Kevin Bales |
| Mende (Nazer) | Sudan | Sudan/UK | 2003 | TPOC | NGO (ASI) |
| Mende Nazer | Sudan | Sudan/UK | 2010 | Autobiography | Coauthored with Damien Lewis |
| Ramphal | India | India | 2004 | TPOC | NGO (Free the Slaves) |
| Ramphal | India | India | 2008 | SOS | NGO (Free the Slaves) |
| Choti | India | India | 2004 | TPOC | NGO (Free the Slaves) |
| Choti | India | India | 2008 | SOS | NGO (Free the Slaves) |
| Shyamkali | India | India | 2004 | TPOC | NGO (Free the Slaves) |
| Sumara | India | India | 2004 | TPOC | NGO (Free the Slaves) |
| Tina | USA | USA | 2005 | TPOC | CT |
| Ruth | Sierra Leone | Liberia | 2006 | TPOC | NGO (Faith Alliance against Slavery & Trafficking) |
| Kwame | Ghana | Ghana | 2006 | TPOC | NGO (Association of People for Practical Life Education) |

(*continued*)

| Survivor's Name/ Pseudonym | Country of Origin | Country of Enslavement | Year | Source | Gathered by: NGO/Journalist/Congress/ Not Known |
|---|---|---|---|---|---|
| Kwasi | Ghana | Ghana | 2006 | TPOC | NGO (Association of People for Practical Life Education) |
| William | Sudan | Sudan | 2006 | TPOC | Arizona State University workshop |
| Mi Sun Bahng | N. Korea | China | 2010 | CT | CT & NGO (318 Partners Mission Foundation) |
| Song-Hyun Choi | N. Korea | China | 2010 | CT | CT & NGO (318 Partners Mission Foundation) |
| Jang Mi Kyung | N. Korea | China | 2010 | CT | CT & NGO (318 Partners Mission Foundation) |
| Keum-Ju Kim | N. Korea | China | 2010 | CT | CT & NGO (318 Partners Mission Foundation) |
| Mi-Kyung Kim | N. Korea | China | 2010 | CT | CT & NGO (318 Partners Mission Foundation) |
| KH Lee | N. Korea | China | 2010 | CT | CT & NGO (318 Partners Mission Foundation) |
| Kim JO | N. Korea | China | 2010 | CT | CT & NGO (318 Partners Mission Foundation) |
| Phuong-Anh Vu | Vietnam | Jordan | 2012 | CT | CT |
| Angela Guanzon | Philippines | USA | 2013 | CT | CT |
| Esther Choe | N. Korea | China | 2013 | CT | CT |

| | | | | |
|---|---|---|---|---|
| Holly Smith | USA | USA | 2014 | CT | CT (SN. 113–177) |
| Shin Don Hyuk | N. Korea | N. Korea | 2014 | CT | CT (SN. 113–197) |
| Karla Jacinto Romero | Mexico | Mexico | 2015 | CT | CT (SN. 114–67) |
| Shandra Woworuntu | Indonesia | USA | 2015 | CT | CT (SN. 114–68) |
| James Kofi Annan | Ghana | Ghana | 2015 | CT | CT (SN. 114–68) |
| Adamou | Niger | Niger | nd | ASI website | NGO |
| Angel | Tanzania | Tanzania | nd | ASI website | NGO |
| Moulkheir | Mauritania | Mauritania | nd | ASI website | NGO |
| Tatinatt | Mauritania | Mauritania | nd | ASI website | NGO |
| Sophia | Tanzania | Tanzania | nd | ASI website | NGO |
| Manisha | "Africa" | UK | nd | Unseen website | NGO |
| Dorina | Romania | UK | nd | Unseen website | NGO |
| Olabisi | Nigeria | UK | nd | Unseen website | NGO |
| Henrick | "E. Europe" | UK | nd | CityHearts website | NGO |
| Agnes | Nigeria | UK | nd | CityHearts website | NGO |
| Jane | North Africa | UK | nd | MigrantHelp website | NGO |
| Katya | Ukraine | USA | 2005 | SOS | US Citizenship & Immigration Services |

(*continued*)

| Survivor's Name/ Pseudonym | Country of Origin | Country of Enslavement | Year | Source | Gathered by: NGO/Journalist/Congress/ Not Known |
|---|---|---|---|---|---|
| O | Albania | Italy | 2005 | SOS | NGO (Association of Albanian Girls and Women) |
| Shamere McKenzie | USA | USA | 2012 | SOS | Self-authored |
| Sopheap | Cambodia | Vietnam | 2003 | SOS | NGO (World Vision International) |
| F | Albania | Italy | 2005 | SOS | NGO (Association of Albanian Girls and Women) |
| Helia Lejaunesse | Haiti | Haiti | 2007 | SOS | NGO (Free the Slaves) |
| Lena | Bulgaria | Macedonia | 2001 & 2003 | SOS | Told to Inge Bell (journalist) |
| Marsha | Russia | Germany | 2000 | SOS | CT (SN. 63–986) |
| Natalya | Moldova | Macedonia | 2001 | SOS | Told to Inge Bell (journalist) |
| VP | Albania | Greece | 2005 | SOS | NGO (Association of Albanian Girls and Women) |
| Elena | Bulgaria | Greece | 2001 | SOS | Told to Inge Bell (journalist) |
| Given Kachepa | Zambia | USA | 2002 | SOS | Combination of visa application, edited by the narrator to include parts of speeches the author made. |
| Shymakali | India | India | 2008 | SOS | NGO (Free the Slaves) |
| Viviana | Romania | Greece/ Macedonia | 2001 | SOS | Told to Inge Bell (journalist) |

| P | | | | | |
|---|---|---|---|---|---|
| James Kofi Annan | Albania | Belgium | 2005 | SOS | NGO (Association of Albanian Girls and Women) |
| Beatrice Fernando | Ghana | Ghana | NK | SOS | Self-authored |
| Beatrice Fernando | Sri Lanka | Lebanon | 2007 | SOS | TV interview |
| Anywar Ricky Richard | Sri Lanka | Lebanon | 2004 | Autobiography | Self-authored |
| Somaly Mam | Uganda | Uganda | 2008 | SOS | NGO (Free the Slaves) |
| Sina Vann | Cambodia | Cambodia | 2008 | SOS | Told to Christopher Shay (journalist) |
| Wati | Vietnam | Cambodia | 2009 | SOS | NGO (Free the Slaves) |
| Kanthi | Indonesia | Singapore & USA | 2009 | SOS | NGO (Coalition to Abolish Slavery and Human Trafficking) |
| Ima | Sri Lanka | USA | 2009 | SOS | NGO (Coalition to Abolish Slavery and Human Trafficking) |
| Flor | Indonesia | USA | 2009 | SOS | NGO (Coalition to Abolish Slavery and Human Trafficking) |
| Flor | Mexico | USA | 2009 | SOS | NGO (Coalition to Abolish Slavery and Human Trafficking) |
| Pasi | Mexico | USA | 2010 | Antislavery.ac.uk | CT |
| Yuni | Indonesia | USA | 2009 | SOS | NGO (Coalition to Abolish Slavery and Human Trafficking) |
| | Indonesia | USA | 2009 | SOS | NGO (Coalition to Abolish Slavery and Human Trafficking) |

*(continued)*

| Survivor's Name/ Pseudonym | Country of Origin | Country of Enslavement | Year | Source | Gathered by: NGO/Journalist/Congress/ Not Known |
|---|---|---|---|---|---|
| Tung | Vietnam | UK | 2017 | AN | Told to Andrea Nicholson, accessed via Palm Cove Society |
| Pranus | Lithuania | UK | 2017 | AN | Told to Andrea Nicholson, accessed via the Police |
| Dwain | Niger | UK | 2018 | AN | Told to Andrea Nicholson |
| Keith | UK | UK | 2018 | AN | Told to Andrea Nicholson, accessed via the NGO Atleu |
| Val | Kenya | Kenya | 2018 | AN | Told to Andrea Nicholson |
| Asia Graves | USA | USA | 2013 | Antislavery.ac.uk | CT |
| Withelma | USA | USA | 2013 | Antislavery.ac.uk | CT |
| Nadia | USA | USA | 2013 | Antislavery.ac.uk | CT |
| Angela Guarzon | Philippines | USA | 2013 | Antislavery.ac.uk | CT |
| Ker Deng | Sudan | Sudan | 2011 | Antislavery.ac.uk | CT |
| Yin Liping | China | China | 2016 | Antislavery.ac.uk | CT |
| Vasanthi | Sri Lanka | Sudan | 2002 | Antislavery.ac.uk | Quaker United Nations Office |
| Evelyn Chumbow | Cameroon | USA | 2016 | Antislavery.ac.uk | CT |
| Leah | USA | USA | 2016 | Antislavery.ac.uk | CT |
| Seba | Mali | France | 1996 | Antislavery.ac.uk | Told to Kevin Bales |
| Almasi | Kenya | Kenya | NK | Antislavery.ac.uk | NGOs (HAART Kenya & Art2be) |
| Edward | NK | UK | NK | Antislavery.ac.uk | NGO (Hope for Justice) |

| | | | | | |
|---|---|---|---|---|---|
| Sabitha-Jayanthi | Sri Lanka | Sri Lanka | 2002 | Antislavery.ac.uk | Quaker United Nations Office |
| Rani | India | India | 2010 | Antislavery.ac.uk | UN |
| Francis Bok | Sudan | Sudan | 2003 | Autobiography | Coauthored with Edward Tivnan |
| China Keitetsi | Uganda | Uganda | 2004 | Autobiography | Self-authored |
| Ishmael Beah | Sierra Leone | Sierra Leone | 2007 | Autobiography | Self-authored |
| Grace Akallo | Uganda | Uganda | 2007 | Autobiography | Coauthored with Faith J. H. McDonnell |
| Sarah Forsyth | UK | Netherlands | 2009 | Autobiography | Self-authored |
| Sarah Forsyth | UK | Netherlands | 2013 | Autobiography | Coauthored with Tim Tate |
| Zana Muhsen | Yemen | Yemen | 2010 | Autobiography | Co-authored with Andrew Crofts |
| Timea E. Nagy | Hungary | Canada | 2010 | Autobiography | Self-authored |
| Rachel Lloyd | UK | Germany | 2011 | Autobiography | Self-authored |
| Sophie Hayes | UK | Italy | 2012 | Autobiography | Self-authored |
| Tina Okpara | Nigeria | France | 2012 | Autobiography | Coauthored with Julie Jodter |
| Monluedee Lueche | Thailand | Thailand | 2012 | Autobiography | Self-authored |
| Theresa Flores | USA | USA | 2013 | Autobiography | Self-authored |
| Katie Taylor | UK | UK | 2013 | Autobiography | Coauthored with Veronica Clark |
| Katariina Rosenblatt | USA | USA | 2014 | Autobiography | Coauthored with Cecil Murphey |
| Barbara Amaya | USA | USA | 2014 | Antislavery.ac.uk | NGO (Richmond Justice Initiative) |
| Barbara Amaya | USA | USA | 2015 | Autobiography | Self-authored |
| Lara McDonell | UK | UK | 2015 | Autobiography | Self-authored |

*(continued)*

| Survivor's Name/ Pseudonym | Country of Origin | Country of Enslavement | Year | Source | Gathered by: NGO/Journalist/Congress/ Not Known |
|---|---|---|---|---|---|
| Farida Khalaf | Iraq | Iraq | 2016 | Autobiography | Coauthored with Andrea C. Hoffmann |
| Anna Ruston | UK | UK | 2016 | Autobiography | Self-authored |
| Nadia Murad | Iraq | Iraq | 2017 | Autobiography | Self-authored |
| Sammy Woodhouse | UK | UK | 2018 | Autobiography | Self-authored |

Variance located in different sources despite same narrative origin
* Denotes the more accurate version – checked against the original source
More than one narrative available from different origins for the same individual

UN: United Nations
CT: Congressional testimony
NGO: Nongovernmental organization
IOM: International Organization for Migration
ASI: Antislavery International
SOS: Laura Murphy, Survivors of Slavery, edited collection
TPOC: Kevin bales & Zoe Trodd, To Plead Our Own Cause, edited collection

# Bibliography

## BOOKS

Allain, Jean. *The Legal Understanding of Slavery: From the Historical to the Contemporary*. Oxford: Oxford University Press, 2012.

Amaya, Barbara. *Nobody's Girl: A Memoir of Lost Innocence, Modern Day Slavery & Transformation*. Pittsburgh: Animal Media Group, 2015.

Andrews, William L. *African American Autobiography: A Collection of Critical Essays*. Upper Saddle River, NJ: Prentice Hall, 1993.

Andrews, William L. *North Carolina Slave Narratives: The Lives of Moses Roper, Lunsford Lane, Moses Grandy, & Thomas H. Jones*. Chapel Hill: The University of North Carolina Press, 2003.

Ayer, Patrick, and Michael Preston-Shoot. *Children's Services at the Crossroads: A Critical Evaluation of Contemporary Policy for Practice*. Lyme Regis: Russell House Publishing, 2010.

Bales, Kevin. *Blood and Earth: Modern Slavery, Ecocide, and the Secret to Saving the World*. New York: Spiegel & Grau, 2016. Kindle.

Bales, Kevin. *Disposable People New Slavery in the Global Economy*. Revised ed. Berkeley and Los Angeles: University of California Press, 2012.

Bales, Kevin. *Ending Slavery: How We Free the World's Slaves*. Berkeley and Los Angeles: University of California Press, 2007.

Bales, Kevin. *Understanding Global Slavery: A Reader*. Berkeley and Los Angeles: University of California Press, 2005.

Bales, Kevin, and Ron Soodalter. *The Slave Next Door: Human Trafficking and Slavery Today*. Berkeley and Los Angeles: University of California Press, 2010. Kindle.

Bales, Kevin, and Zoe Trodd. *To Plead Our Own Cause: Personal Stories by Today's Slaves*. New York: Cornell University Press, 2008.

Bales, Kevin, Zoe Trodd, and Alex Kent Williamson. *Modern Slavery: The Secret World of 27 Million People*. Oxford: Oneworld Publications, 2009.

Barry, Kathleen. *Female Sexual Slavery*. New York and London: New York University Press, 1979.

Beah, Ishmael. *A Long Way Gone: The True Story of a Child Soldier*. London: Harper Perennial, 2008.
Bernier, Celeste-Marie. *Public Art, Memorials and Atlantic Slavery*. Abingdon: Routledge, 2009.
Bibb, Henry. *Narrative of the Life and Adventures of Henry Bibb, an American Slave, Written by Himself*. New York: Published by the Author, 1849. http://docsouth.unc.edu/neh/bibb/bibb.html
Black, Toban, Stephen D'Arcy, Tony Weis, and Joshua Kahn Russell. *A Line in the Tar Sands: Struggles for Environmental Justice*. Oakland: PM Press, 2014.
Bland, Sterling Lecater. *African American Slave Narratives: An Anthology*. Westport: Greenwood Press, 2001.
Blassingame, John. *The Frederick Douglass Papers: Series One–Speeches, Debates, and Interviews*. New Haven: Yale University Press, 1979.
Blassingame, John. *Slave Testimony, Two Centuries of Letters, Speeches, Autobiographies and Interviews*. Baton Rouge: Louisiana State University Press, 1977.
Blight, David W. *A Slave No More. Two Men Who Escaped to Freedom, Including Their Own Narratives of Emancipation*. Boston and New York: Mariner Books, 2009. Kindle.
Bodel, John, and Walter Scheidel. *On Human Bondage: After Slavery and Social Death*. Oxford: John Wiley & Sons, Inc., 2017. Kindle.
Bok, Francis, and Edward Tivnan. *Escape from Slavery: The True Story of My Ten Years in Captivity and My Journey to Freedom in America*. New York: St. Martin's Press, 2007. Kindle.
Borrego, Silvia Pilar Castro, and Maria Isabel Romero Ruiz. *Identities on the Move*. Lanham, MD: Lexington Books, 2015.
Braxton, Joanne M. *Black Women Writing Autobiography: A Tradition within a Tradition*. Philadelphia: Temple University Press, 1989.
Brennan, Denise. *Life Interrupted. Trafficking into Forced Labor in the United States*. Durham and London: Duke University Press Books, 2014. Kindle.
Bruner, Peter. *A Slave's Adventures toward Freedom. Not Fiction, but the True Story of a Struggle*. Oxford, OH: S.n., 1918. http://docsouth.unc.edu/neh/bruner/menu.html
Burke, Mary C. *Human Trafficking: Interdisciplinary Perspectives*. New York: Routledge, 2013.
Butterfield, Stephen. *Black Autobiography in America*. Amherst, MA: University of Massachusetts Press, 1974.
Brysk, Alison, and Austin Choi-Fitzpatrick. *From Human Trafficking to Human Rights: Reframing Contemporary Slavery*. Philadelphia: University of Pennsylvania Press, 2012. Kindle.
Cadet, Jean-Robert, and Jim Luken. *My Stone of Hope: From Haitian Slave Child to Abolitionist*. Austin: University of Texas Press, 2011. Kindle.
Cadet, Jean-Robert. *Restavec: From Haitian Slave Child to Middle-Class American*. Austin: University of Texas Press, 1998. Kindle.
Caruth, Cathy. *Unclaimed Experience, Trauma, Narrative and History*. Baltimore: Johns Hopkins University Press, 1996.
Caruth, Cathy. *Listening to Trauma: Conversations with Leaders in the Theory & Treatment of Catastrophic Experience*. Baltimore: John Hopkins University Press, 2014.

Caruth, Cathy. *Critical Encounters: Reference and Responsibility in Deconstructive Writing*. New Brunswick, NJ: Rutgers University Press, 1995.
Caruth, Cathy. *Trauma: Explorations in Memory*. Baltimore and London: The John Hopkins University Press, 1995.
Charmaz, Kathy. *Constructing Grounded Theory: A Practical Guide through Qualitative Analysis*. London: Sage, 2006.
Choi-Fitzpatrick, Austin. *What Slaveholders Think: How Contemporary Perpetrators Rationalize What They Do*. New York: Columbia University Press, 2017.
Chouliaraki, Lilie. *Spectatorship of Suffering*. London: Sage, 2006.
Connell, Noreen, and Cassandra Wilson. *Rape: The First Sourcebook for Women by New York Radical Feminists*. New York: The New American Library, 1974.
Cowling, Camelia. *Conceiving Freedom Women of Color, Gender, and the Abolition of Slavery in Havana and Rio de Janeiro*. Chapel Hill: The University of North Carolina Press, 2013. Kindle.
Creswell, John W., and Cheryl N. Poth. *Qualitative Inquiry and Research Design: Choosing among Five Approaches*. 4th ed. Thousand Oaks, CA: Sage, 2018.
Dahl, Luke. G. *Daddy's Curse: A Sex Trafficking True Story of an 8-Year Old Girl*. Stockholm: Cedenheim Publishing, 2017. Kindle.
Davidson, Julia O'Connell. *Modern Slavery: The Margins of Freedom*. Basingstoke: Palgrave Macmillan, 2015. Kindle.
Davis, David Brion. *Slavery and Human Progress*. Oxford: Oxford University Press, 1984.
Davis, David Brion. *Black Is the Color of the Cosmos: Essays on Afro-American Literature and Culture, 1942–1981*. New York: Garland Publishing, Inc., 1982.
Davis, Charles T., and Henry Louis Gates Jr. *The Slave's Narrative*. Oxford: Oxford University Press, 1985.
Degruy, Joy. *Post Traumatic Slave Syndrome: America's Legacy of Enduring Injury and Healing*. Self-published, Joy Degruy Publications Inc., 2017. Kindle.
Dimsdale, Joel E. *Survivors, Victims, and Perpetrators: Essays on the Nazi Holocaust*. Baskerville, VA: Hemisphere Publishing Corporation, 1980.
Dirie, Waris, and Cathleen Miller. *Desert Flower: The Extraordinary Journey of a Desert Nomad*. n.p.: Harper Collins Publishers, 2009. Kindle.
Douglass, Frederick. *My Bondage and My Freedom. Part I. Life as a Slave. Part II. Life as a Freeman*. New York: Miller, Orton & Mulligan, 1855. [New York: Penguin Group, 2003.]
Douglass, Frederick. *Narrative of the Life of Frederick Douglass, an American Slave*. Dublin: Webb and Chapman, 1845.
Downs, Jim. *Sick from Freedom: African-American Illness and Suffering during the Civil War and Reconstruction*. Oxford: Oxford University Press, 2012. Kindle.
Drew, Benjamin. *A North-Side View of Slavery. The Refugee: Or the Narratives of Fugitive Slaves in Canada. Related by Themselves, with an Account of the History and Condition of the Colored Population of Upper Canada*. Boston: John P. Jewett and Company, 1855. Electronic edition available at http://docsouth.unc.edu/neh/drew/drew.html
Dreyfus, Hubert L. *Being-in-the-World: A Commentary on Heidegger's Being and Time*. Cambridge, MA: MIT Press, 1995.

Durrant, Sam. *Postcolonial Narrative and the Work of Mourning: J. M. Coetzee, Wilson Harris, and Toni Morrison*. Albany: NY. SUNY Press, 2004.
Eagleton, Terry. *Literary Theory: An Introduction*. 2nd ed. Minneapolis: University of Minnesota Press, 1996.
Fleman, Shoshana, and Dori Laub. *Testimony: Crisis of Witnessing in Literature, Psychoanalysis, and History*. New York: Routledge, 1992.
Fernando, Beatrice. *In Contempt of Fate: The Tale of a Sri Lankan Sold into Servitude, Who Survived to Tell It*. Merrimac, MA: Bearo Publishing, 2005.
Fisch, Audrey. *The Cambridge Companion to the African American Slave Narrative*. Cambridge: Cambridge University Press, 2007.
Fisher, Ronald P., and R. Edward Geiselman. *Memory-Enhancing Techniques for Investigative Interviewing: The Cognitive Interview*. Springfield, IL: Charles C Thomas Pub Ltd, 1992.
Fleishner, Jennifer. *Mastering Slavery: Memory, Family and Identity in Women's Slave Narratives*. New York: New York University Press, 1996.
Flores, Theresa. *The Slave across the Street: How a 15-Year-Old Girl Became a Sex Slave*. London: Arrow books, 2013.
Flyvberg, Bent, Todd Landman, and Sandford Schram. *Real Social Science*. Cambridge: Cambridge University Press, 2012.
Forsyth, Sarah, and Tim Tate. *Slave Girl – Return to Hell: Ordinary British Girls Are Being Sold into Sex Slavery; I Escaped, but Now I'm Going to Help Free Them. This Is My True Story*. London: John Blake Publishing, 2013.
Foster, Frances Smith. *Witnessing Slavery: The Development of Ante-Bellum Slave Narratives*. 2nd ed. Madison, WI: The University of Wisconsin Press, 1994.
Foucault, Michel. *The Archaeology of Knowledge*. Trans. A. M. Sheridan Smith. New York: Pantheon, 1972.
Gates, Henry Louis Jr. *The Classic Slave Narratives*. New York: Penguin, 1987.
Gates, Henry Louis, and William L. Andrews. *The Civitas Anthology of African American Slave Narratives*. Washington: Counterpoint, 1999.
Gates, Henry Louis. *Figures in Black: Words, Signs, and the "Racial" Self*. New York: Oxford University Press, 1987.
Ghandi, Leela. *Postcolonial Theory: An Introduction*. Edinburgh: Edinburgh University Press, 1998.
Gotschall, Jonathan. *The Storytelling Animal: How Stories Make Us Human*. New York: First Mariner Books, 2013.
Gready, Paul. *The Era of Transitional Justice: The Aftermath of the Truth and Reconciliation Commission in South Africa and Beyond*. Oxford: Routledge, 2017.
Greenspan, Henry. *On Listening to Holocaust Survivors: Beyond Testimony*. 2nd ed. St. Paul, MN: Paragon House, 2011. Kindle.
Gupta, Rahila. *Enslaved: The New British Slavery*. London: Portobello Books, 2007. Kindle.
Hager, Christopher. *Word by Word: Emancipation and the Act of Writing*. Cambridge, MA, and London: Harvard University Press, 2013.
Hall, Shyima, and Lisa Wysocky. *Hidden Girl: The True Story of a Modern-Day Child Slave*. New York: Simon & Schuster Books, 2014.
Hamilton, Douglas, Kate Hodgson, and Joel Quirk. *Slavery, Memory and Identity: National Representations and Global Legacies*. Abdingon: Routledge, 2016.

Hawthorn, Jeremy. *Narrative: From Malory to Motion Pictures*. London: Edward Arnold, 1985.
Hayes, Sophie. *Trafficked: The Terrifying True Story of a British Girl Forced into the Sex Trade*. London: Harper Collins, 2012. Kindle.
Hendry, Sharon. *Radhika's Story: Surviving Human Trafficking*. London: New Holland Publishers (UK) Ltd., 2011. Kindle.
Herman, Judith. *Trauma and Recovery: The Aftermath of Violence – From Domestic Abuse to Political Terror*. New York: Basic Books, 2015.
Jackson, Andrew B. *Narrative and Writings of Andrew Jackson, of Kentucky; Containing an Account of His Birth, and Twenty-Six Years of His Life While a Slave; His Escape; Five Years of Freedom, Together with Anecdotes Relating to Slavery; Journal of One Year's Travels; Sketches, etc. Narrated by Himself; Written by a Friend*. Syracuse: Daily and Weekly Star Office, 1847. https://docsouth.unc.edu/neh/jacksona/menu.html
Jacobs, Harriet Ann, and Lydia Maria Frances Child. *Incidents in the Life of a Slave Girl*. Boston: Published for the Author, 1861. http://docsouth.unc.edu/fpn/jacobs/menu.html
James, Joy. *New Abolitionists: (Neo) Slave Narratives and Contemporary Prison Writings*. New York: State University of New York Press, 2015.
Jordan, Mary, Carina Buckley, and David Mossop. *Destiny of Choice*. Southampton: Dolphin Marketing Press Ltd., 2014.
Judy, Ronald A. T. *(Dis)Forming the American Canon*. Minneapolis: University of Minnesota Press, 1993.
Kara, Siddharth. *Modern Slavery: A Global Perspective*. New York: Columbia University Press, 2017.
Kara, Siddharth. *Sex Trafficking: Inside the Business of Modern Slavery*. New York: Columbia University Press, 2009.
Keitetsi, China. *Child Soldier*. London: Souvenir Press, 2011. Kindle.
Khalaf, Farida, and Andrea C. Hoffmann. *The Girl Who Escaped ISIS: Farida's Story*. London: Vintage Digital, 2016. Kindle.
Lane, Lunsford. *The Narrative of Lunsford Lane, Formerly of Raleigh, N.C. Embracing an Account of His Early Life, the Redemption by Purchase of Himself and Family from Slavery, and His Banishment from the Place of His Birth for the Crime of Wearing a Colored Skin*. Self-published. Boston: Published by Himself, 1842. http://docsouth.unc.edu/neh/lanelunsford/menu.html
Lester, Julius. *To Be a Slave: Paintings by Tom Feelings*. New York: Puffin Books, 2000.
Leys, Ruth. *Trauma: A Genealogy*. Chicago: University of Chicago Press, 2000. Kindle.
Lifton, Robert Jay. *Death in Life: The Survivors of Hiroshima*. London: Weidenfield & Nicholson, 1967.
Lifton, Robert Jay. *The Protean Self: Human Resilience in an Age of Fragmentation*. Chicago: University of Chicago Press, 1993.
Lloyd, Rachel. *Girls Like Us: A Memoir*. New York: Harper Collins Publishers, 2011.
Lueche, Monluede. *Child Sex Slave: A Memoir*. North Charleston, South Carolina: CreateSpace Independent Publishing Ltd., 2012.

Lussana, Sergio A. *My Brother Slaves: Friendship, Masculinity, and Resistance in the Antebellum South*. Kentucky: University Press of Kentucky, 2016.

Lutnick, Alexandra. *Domestic Minor Sex Trafficking: Beyond Victims & Villains*. New York. Columba University Press (2016).

Maurois, Andre. *Aspects of Autobiography*. New York: Appleton & Co., 1929.

McDonell, Faith J. H., and Grace Akallo. *Girl Soldier: A Story of Hope for Northern Uganda's Children*. Grand Rapids, MI: Chosen Books, 2007.

McDonnell, Lara. *Girl for Sale: The Shocking True Story from the Girl Trafficked and Abused by Oxford's Evil Sex Ring*. London: Ebury Press, 2015. Kindle.

Moses, Wilson Jeremiah. *Creative Conflict in African American Thought: Frederick Douglass, Alexander Crummell, Booker T. Washington, W.E.B Du Bois, and Marcus Garvey*. Cambridge, UK: Cambridge University Press, 2004.

Moya, Paula M. L., and R. Hames-Garcia Michael. *Reclaiming Identity: Realist theory and the Predicament of Postmodernism*. Berkeley and Los Angeles: University of California Press, 2000.

Muhsen, Zana, and Crofts, Andrew. *Sold: One Woman's Heartbreaking, True Account of Modern Slavery*. London: Sphere Publishing, 2010.

Murad, Nadia. *Last Girl: My Story of Captivity, and My Fight against the Islamic State*. London: Virago, 2017. Kindle.

Murphy, Laura T. *The New Slave Narrative: The Battle over Representations of Contemporary Slavery*. New York: Columbia University Press, 2019.

Murphy, Laura T. *Survivors of Slavery: Modern-Day Slave Narratives*. New York: Columbia University Press, 2014.

Myers, John E. B. *Myers on Evidence in Child, Domestic and Elder Abuse Cases, Vol. 1*. 4th ed. New York: Aspen Publishers, 2005.

Nagy, Timea. *Memoirs of a Sex Slave Survivor*. Toronto: Communication Dynamics Publishing, 2010.

Nazer, Mende, and Damien Lewis. *Slave: The True Story of a Girl's Lost Childhood and Her Fight for Survival*. London: Virago, 2010. Kindle.

Okpara, Tina, and Julie Jodter. *My Life Has a Price: A Memoir of Survival and Freedom*. Dakar: Amalion, 2012. Kindle.

Olney, James. *Memory & Narrative: The Weave of Life-Writing*. Chicago: University of Chicago Press, 1998.

Olney, James. *Metaphors of Self*. Princeton: Princeton University Press, 1972.

Olney, James. *Tell Me Africa: An Approach to African Literature*. Princeton: Princeton University Press, 1973.

Patterson, Orlando. *Slavery and Social Death: A Comparative Study*. Cambridge, MA: Harvard University Press, 1982.

Phillips, Ulrich B. *Life and Labour in the Old South*. Boston: Little, Brown and Company, 1929.

Pike, Godfrey H. *From Slave to College President, Being the Life Story of Booker T Washington*. Cabin John, MD: Wildside Press, 2009.

Pitts, Victoria. *In the Flesh: The Cultural Politics of Body Modification*. London: Palgrave Macmillan, 2003.

Priest, Josiah. *Bible Defence of Slavery*. Kentucky: W. S. Brown, 1852. http://babel.hathitrust.org/cgi/pt?id=miun.aev3898.0001.001;view=1up;seq=7

Prum, Vannak Anan, Pederick Ben, and Pederick Jocelyn. *The Dead Eye and the Deep Blue Sea: The World of Slavery at Sea – A Graphic Memoir*. New York: Seven Stories Press, 2018.

Quirk, Joel. *The Anti-Slavery Project: From the Slave Trade to Human Trafficking*. Philadelphia: University of Pennsylvania Press, 2011. Kindle.

Rawick, George P. *The American Slave: A Composite Autobiography*. Westport, CT: Greenwood Publishing Company, 1972.

Reed, Angela, and Marietta Latonio. *I Have a Voice: Trafficked Women – In Their Own Words*. Victoria, Melbourne: Our Community Pty Ltd., 2015.

Risman, Barbara J. *Gender Vertigo: American Families in Transition*. New Haven: Yale University Press, 1999.

Risse, Thomas, Stephen C. Ropp, and Kathryn Sikkink. *The Power of Human Rights: International Norms and Domestic Change*. Cambridge: Cambridge University Press, 1999.

Rosenblatt, Katarina, and Cecil Murphey: *Stolen: The True Story of a Sex Trafficking Survivor*. Grand Rapids, MI: Revell, 2014. Kindle.

Ruston, Anna. *Secret Slave: Kidnapped and Abused for 13 Years. This Is My Story of Survival*. London: Blink Publishing, 2016. Kindle.

Sage, Jesse, and Kasten Liora. *Enslaved: True Stories of Modern Day Slavery*. New York: Palgrave Macmillan, 2006. Kindle.

Schaffer, Kay, and Smith Sidonie. *Human Rights and Narrated Lives: The Ethics of Recognition*. New York: Palgrave Macmillan, 2004.

Skinner, E. Benjamin. *A Crime So Monstrous. A Shocking Expose of Modern-Day Sex Slavery, Human Trafficking and Urban Child Markets*. Edinburgh: Mainstream Publishing, 2008.

Smith, Jonathan A., Paul Flowers, and Larkin Michael. *Interpretative Phenomenological Analysis: Theory, Method and Research*. Los Angeles: Sage, 2009.

Smith, Jonathan A. *Qualitative Psychology: A Practical Guide to Research Methods*. 2nd ed. London: Sage. 2008.

Spence, Donald P. *Narrative Truth and Historical Truth: Meaning and Interpretation in Psychoanalysis*. New York: W. W. Norton & Company, 1982.

Stauffer, John, Zoe Trodd, Celeste Marie-Bernier, Louis Gates Henry, and Kenneth B. Morris. *Picturing Frederick Douglass: An Illustrated Biography of the Nineteenth Century's Most Photographed American*. New York: Liveright, 2015.

Stauffer, John, and Louis Gates Henry. *The Portable Frederick Douglass*. New York: Penguin, 2016.

Stewart, Catherine A. *Long Past Slavery: Representing Race in the Federal Writers' Project*. Chapel Hill: The University of North Carolina Press, 2016.

Storr, Anthony. *The Essential Jung*. Princeton: Princeton University Press, 1983.

Stowe, Harriet Beecher. *A Key to Uncle Tom's Cabin; Presenting the Original Facts and Documents upon Which the Story Is Founded, Together with Corroborative Statements Verifying the Truth of the Work*. Boston: John P. Jewett & Co., 1853.

Swift, Graham. *Waterland*. London: Picador, 2010.

Taylor, Katie, and Clark Veronica. *Stolen Girl: I Was an Innocent Schoolgirl. I Was Targeted, Raped and Abused by a Gang of Sadistic Men. But That Was Just the Beginning ... This Is My Terrifying True Story*. London: John Blake Publishing Ltd., 2013. Kindle.

Tomich, Dale W. *Through the Prism of Slavery: Labor, Capital and World Economy*. Lanham, MD: Rowman & Littlefield Publishers, Inc, 2004.
Trodd, Zoe. *American Protest Literature*. Cambridge, MA: Harvard University Press, 2008.
Van Der Kolk, Bessel A. *The Body Keeps the Score*. London: Penguin Books, 2015.
Weld, Theodore Dwight. *American Slavery as It Is: Testimony of a Thousand Witnesses*. New York: The American Slavery Society, 1839.
Wexler, David, and Winick Bruce. *Law in a Therapeutic Key: Developments in Therapeutic Jurisprudence*. Durham, North Carolina: Carolina Academic Press, 1996.
White, Hayden. *The Content of the Form: Narrative Discourse and Historical Representation*. Baltimore: The Johns Hopkins University Press, 1990.
Whitman, Ivy G. *At the Dusk of Dawn, Selected Poetry and Prose of Albery Allson Whitman*. Boston: Northeastern University Press, 2009.
Woodhouse, Sammy. *Just a Child*. London: Blink Publishing, 2018.
Yetman, Norman R. *Life under the "Peculiar Institution": Selections from the Slave Narrative Collection*. New York: Robert E. Kreiger Publishing Company, 1976.
Yetman, Norman R. *Voices from Slavery: 100 Authentic Slave Narratives*. New York: Dover Publications Inc., 2000.
Yung, Carl, translated from the German by R. F. C. Hull. *The Undiscovered Self*. London: Routledge & Kegan, 1975.

### ARTICLES AND CHAPTERS IN BOOKS

Abayneh, Sisay, Heidi Lempp, Jill Manthorpe, and Charlotte Hanlon. "Development of Programme Theory for Integration of Service User and Caregiver Involvement in Mental Health System Strengthening: Protocol for Realist Systematic Review." *International Journal of Mental Health Systems* 12, no. 1 (2018): 12–41.
Adams, Cherish. "Re-trafficked Victims: How a Human Rights Approach Can Stop the Cycle of Re-victimization of Sex Trafficking Victims." *George Washington International Law Review* 43 (2011): 201–34.
Adorno, Theodor W. "Meditations on Metaphysics from Negative Dialektik." trans. by Simon Jarvis: 1–48. https://readinggroupcork.files.wordpress.com/2012/07/simon-jarvis-translation-of-tw-adorno-_meditations-on-metaphysics-word-97.pdf
Aje, Lawrence. "Fugitive Slave Narratives and the (Re)presentation of the Self? The Cases of Frederick Douglass and William Brown." *L'Ordinaire des Amériques* 215 (2013): 1–22. http://journals.openedition.org/orda/507
Alcoff, Linda, and Laura Gray. "Survivor Discourse: Transgression or Recuperation?" *Journal of Women in Culture & Society* 18, no. 2 (1993): 260–90.
Allain, Jean, and Kevin Bales. "Slavery and Its Definition," in *The Law and Slavery*, ed. Jean Allain, 502–12. Human Rights and Humanitarian Law E-Books Online, Collection 2015. Leiden: Brill and Nijhoff, 2015.
Allain, Jean. "Conceptualizing the Exploitation of Human Trafficking," in *The SAGE Handbook of Human Trafficking and Modern Day Slavery*, ed. Jennifer

Bryson Clark and Sasha Poucki, 3–17. London: SAGE Publications Ltd., 2019. www.researchgate.net/publication/325846087

Allain, Jean, and Robin Hickey. "Property and the Definition of Slavery." *International and Comparative Law Quarterly* 61, No. 4 (2012): 915–38.

Angueira, Katherine. "To Make the Personal Political: The Use of Testimony as a Consciousness-Raising Tool against Sexual Aggression in Puerto Rico." *Oral History Review* 16, No. 2 (1988): 65–93.

Balaev, M. "Literary Trauma Theory Reconsidered," in *Contemporary Approaches in Literary Trauma Theory*, ed. M. Balaev, 1–14. London: Palgrave Macmillan, 2014.

Bales, Kevin. "Slavery and the Human Right to Evil." *Journal of Human Rights* 3, No. 1 (2004): 53–63.

Bandes, Susan A. "Victims, Closure, and the Sociology of Emotion." *Law & Contemporary Problems* 72, No. 1 (2009): 1–26.

Bernard-Donals, Michael. "Beyond the Question of Authenticity: Witness and Testimony in the Fragments Controversy." *PMLA* 116, No. 5 (2001): 1302–15.

Bernstein, Dorthe, and David C. Rubin. "The Centrality of Event Scale: A Measure of Integrating a Trauma into One's Identity and Its Relation to Post-Traumatic Stress Disorder Symptoms." *Behaviour Research and Therapy* 44, No. 2 (2006): 219–31.

Best, Joel. "Victimization and the Victim Industry." *Society* 34, No. 4 (1997): 9–17.

Biggerstaff, Deborah, and Andrew R. Thompson. "Interpretative Phenomenological Analysis (IPA): A Qualitative Methodology of Choice in Healthcare Research." *Qualitative Research in Psychology* 5, No. 3 (2008): 173–83.

Blassingame, John W. "Using the Testimony of Ex-Slaves: Approaches and Problems." *The Journal of Southern History* 41, No. 4 (1975): 473–92.

Blume, Saskia. "Masculinity and the 'Ideal Victim' in the US Trafficking Discourse." *Centre on Migration, Policy and Society*. Working Paper. University of Oxford, 2015: 1–36. www.compas.ox.ac.uk/media/WP-2015-124-Sassen_Masculinity_Ideal_Victim.pdf

Brockmeier, Jens. "Reaching for Meaning: Human Agency and the Narrative Imagination." *Theory & Psychology* 19, No. 2 (2009): 213–33.

Brown, Laura S. "Not Outside the Range: One Feminist Perspective on Psychic Trauma," in *Trauma: Explorations in Memory*, ed. Cathy Caruth, 100–3. Baltimore and London: The John Hopkins University Press, 1995.

Brubaker, Rogers, and Frederick Cooper. "Beyond 'Identity'." *Theory & Society* 29, No. 1 (2000): 1–47.

Burns, Tony. "Hegel, Identity Politics and the Problem of Slavery." *Culture, Theory and Critique* 47, No. 1 (2006): 87–104.

Bump, Micah, Julianne Duncan, Elzbieta Gozdziak, and Margaret MacDonnell. "Second Conference on Identifying and Serving Child Victims of Trafficking." *International Migration* 43, No. 1/2 (2005): 344–63.

Cade, John B. "Out of the Mouths of Ex-slaves." *The Journal of Negro History* 20, No. 3 (1935): 294–337.

Carr, Bridgette A. "When Federal and State Systems Converge: Foreign National Human Trafficking Victims within Juvenile and Family Courts." *Juvenile & Family Court Journal* 63, No. 1 (2012): 77–90.

Cash, Floris Barnett. "Kinship and Quilting: An Examination of an African-American Tradition." *The Journal of Negro History* 80, No. 1 (1995): 30–41.

Chacón, Jennifer M. "Tensions and Trade-Offs: Protecting Trafficking Victims in the Era of Immigration Enforcement." *University of Pennsylvania Law Review* 158 (2010): 1609–53.

Chase, Elaine. "Agency and Silence: Young People Seeking Asylum Alone in the UK." *British Journal of Social Work* 40, No. 7 (2010): 2050–68.

Cohen, Oryx. "How Do We Recover? An Analysis of Psychiatric Survivor Oral Histories." *Journal of Humanistic Psychology* 45, No. 3 (2005): 333–54.

Conway, Martin A., and Mark L. Howe. "Memory and the Law: Insights from Case Studies." *Memory* 21, No. 5 (2013): 545–46.

Conway, Martin A., and Catherine Loveday. "Remembering, Imagining, False Memories and Personal Meanings." *Consciousness and Cognition* 33 (2014): 574–81.

Countryman-Roswurm, Karen, and Patton Brackin Bailey. "Awareness without Re-exploitation: Empowering Approaches to Sharing the Message about Human Trafficking," *Journal of Human Trafficking* 3, No. 4 (2017): 327–34.

Cowling, Camelia. "'As a Slave Woman and as a Mother': Women and the Abolition of Slavery in Havana and Rio De Janeiro." *Social History* 36, No. 3 (2011): 294–311.

Cowling, Camelia. "Debating Womanhood, Defining Freedom: The Abolition of Slavery in 1880s Rio de Janeiro." *Gender & History* 22, No. 2 (2010): 284–301.

Crenshaw, Kimberle. "Mapping the Margins: Intersectionality, Identity Politics, and Violence against Women of Color." *Stanford Law Review* 43, No. 6 (1991): 1241–99.

Crossley, Michele L. "Narrative Psychology, Trauma and the Study of Self/Identity." *Theory and Psychology* 10, No. 4 (2000): 527–46.

Cutler, Brian L., Steven D. Penrod, and Todd K. Martens. "Improving the Reliability of Eyewitness Identifications: Putting Context into Context." *Journal of Applied Psychology* 72, No. 4 (1987): 629–37.

Dang, Minh. "Epistemology of Survival: A Working Paper" (2021). www.minh-dang.com/publications

Dang, Minh, and Lutnick Alexandra. "Forging Partnerships between Researchers and the Researched: A Community Based Anti-Trafficking Response" (2017). https://sftaskforceeval.files.wordpress.com/2018/02/danglutnick_sswr2018_forgingpartnerships_final.pdf

Dang, Minh. "Paradox of Survivor Leadership," in *Wicked Problems: The Ethics of Action for Peace, Rights, and Justice*, ed. Douglass Irvin-Erickson, Austin Choi-Fitzpatrick, and Ernesto Verdeja. Oxford: Oxford University Press, In Press.

Dang, Minh. "Survivors Are Speaking: Are We Listening?" (2018). www.minh-dang.com/publications

Davis, Terri. "Images of Healing and Learning. Art Therapy Exhibitions: Exploitation or Advocacy?" *AMA Journal of Ethics* 19, No. 1 (2017): 98–106.

Dawes, James. "Human Rights in Literary Studies." *Human Rights Quarterly* 31, No. 2 (2009): 394–409.

De Angelis, Maria. "Narratives of Human Trafficking: Ways of Seeing and Not Seeing the Real Survivors and Stories." *Narrative Works* 7, No. 1 (2017): 44–63.

De Lauri, Antonio. "The Absence of Freedom: Debt, Bondage and Desire among Pakistani Brick Kiln Workers." *Journal of Global Slavery* 2, No. 1–2 (2017): 122–38.

DeRoche, Kathryn K., and Maria K. E. Lahman. "Methodological Considerations for Conducting Qualitative Interviews with Youth Receiving Mental Health Services." *Qualitative Social Research* 9, No. 3, Art. 17 (2008), online publication: www.qualitative-research.net/index.php/fqs/article/view/1016/2189

Dell, Nathaniel A., Brandy R. Maynard, Kara R. Born, Elizabeth Wagner, Bonnie Atkins, and Whitney House. "Helping Survivors of Human Trafficking: A Systematic Review of Exit and Postexit Interventions." *Trauma, Violence and Abuse* (2017): 1–14.

Doezma, Jo. "Loose Women or Lost Women? The Re-emergence of the Myth of White Slavery in Contemporary Discourse of Trafficking in Women." *Gender Issues* (2000): 23–50.

Dovydaitis T. "Human Trafficking: The Role of the Health Care Provider." *Journal of Midwifery & Women's Health* 55, No. 5 (2010): 462–67.

Doychak, Kendra, and Raghavan Chitra. "'No Voice or Vote:' Trauma-Coerced Attachment in Victims of Sex Trafficking," *Journal of Human Trafficking* 6, No. 3 (2020): 339–57.

Dunn, Jennifer. "'Victims' and 'Survivors': Emerging Vocabularies of Motive for 'Battered Women Who Stay'." *Sociological Inquiry* 75, No. 1 (2005): 1–30.

Dunn, Jennifer. "The Politics of Empathy: Social Movements and Victim Repertoires." *Sociological Focus* 37, No. 3 (2004): 235–50.

Earley, Samantha. "Writing from the Centre or the Margins? Olauduh Equiano's Writing Life Reassessed." *African Studies Review* 46, No. 3 (2003): 1–16.

Echeverri, Marcela. "'Enraged to the Limit of Despair': Infanticide and Slave Judicial Strategies in Barbacoas, 1788-98." *Slavery & Abolition* 30, No. 3 (2009): 403–26.

Eyal, Gil. "Identity and Trauma: Two Forms of the Will to Memory." *History and Memory* 16, No. 1 (2004): 5–36.

Farmer, Alice. "Refugee Responses, State-Like Behavior, and Accountability for Human Rights Violations: A Case Study of Violence in Guinea's Refugee Camps." *Yale Human Rights & Development Law Journal* 9, No. 1 (2006): 44–84.

Fisher, Ronald P., Stephen J. Ross, and Brian S. Cahill. "Interviewing Witnesses and Victims." (working paper, n.p., n.d.). https://pdfs.semanticscholar.org/3842/61136770c611fd3e4a04014263285 1d8ceab.pdf

Fong, Rowena, and Jodi Berger Cardoso. "Child Human Trafficking Victims: Challenges for the Child Welfare System." *Evaluation & Program Planning* 33, No. 3 (2010): 311–16.

Gallagher, Anne T. "Human Rights and Human Trafficking: Quagmire or Firm Ground? A Response to James Hathaway." *Virginia Journal of International Law* 50, No. 1 (2008): 789–848.

Gallagher, Anne T., and Elaine Pearson. "The High Cost of Freedom: A Legal and Policy Analysis of Shelter Detention for Victims of Trafficking." *Human Rights Quarterly* 32 (2010): 73–114.

Gallagher, Anne T., and Paul Holmes. "Developing an Effective Criminal Justice Response to Human Trafficking: Lessons from the Front Line." *International Criminal Justice Review* 18, No. 3 (2008): 318–43.

Gilfus, Mary E. "The Price of the Ticket: A Survivor-Centred Appraisal of Trauma Theory," *Violence Against Women* 5, No. 11 (1999): 1238–57.

Goodman, A., and K. Bales,. *The Slave Next Door: Human Trafficking and Slavery in America Today*. Democracy Now, September 9, 2009. www.democracynow.org/2009/9/9/the_slave_next_door_human_trafficking

Gould, Philip. "The Rise of the Slave Narrative." in *The Cambridge Companion to the African American Slave Narrative*, ed. Audrey Fisch, 11–27. Cambridge: Cambridge University Press, 2007.

Gready, Paul. "Introduction – Responsibility to the Story." *Journal of Human Rights Practice* 2, No. 2 (2010): 177–90.

Gross, Ariela. "When Is the Time of Slavery? The History of Slavery in Contemporary Legal and Political Argument." *California Law Review* 96, No. 1 (2008): 283–321

Gunn, Jeffrey. "Literacy and the Humanizing Project in Olaudah Equiano's *The Interesting Narrative* and Ottobah Cugoano's *Thoughts and Sentiments*." *Orality & History*, No. 10 (2007): 1–19.

Habermas, Tilmann. "Autobiographical Reasoning: Arguing and Narrating from a Biographical Perspective." *New Directions for Child and Adolescent Development*, No. 131 (Spring 2010): 1–17.

Habermas, Tilmann. "History and Life Stories: A Commentary on Grob, Krings, and Bangerter." *Human Development* 44, No. 4 (2001): 191–94.

Hanna, Cheryl. "No Right to Choose: Mandated Victim Participation in Domestic Violence Prosecutions," *Harvard Law Review* 109, No. 8 (1996): 1849–910.

Harding, Sandra. "Rethinking Standpoint Epistemology: What Is 'Strong Objectivity?'" *The Centennial Review* 36, No. 3 (Fall 1992): 437–70.

Hart, Catie, Roberts Celia, Geneviève T. Tiangco, Baybie Kae, Anderson Monica, Hang Ummra, Lutnick Alex, and Dang Minh. "Tips for Anti-Trafficking Professionals When Working with Survivor Leaders" (n.d.). www.survivoralliance.org/survivor-engagement-resources

Hartman, Geoffrey H. "Learning from Survivors: The Yale Testimony Project." *Holocaust and Genocide Studies* 9, No. 2 (1995): 192–207.

Hartman, Geoffrey H. "The Humanities of Testimony: An Introduction." *Poetics Today* 27, No. 2 (2006): 249–60.

Horowitz, Mardi J. "Self-Identity Theory and Research Methods." *Journal of Research Practice* 8, No. 2 (2012): 1–9. http://jrp.icaap.org/index.php/jrp/article/view/296/26

Huehls, Mitchum. "Referring to the Human in Contemporary Human Rights Literature." *Modern Fiction Studies* 58, No. 1 (2012): 1–21.

Hugman, Richard, Eileen Pittaway, and Linda Bartolomei. "When 'Do No Harm' Is Not Enough: The Ethics of Research with Refugees and Other Vulnerable Groups." *The British Journal of Social Work* 41, No. 7 (2011): 1271–87.

Hutchinson, Kimberley, KJ, Esiovwa Nancy, with additional support and editing by Sereni, Anna. "Agents for Change: Survivor Peer Researchers Bridge the Evidence and Inclusion Gap," Anti-Trafficking Monitoring Group (2020).

Jobson, Laura, Alireza Moradi, Vafa Rahimi-Movaghar, Martin Conway, and Tim Galgleish. "Culture and the Remembering of Trauma." *Clinical Psychological Science* 2, No. 6 (2014): 696–713.
Johnson, Kelli Lyon. "The New Slave Narrative: Advocacy and Human Rights in Stories of Contemporary Slavery." *Journal of Human Rights* 12, No. 2 (2013): 242–58.
Kafle, Narayan Prasad. "Hermeneutic Phenomenological Research Method Simplified." *Bodhi* 5, No. 1 (2011): 181–200.
Kapstein, Ethan B. "The New Global Slave Trade." *Foreign Affairs* 85, No. 6 (2006): 103–15.
Kaoma, Kaelyn. "Child Soldier Memoirs and the 'Classic' Slave Narrative: Tracing the Origins." *Life Writing* 15, No. 2 (2018): 195–210.
Kidder, Louise H., and Michelle Fine. "Qualitative Inquiry in Psychology: A Radical Tradition," in *Critical Psychology: An Introduction*, ed. Dennis Fox and Isaac Prilleltensky, 34–50. Thousand Oaks, CA: Sage Publications, Inc., 1998.
King, Sigrid. "Naming and Power in Zora Neale Hurston's Their Eyes Were Watching God." *Black American Literature Forum* 24, No. 4 (1990): 683–96.
Klug, Francesca, and Helen Wildbore. "Breaking New Ground: The Joint Committee on Human Rights and the Role of Parliament in Human Rights Compliance." *European Human Rights Law Review* 3 (2007): 231–50.
Kopytoff, Igor. "Slavery." *Annual Review of Anthropology* 11 (1982): 207–30.
Landman, Todd, and Bernard W. Silverman. "Globalization and Modern Slavery." *Politics and Governance* 7, No. 4 (2019): 275–90.
Larkin, Michael, Simon Watts, and Elizabeth Clifton. "Giving Voice and Making Sense in Interpretative Phenomenological Analysis." *Qualitative Research in Psychology* 3, No. 2 (2006): 102–20.
Larson, Pier M. "Reconsidering Trauma, Identity, and the African Diaspora: Enslavement and Historical Memory in Nineteenth-Century Highland Madagascar." *The William and Mary Quarterly* 56, No. 2 (1999): 335–62.
Laub, Dori, and Susanna Lee. "Thanatos and Massive Psychic Trauma: The Impact of the Death Instinct on Knowing, Remembering, and Forgetting." *Journal of the American Psychoanalytic Association* 51, No. 2 (2003): 433–64.
Laub, Dori. "Truth and Testimony the Process and the Struggle." *American Imago* 48, No. 1 (1991): 75–91.
Liévana, Gema Fernández Rodrıguez de, and Viviana Waisman. "'Lost in Translation': Assessment of the (Non)-Implementation of the Trafficking Directive from a Gender Perspective in Spain." *Journal of Human Rights Practice* 9, No. 3 (2017): 504–25.
Lifton, Robert Jay. "The Concept of the Survivor," in *Survivors, Victims, and Perpetrators: Essays on the Nazi Holocaust*, ed. Joel E. Dimsdale. Baskerville, VA: Hemisphere Publishing Corporation, 1980.
Lisak, David. "The Psychological Impact of Sexual Abuse: Content Analysis of Interviews with Male Survivors." *Journal of Traumatic Stress* 7, No. 4 (1994): 525–48.
Lloyd, Rachel. "At What Cost? The Road to Anti-Trafficking Is Paved with Good Intentions," *Canadian Women's Foundation* (2014). https://canadianwomen.org/blog/what-cost-trafficking/

Lockyer, Sue. "Beyond Inclusion: Survivor-Leader Voice in Anti-Human Trafficking Organizations." *Journal of Human Trafficking* (online, 2020): 1–22.

Lovejoy, Paul E. "'Freedom Narratives' of Transatlantic Slavery." *Slavery & Abolition* 32, No. 1 (2011): 91–107.

Lusk, Mark, and Faith Lucas. "The Challenge of Human Trafficking and Contemporary Slavery." *Journal of Comparative Social Welfare* 25, No. 1 (2009): 49–57.

Lutnick, Alexandra, and Minh Dang. "Forging Communities of Sex Worker and Anti-Trafficking Activists." *The American Society of Criminology Annual Meeting* (2017). Philadelphia, PA. https://sftaskforceeval.files.wordpress.com/2018/02/forgingcommunities_asc.pdf

Lutnick, Alexandra, and Minh Dang. "Researcher-Survivor-Ally Evaluation of the Mayor's Task Force on Anti-Human Trafficking Draft Final Summary Report" (2018), Prepared for the National Institute of Justice, Washington, DC.

Malkani, Bharat. "Voices of the Condemned: A Comparative Study of the Testimonies of Death Row Exonerees and Slave Narratives." *Law, Culture and the Humanities*. Published online, October 27, 2014: 1–21. http://lch.sagepub.com/content/early/2014/10/23/1743872114556435

Marren, Susan M. "Between Slavery and Freedom: The Transgressive Self in Olaudah Equiano's Autobiography." *PMLA* 108, No. 1 (1993): 94–105.

Marshall, Jill. "Human Rights Law and Personal Identity." University of Leicester School of Law Legal Studies Research Paper Series, Research Paper No. 14-30, November 11, 2014. https://papers.ssrn.com/sol3/papers.cfm?abstract_id=2521117##

Martins, Angelo Jr. "Interview with Julia O'Connell Davidson on Modern Slavery." *Theory, Culture and Society* 33, No. 7–8 (2016): 381–90.

Memom, Amina, and Ray Bull. "The Cognitive Interview – Its Origins, Empirical Support, Evaluation and Practical Implications." *Journal of Community & Applied Social Psychology* 1, No. 4 (1991): 291–307.

Miccio, G. Kristian. "A House Divided: Mandatory Arrest, Domestic Violence, and the Conservatization of the Battered Women's Movement." *Houston Law Review* 42 (2005): 237–323.

Mills, Linda G. "Killing Her Softly: Intimate Abuse and the Violence of State Intervention." *Harvard Law Review* 113 (1999): 570–71.

Mockus, Suan, Laura Cinq, Mars, Dorothy Guazzo Ovard, Ruta Mazelis, Paula Bjelajac, Janice Grady, Christine LaClair, Cardenia Livingston, Sharon Slavin, Susan Williams, and Jacki McKinney. "Developing Consumer/Survivor/Recovering Voice and Its Impact on Services and Research: Our Experience with the SAMHSA Women, Co-occurring Disorders and Violence Study." *Journal of Community Psychology* 33, No. 4 (2005): 513–25.

Mohanty, S. P. "Us and Them: On the Philosophical Bases of Political Criticism." *The Yale Journal of Criticism* 2, No. 2 (1989): 1–31.

Moynagh, Maureen. "Human Rights, Child-Soldier Narratives, and the Problem of Form." *Research in African Literatures* 42, No. 4 (2011): 39–59.

Murphy, Laura. "Black Face Abolition and the New Slave Narrative." *Cambridge Journal of Postcolonial Literary Inquiry* 2, No. 1 (2015): 93–113.

Murphy, Laura. "The New Slave Narrative and the Illegibility of Modern Slavery." *Slavery & Abolition* 36, No. 2 (2015): 382–405.
Murray, Hannah Rose. "Voices: Ideas for Using Survivor Testimony in Antislavery Work." October 2019, Rights Lab, Nottingham.
Newlin, Chris, Linda Cordisco Steele, Andra Chamberlin, Jennifer Anderson, Julie Kenniston, Amy Russell, Heather Stewart, and Viola Vaughan-Eden. "Child Forensic Interviewing: Best Practices." *Juvenile Justice Bulletin* (2015): 2–17.
Nicholson, Andrea, Minh, Dang, and Zoe, Trodd. "A Full Freedom: Contemporary Survivors' Definitions of Slavery." *Human Rights Law Review* 18, No. 4 (2018): 689–704.
O'Connell, Jamie. "Gambling with the Psyche: Does Prosecuting Human Rights Violators Console Their Victims?" *Harvard international Law Journal* 46, No. 2 (2005): 295–345
O'Connell Davidson, Julia. "New Slavery, Old Binaries: Human Trafficking and the Borders of 'Freedom'." *Global Networks* 10, No. 2 (2010): 244–61
Olney, James. "'I Was Born': Slave Narratives, Their Status as Autobiography and as Literature." *Callaloo* 20 (1984): 46–73
Pals, Jennifer L., and Dan P. McAdams. "The Transformed Self: A Narrative Understanding of Posttraumatic Growth." *Psychological Inquiry* 15, No. 1 (2004): 65–69.
Patterson, Orlando. "Trafficking, Gender and Slavery: Past and Present," in *The Legal Understanding of Slavery*, ed. Jean Allain, 323–29. Oxford: Oxford University Press, 2012.
Pearce, Jenny J. "Working with Trafficked Children and Young People: Complexities in Practice." *British Journal of Social Work* 41, No. 8 (2011): 1424–41.
Pietkiewicz, Igor, and Jonathan A. Smith. "A Practical Guide to Using Interpretative Phenomenological Analysis in Qualitative Research Psychology." *Psychological Journal* 18, No. 2 (2912): 361–69.
Pimenta, Sherline, and Ravi Poovaiah. "*On Defining Visual Narratives*." Bombay: Industrial Design Centre (2010): 25–46. www.idc.iitb.ac.in/resources/dt-aug-2010/On%20Defining%20Visual%20Narratives.pdf
Pinto-Gouveia, José, and Marcela Matos. "Can Shame Memories Become a Key to Identity? The Centrality of Shame Memories Predicts Psychopathology." *Applied Cognitive Psychology* 25, No. 2 (2011): 281–90.
Popkin, Jeremy D. "Ka-Tzetnik 135633: The Survivor as Pseudonym." *New Literary History* 33, No. 2 (2002): 343–55.
Potocky, Miriam. "Effectiveness of Services for Victims of International Human Trafficking: An Exploratory Evaluation." *Journal of Immigrant and Refugee Studies* 8, No. 4 (2010): 359–85.
Pourmokhtari, Navid. "Global Human Trafficking Unmasked: A Feminist Rights-Based Approach." *Journal of Human Trafficking* 1, No. 2 (2015): 156–66.
Puggioni, Raffaela. "Speaking through the Body: Detention and Bodily Resistance in Italy." *Citizenship Studies* 18, No. 5 (2014): 562–77.
Pyrou, Spyros. "The Limits of Children's Voices: From Authenticity to Critical, Reflexive Representation." *Childhood* 18, No. 2 (April 2011): 151–65.

Quirk, Joel. "Inventing Modern Slavery: From the Slave Trade to Human Trafficking." (Working Paper n.p., n.d.). www.tubmaninstitute.ca/sites/default/files/file/Quirk,%20Inventing%20Modern%20Slavery.pdf

Quirk, Joel, and Julia O'Connell Davidson. "Moving beyond Popular Representations of Trafficking and Slavery." *Open Democracy* (2015).

Quirk, Joel. "The Rhetoric and Reality of 'Ending Slavery in Our Lifetime'." *Open Democracy* (2015).

Risan, Patrick, Per-Einar Binder, and Rebecca Jane Milne. "Establishing and Maintaining Rapport in Investigative Interviews of Traumatized Victims: A Qualitative Study." *Policing: A Journal of Policy and Practice* 12, No. 4 (2018): 372–87.

Robson, Kathryn. "Curative Fictions: The 'Narrative Cure' in Judith Herman's Trauma and Recovery and Chantal Chawaf's Le Manteau Noir." *Journal for Cultural Research* 5, No. 1 (2001): 115–30.

Ryan, Gerry W., and H. Russell Bernard. "Techniques to Identify Themes in Qualitative Data." *Field Methods* 15, No. 1 (2003): 85–109.

Ryff, Carol D. "Psychological Well-Being in Adult Life." *Current Directions in Psychological Science* 4, No. 4 (1995): 99–104.

Sarich, Jody, Michele Oliver, and Kevin Bales. "Forced Marriage, Slavery, and Plural Legal Systems: An African Example." *Human Rights Quarterly* 38, No. 2 (2016): 450–76.

Schwarz, Katarina, and Andrea Nicholson. "Collapsing the Boundaries between De Jure and De Facto Slavery: The Foundations of Slavery beyond the Transatlantic Frame." *Human Rights Review* 20, No. 4 (2020): 391–414.

Schweitzer, Robert, and Zachary Steel. "Researching Refugees: Methodological and Ethical Considerations," in *Doing Cross-Cultural Research: Ethical and Methodological Perspectives*, ed. Pranee Liamputtong, 87–101. Netherlands: Springer, 2008.

Scully, Pamela. "Narratives of Infanticide in the Aftermath of Slave Emancipation in the Nineteenth-Century Cape Colony, South Africa." *Canadian Journal of African Studies/Revue Canadienne des Études Africaines* 30, No. 1 (1996): 88–105.

Sen, Amartya. "More Than 100 Million Women Are Missing." *New York Review of Books* (1990). www.nybooks.com/articles/1990/12/20/more-than-100-million-women-are-missing/

Sekora, John. "Black Message/White Envelope: Genre, Authenticity, and Authority in the Antebellum Slave Narrative." *Callaloo* 32 (1987): 482–515.

Shigekane, Rachel. "Rehabilitation and Community Integration of Trafficking Survivors in the United States." *Human Rights Quarterly* 29, No. 1 (2007): 112–36.

Sigmon, Jane Nady. "Combatting Modern-Day Slavery: Issues in Identifying and Assisting Victims of Human Trafficking Worldwide." *Victims and Offenders* 3, No. 2/3 (2008): 245–57.

Slaughter, Joseph R. "Life, Story, Violence: What Narrative Doesn't Say." *Humanity* 8, No. 3 (2007): 467–83.

Snajdr, Edward. "Beneath the Master Narrative: Human Trafficking, Myths of Sexual Slavery and Ethnographic Realities." *Dialectical Anthropology* 37, No. 2 (2013): 229–56.

Spry, Tami. "In the Absence of Word and Body: Hegemonic Implications of 'Victim' and 'Survivor' in Women's Narratives of Sexual Violence." *Women and Language* 13, No. 2 (1995): 27–37.

Spyrou, Spyros. "The Limits of Children's Voices: From Authenticity to Critical, Reflexive Representation." *Childhood* 18, No. 2 (2011): 151–65.

Srikantiah, Jayashri. "Perfect Victims and Real Survivors: The Iconic Victim in Domestic Human Trafficking Law." *Immigration and Nationality Law Review* 28 (2007): 741–798.

Starks, Helene, and Susan Brown. "Choose Your Method: A Comparison of Phenomenology, Discourse Analysis, and Grounded Theory." *Trinidad Qualitative Health Research* 17, No. 10 (2007): 1372–80.

Stauffer, John. "Foreword," in *American Protest Literature*, ed. Zoe Trodd, xi–xviii. Cambridge, MA: First Harvard University Press, 2008.

Stepnitz, Abigail. "A Lie More Disastrous than the Truth: Asylum and the Identification of Trafficked Women in the UK." *Anti-Trafficking Review* 1, No. 1 (2012): 104–19.

"The Rights of a Witness before a Congressional Committee." *Fordham Law Review* 29, No. 2 (1960) 357–74. http://ir.lawnet.fordham.edu/flr/vol29/iss2/4

Thomsen, Dorthe Kirkegaard, and Dorthe Bernsten. "The Long-Term Impact of Emotionally Stressful Events on Memory characteristics and Life Story." *Applied Cognitive Psychology* 23, No. 4 (2009): 579–98.

Todres, Jonathan. "Widening Our Lens: Incorporating Essential Perspectives in the Fight against Human Trafficking." *Michigan Journal of International Law* 33, No. 1 (2011): 53–76.

Törnberg, Anton. "Combining Transition Studies and Social Movement Theory: Towards a New Research Agenda." *Theory and Society* 47, No. 3 (2018): 381–408.

Tyldum, Guri, and Anette Brunovskis. "Describing the Unobserved: Methodological Challenges in Empirical Studies on Human Trafficking." *International Migration* 43, No. 1/2 (2005): 17–34.

Vinthagen, Stellan. "Understanding 'Resistance': Exploring Definitions, Perspectives, Forms and Implications." *Resistance Studies Magazine* 1, No. 2 (2013):1–46.

Visser, Irene. "Decolonizing Trauma Theory: Retrospect and Prospects." *Humanities* 4, No. 2 (2015): 250–65.

Waddington, P. A. J., and Ray Bull. "Cognitive Interviewing as a Research Technique." *Social Research Update* 50, No. 50 (2007): 1–5.

Ward, Abigail. "Understanding Postcolonial Traumas." *Journal of Theoretical and Philosophical Psychology* 33, No. 3 (2013): 170–84.

Ward, Abigail. "'Word People': A Conversation with David Dabydeen." *Atlantic Studies* 11, No. 1 (2014): 30–46.

Ward, Abigail. "Servitude and Slave Narratives: Tracing 'New Slaveries' in Mende Nazer's Slave and Zadie Smith's the Embassy of Cambodia'." *Wasafari* 31, No. 3 (2016): 42–48.

Webster, Crystal Lynn. "In Pursuit of Autonomous Womanhood: Nineteenth-Century Black Motherhood in the U.S. North." *Slavery & Abolition* 38, No. 2 (2017): 425–40.

Weiner, Marion. "Child Labour in Developing Countries: The Indian Case." *International Journal of Children's Rights,* No. 2 (1994): 121–28.
Welch, Jr., Claude E. "Defining Contemporary Forms of Slavery: Updating a Venerable NGO." *Human Rights Quarterly* 31, No. 1 (2009): 70–128.
Young, James E. "Interpreting Literary Testimony: A Preface to Rereading Holocaust Diaries and Memoirs." *New Literary History* 18, No. 2 (1987): 403–23.
Zimmerman, Cathy, Mazeda Hossain, and Charlotte Watts. "Human Trafficking and Health: A Conceptual Model to Inform Policy, Intervention and Research." *Social Science & Medicine* 73, No. 2 (2011): 327–35.
Zimmerman, Cathy, and Nicola Pocock. "Human Trafficking and Mental Health: 'My Wounds Are Inside; They Are Not Visible'." *Brown Journal of World Affairs* 11, No. 2 (2013): 265–80.

### THESES/DISSERTATIONS

Fitzpatrick, Liseli A. "African Names and Naming Practices: The Impact Slavery and European Domination Had on the African Psyche, Identity and Protest." Masters Thesis. The Ohio State University 2012.
Murray, Hannah-Rose. "'It Is Time for the Slaves to Speak:' Transatlantic Abolitionism and African American Activism in Britain 1835–1895." PhD Diss., University of Nottingham, 2018. Not yet publicly available.
Reed, Shelly. "The Rhetorical Possibilities of Representation: How Survivor Narratives Frame Sex Trafficking." Masters Thesis, Colorado State University, 2015. ProQuest Number: 1597935.
Sandeen, Loucynda Elayne. "Who Owns This Body? Enslaved Women's Claim on Themselves." Masters Thesis, Portland State University, 2013. 10.15760/etd.1491

### PAPERS, REPORTS, AND GUIDELINES

American Professional Society on the Abuse of Children. *Practice Guidelines: Forensic Interviewing in Cases of Suspected Child Abuse* (Chicago, IL: APSAC, 2012).
Annison, Rachel. *In the Dock: Examining the UK's Criminal Justice Response to Trafficking* (Anti-Slavery International, for the Anti-Trafficking Monitoring Group, June 2013).
Anti-Slavery International. *Home Truths: Wellbeing and Vulnerabilities of Child Domestic Workers* (London: Anti-Slavery International, March 2013).
Anti-Trafficking Review. *Life after Trafficking.* Issue 10 (April 2018).
Armstrong, Helen C. *Rebuilding Lives: An Introduction to Promising Practices in the Rehabilitation of Freed Slaves* (Washington, DC: Free the Slaves, March 2008). www.freetheslaves.net/wp-content/uploads/2015/03/RebuildingLives2008.pdf
Balch, Alex, and City Hearts. *Fresh Start. Integrating Survivors of Modern Slavery. Centre for the Study of International Slavery* (Liverpool: University of Liverpool; Sheffield: City Hearts, February 2017).

Balch, Alex. *One Step Forward, Two Steps Back? Modern Slavery and Victim Protection in the UK*. FLMG Briefing Statement on Victim protection and Support (January 2016).

Beddoe, Christine, Lara Bundock, and Tatiana Jardan. *Life Beyond the Safehouse for Survivors of Modern Slavery in London: Gaps and Options Review* (Human Trafficking Foundation, July 2015). https://static1.squarespace.com/static/599abfb4e6f2e19ff048494f/t/599eeb28914e6b9ddcceace2/1503587117886/Web_Life+Beyond+the+Safe+House.pdf

Caspar, Rachel A., Judith T. Lessler, and Gordon B. Willis. *Cognitive Interviewing: A 'How To' Guide: Reducing Survey Error through Research on the Cognitive and Decision Processes in Surveys* (Research Triangle Institute, 1999).

City Hearts. *Integration Support Programme Interim Report: January–March 2017* (Sheffield: City Hearts, April 2017).

City Hearts. *What Happens Next? Pathways Out of the Post NRM Maze. City Hearts Integration Support Programme Six Month Review: January–June 2017* (Sheffield: City Hearts, September 2017).

Clawson, Heather J., and Lisa Goldblatt Grace. *Finding a Path to Recovery: Residential Facilities for Minor Victims of Domestic Sex Trafficking* (US Department of Health and Human Services, Office of the Assistant Secretary for Planning and Evaluation, January 2007). http://digitalcommons.unl.edu/humtraffdata/10

Clawson, Heather J., Nicole M. Dutch, Amy Salomon, and Lisa Goldblatt Grace. *Study of HSS Programs Serving Human Trafficking Victims: Final Report* (U.S. Department of Health and Human Services, Office of the Assistant Secretary for Planning and Evaluation, December 2009).

Conway, Martin A., and Emily A. Holmes. *Guidelines on Memory and the Law: Recommendations from the Scientific Study of Human Memory* (Leicester: The British Psychological Society, June 2008).

Davis, Jarrett, James Havey, Lim Vanntheary, Nhanh Channtha, and Sreang Phaly. *The Forgotten Cohort. An Exploration of Themes and Patterns among Male Survivors of Sexual Exploitation & Trafficking. The Butterfly Longitudinal Research Project: A Chab Dai Study on (Re)integration: Researching the Lifecycle of Sexual Exploitation & Trafficking in Cambodia* (Phnom Penh: Chab Dai, 2016).

Elliott, Jessica, and Kate Garbers. *The National Referral Mechanism Pilots: A Review of The Training* (Unseen.org, n.p., n.d.). www.unseenuk.org/uploads/20160609115454807.pdf

Engerman, Stanley L. *Collective Degradation: Slavery and the Construction of Race. Proceedings of the Fifth Annual Gilder Lehrman Center International Conference at Yale University* (New Haven, CT: Yale University, November 7–8, 2003). https://glc.yale.edu/sites/default/files/files/events/race/Engerman.pdf

Faulkner, Alison. *The Guidelines for the Ethical Conduct of Research Carried Out by Mental Health Service Users and Survivors* (Bristol: The Policy Press, 2004).

Ferrell-Schweppenstedde, Samantha. *Day 46: Is There Life after the Safehouse for Survivors of Modern Slavery?* (The Human Trafficking Foundation, October 2016). https://snowdropproject.co.uk/wp-content/uploads/2018/02/Day-46.pdf

Gallagher, Anne T., and Nicole Karlebach. Prosecution of Trafficking in Persons Cases: Integrating a Human Rights-Based Approach in the Administration of Criminal Justice (Geneva: Expert Meeting of the United Nations Special Rapporteur on Trafficking in Persons, Especially Women and Children, July 4, 2011).

Gallagher, Anne T. *The Right to an Effective Remedy for Victims of Trafficking in Persons: A Survey of International Law and Policy* (Bratislava: Consultation of the United Nations Special Rapporteur on Trafficking in Persons, Especially Women and Children, November 22–23, 2010).

Haughey, Caroline. *The Modern Slavery Act Review* (London: Home Office, July 31, 2016). https://assets.publishing.service.gov.uk/government/uploads/system/uploads/attachment_data/file/542047/2016_07_31_Haughey_Review_of_Modern_Slavery_Act_-_final_1.0.pdf

Hestia. *Underground Lives: The Reality of Modern Slavery in London* (Hestia, November 2017). www.hestia.org/Handlers/Download.ashx?IDMF=-68f44ab0-fa94-49eb-ac4d-d4ae2b1f8586

Home Office. *Review of the National Referral Mechanism for Victims of Human Trafficking* (London: Home Office, November 2014). http://webarchive.nationalarchives.gov.uk/20141202113228/https://nrm.homeoffice.gov.uk/documents/2014/11/nrm-final-report.pdf

House of Commons Work and Pensions Committee. *Victims of Modern Slavery: Twelfth Report of Session 2016–17* (London: House of Commons, HC 803, April 30, 2017).

Human Rights Watch. *The Education Deficit: Failures to Protect and Fulfill the Right to Education in Global Development Agendas* (USA: Human Rights Watch, June 2016).

Human Trafficking Foundation. *The Slavery and Trafficking Survivor Care Standards* (2018). www.gla.gov.uk/media/2607/trafficking-survivor-care-standards-pdf.pdf

Human Trafficking Foundation Online Forum, "The Voice of British Survivors of Human Trafficking," (January 25, 2021): https://static1.squarespace.com/static/599abfb4e6f2e19ff048494f/t/601be6342f537f095a0763a3/1612441143314/British+survivors+online+forum_25+January_minutes.pdf

Independent Anti-Slavery Commissioner. *Annual Report 2016–17: Annual Report for the Period 1 October 2016 to 30 September 2017, Presented to Parliament pursuant to Section 42 (10) (b) of the Modern Slavery Act 2015* (October 2017). https://assets.publishing.service.gov.uk/government/uploads/system/uploads/attachment_data/file/654162/iasc_annual_report_2016_2017_web_new.pdf

Independent Anti-Slavery Commissioner. *Strategic Plan 2015–2017. Annual Report for the Period 1 October 2016 to 30 September 2017, Presented to Parliament pursuant to Section 42 (10) (a) of the Modern Slavery Act 2015* (October 2015).

International Women's Human Rights Clinic. *Criminalization of Trafficking Victims* (City New York: University of New York Law School Trafficking Victims Advocacy Project, Legal Aid Society of New York, Submission to the United National Universal Periodic Review of United States of America, second cycles, 22nd Session of the UPR. Human Rights Council, April–May 2015).

Iphofen, Ron. *Research Ethics in Ethnography/Anthropology* (Ethics Unit B6, DG Research and Innovation of the European Commission, June 30, 2015). http://ec.europa.eu/research/participants/data/ref/h2020/other/hi/ethics-guide-ethnog-anthrop_en.pdf

Katona, Cornelius, Katy Robjant, Rachel Shapcott, and Rachel Witkin. *Addressing Mental Health Needs in Survivors of Modern Slavery: A Critical Review and Research Agenda* (London: Helen Bamber Foundation and The Freedom Fund, 2015). https://d1r4goyjvcc7lx.cloudfront.net/uploads/2015-Addressing-the-Mental-Health-Needs-in-Survivors-of-Modern-Slavery.pdf

Lam, J., and K. Skrivankova. *Opportunities and Obstacles: Ensuring Access to Compensation for Trafficked Persons in the UK* (London: Anti-Slavery International, 2009).

Members of the Research Network on the Legal Parameters of Slavery. *Bellagio-Harvard Guidelines on the Legal Parameters of Slavery* (March 3, 2012). www.law.qub.ac.uk/schools/SchoolofLaw/FileStore/Filetoupload,651854,en.pdf

Ministry of Justice. *Achieving Best Evidence in Criminal Proceedings: Guidance on Interviewing Victims and Witnesses, and Guidance on Using Special Measures* (London: Ministry of Justice, March 2011).

Murphy, Carole. *A Game of Chance? Long-Term Support for Survivors of Modern Slavery* (London: Centre for the Study of Modern Slavery, St Mary's University, 2018).

National Audit Office Report by the Comptroller and Auditor General. *Reducing Modern Slavery* (London: Home Office, HC 630 Session 2017–2019, December 15, 2017). www.nao.org.uk/wp-content/uploads/2017/12/Reducing-Modern-Slavery.pdf

*National Referral Mechanism Statistics – End of Year Summary 2016* (London: Modern Slavery Human Trafficking Unit, version number: 2.0, 0380-MSHT, April 4, 2017).

Newlin, Chris, Linda Cordisco Steele, Andra Chamberlin, Jennifer Anderson, Julie Kenniston, Amy Russell, Heather Stewart, and Viola Vaughan-Eden. *Child Forensic Interviewing: Best Practices* (US Dept. of Justice Office of Juvenile Justice and Delinquency Prevention, Juvenile Justice Bulletin, September 2015). www.ojjdp.gov/pubs/248749.pdf

Office of the High Commissioner for Human Rights. *Recommended Principles and Guidelines on Human Rights and Human Trafficking.* Addendum to the Report of the United Nations High Commissioner for Human Rights (United Nations, E/2002/68/Add. 1, 2002).

Quirk, Joel. *Unfinished Business: A Comparative Survey of Historical and Contemporary Slavery* (Hull: Wilberforce Institute for the Study of Slavery and Emancipation, University of Hull, 2008).

Report of the Director-General. *Accelerating Action against Child Labour. Global Report under the Follow-Up to the ILO Declaration on Fundamental Principles and Rights at Work* (Geneva: International Labour Office, Report I(B), 2010).

Report of the Director-General. The End of Child Labour: Within Reach. *Global Report under the Follow-Up to the ILO Declaration on Fundamental Principles and Rights at Work* (Geneva: International Labour Office, Report I(B), 2006).

Richard, Stephanie. *Victims of Human Trafficking Should Not Be Arrested for Crimes Their Traffickers Force Them to Commit: A Study of Data from the Coalition to Abolish Slavery & Trafficking (CAST)* (The Coalition to Abolish Slavery & Trafficking, January 2016). http://castla.org/assets/files/arrest_is_not_the_answer.pdf

Schulze, Erika, Sandra Isabel Novo Canto, Mason Peter, and Maria Skalin. *Gender Equality, 'Sexual Exploitation and Prostitution and Its Impact on Gender Equality* (Brussels: European Parliament, Directorate General for Internal Policies Policy Department C: Citizens' Rights and Constitutional Affairs, PE 493.040, 2014).

Shahinian, Gulnara. *Report of the Special Rapporteur on Contemporary Forms of Slavery, Including Its Causes and Consequences* (Human Rights Council, 15th session, United Nations General Assembly, A7HRC/15/20, June 18, 2010).

Smith, Holly. *Interviewing Victims of Human Trafficking: Survivors Offer Advice* (Communities Digital News, March 2, 2014). www.commdiginews.com/life/interviewing-victims-of-human-trafficking-survivors-offer-advice-11238/

The Anti-Trafficking Monitoring Group (ATMG) & Human Trafficking Foundation. *Submission to the UN Special Rapporteur on Contemporary Forms of Slavery: Questionnaire on Access to Justice and Remedy* (March 2017). www.kalayaan.org.uk/wp-content/uploads/2014/09/ATMG-HTF-submission-to-Special-Rap-Contemporary-Slavery_Justice-Remedies_Final.pdf

The Anti-Trafficking Monitoring Group. *Hidden in Plain Sight – Three Years on: Updated Analysis of UK Measures to Protect Trafficked Persons* (London: Anti-Slavery International, 2013).

The Anti-Trafficking Monitoring Group. *Proposal for a Revised National Referral Mechanism (NRM) for Adults* (September 2014). www.antislavery.org/wp-content/uploads/2017/01/atmg_national_referral_mechanism_for_adults.pdf

The British Psychological Society. *Guidelines on Memory and the Law: Recommendations from the Scientific Study of Human Memory. A Report from the Research Board, June 2008* (Leicester: The British Psychological Society, June 2008). www.forcescience.org/articles/Memory&TheLaw.pdf

*The IOM Handbook on Direct Assistance for Victims of Trafficking* (Geneva: International Organization for Migration, 2007). http://publications.iom.int/system/files/pdf/iom_handbook_assistance.pdf

The Slavery Working Group. *It Happens Here: Equipping the United Kingdom to Fight Modern Slavery* (London: The Centre for Social Justice, March 11, 2013). www.centreforsocialjustice.org.uk/library/happens-equipping-united-kingdom-fight-modern-slavery.

UN Office of the High Commissioner for Human Rights (OHCHR). *Recommended Principles and Guidelines on Human Rights and Human Trafficking* (United Nations, E/2002/68/Add.1, May 20, 2002). www.refworld.org/docid/3f1fc60f4.html

UNICEF. *Victim, Not Criminal: Trafficked Children and the Non-punishment Principle in the UK* (Unicef UK, 2017). https://downloads.unicef.org.uk/wp-content/uploads/2017/05/Unicef-UK-Briefing_Victim-Not-Criminal_2017.pdf

US Department of Health and Human Services, National Human Trafficking Training and Technical Assistance Center. "Toolkit for Building Survivor-Informed Organizations: Trauma-Informed Resources and Survivor-Informed Practices to Support and Collaborate with Survivors of Human Trafficking as Professionals." (2018). www.hsdl.org/?abstract&did=818548

Weissbrodt, David, and Anti-Slavery International. *Abolishing Slavery and Its Contemporary Forms* (New York and Geneva: United Nations, Office of the United Nations High Commissioner for Human Rights, HR/PUB/02/4, 2002).

Wiggall, Stacey, and Alicia Boccellari, produced in collaboration with Allen/Loeb Associates. *The UC San Francisco Trauma Recovery Center Manual: A Model for Removing Barriers to Care and Transforming Services for Survivors of Violent Crime* (San Francisco: The UC San Francisco Trauma Recovery Center, University of California, 2017). http://traumarecoverycenter.org/wp-content/uploads/2017/05/TRC-Manual-v1-5-10-17.pdf

### LEGAL DOCUMENTS

Supplementary Convention on the Abolition of Slavery, the Slave Trade, and Institutions and Practices Similar to Slavery, April 30, 1956.

The Slavery Convention, September 25, 1926.

Protocol to Prevent, Suppress and Punish Trafficking in Persons Especially Women and Children, supplementing the United Nations Convention against Transnational Organized Crime, November 15, 2000.

EU directive 2011/36/EU on Prevention and Combating Trafficking in Human Beings and Protecting its Victims (OJ L 101, 1 15.4.2011), April 5, 2011.

The Modern Slavery Act, 2015, c.30.

The Modern Slavery (Victim Support) Bill [HL] 2017–19.

### CONGRESSIONAL TESTIMONY

*The Construction of the United States Capitol: Recognizing the Contributions of Slave Labor. Hearing before the Committee on House Administration, House of Representatives*, 110th Cong., First Session, November 7, 2007.

*Escaping North Korea. Hearing before the Tom Lantos Human Rights Commission, House of Representatives*, 111th Cong., Second Session, September 23, 2010.

*Examining Ongoing Human Rights Abuses in Vietnam. Hearing before the Subcommittee on Africa, Global Health, and Human Rights of the Committee on Foreign Affairs House of Representatives*, 112th Cong., Second Session, January 24, 2012.

*Regional Perspectives in the Global Fight against Human Trafficking. Hearing before the Committee on Foreign Affairs House of Representatives*, 113th Cong., First Session, November 4, 2013.

*Tier Rankings in the Fight against Human Trafficking. Hearing before the Subcommittee on Africa, Global Health, Global Human Rights, and International*

*Organizations of the Committee on Foreign Affairs House of Representatives*, 113th Cong., First Session, April 18,
*Highlighting Vietnamese Government Human Rights Violations in Advance of the U.S.-Vietnam Dialogue. Hearing before the Subcommittee on Africa, Global Health, Global Human Rights, and International Organizations of the Committee on Foreign Affairs House of Representatives*, 113th Cong., First Session, April 11, 2013.
*A Pathway to Freedom: Rescue and Refuge for Sex Trafficking Victims. Hearing before the Subcommittee on Africa, Global Health, Global Human Rights, and International Organizations of the Committee on Foreign Affairs House of Representatives*, 114th Cong., First Session, May 14, 2015.
*Ending Modern Slavery: What Is the Best Way Forward? Hearings before the Committee on Foreign Relations United States Senate*, 114th Cong., First Session, February 4 And February 11, 2015.
*Accountability and Transformation: Tier Rankings in the Fight against Human Trafficking. Hearing before the Subcommittee on Africa, Global Health, Global Human Rights, and International Organizations of the Committee on Foreign Affairs House of Representatives*, 114th Cong., First Session, April 22, 2015.
*Women Under ISIS Rule: From Brutality to Recruitment. Hearing before the Committee on Foreign Affairs House of Representatives*, 114th Cong., First Session, July 29, 2015.

### INTERVIEWS

Dwain, interviewed by Andrea Nicholson, November 3, 2017.
Keith, interviewed by Andrea Nicholson, May 17 and 19, 2018.
Pranus, interviewed by Andrea Nicholson, January 20, 2017.
Tung, interviewed by Andrea Nicholson, February 9, 2017.
Val, interviewed by Andrea Nicholson, April 15, 2018.

### LECTURES, BLOGS, NEWSPAPERS, AND SOCIAL MEDIA

Bernier, Celeste-Marie. *Stories That Stick to the Skin: Quilting Traditions, Slavery's Stories and the Fight for Civil Rights*. University of Nottingham: Department of American & Canadian Studies [Lecture]. University of Nottingham, April 25, 2016.
Campbell, Donna M. *The Slave, Freedom, or Liberation Narrative*.Washington State University. https://public.wsu.edu/~campbelld/amlit/slave.htm
Cohen, David. "My Life as a London Slave." *The Evening Standard*, January 21, 2004. www.standard.co.uk/news/my-life-as-a-london-slave-7298724.html
Dang, Minh. "Language Matters: Defining Human Trafficking and Slavery." *End Slavery Now*, blog, October 2, 2014. www.endslaverynow.org/blog/articles/language-matters-defining-human-trafficking-and-slavery
Douglass, Frederick "Give Us the Freedom Intended for Us." *The New National Era*, December 5, 1872. https://chroniclingamerica.loc.gov/lccn/sn84026753/

# Bibliography

Douglass, Frederick. "Our Paper and Its Prospects." *The North Star*, December 3, 1847. https://docsouth.unc.edu/neh/douglass/support15.html

Freedmen & Southern Society Project, *A Documentary History of Emancipation, 1861–1867*. Part of the History Department of the University of Maryland: www.freedmen.umd.edu/sampdocs.htm

Nicholson, Andrea. "Survivors' Solutions: The Value of Survivors' Voices in the Antislavery Movement." *The Rights Lab, University of Nottingham*, blog, October 27, 2017. http://blogs.nottingham.ac.uk/rights/2017/10/27/walkfree8/

Smith-Spark, Laura. *Ex-Child Soldier's Path to Hope*. BBC news online, May 25, 2004. http://news.bbc.co.uk/1/hi/uk/3733349.stm.

## WEBSITES

Aesop Agency: A creative agency powered by narrative thinking: https://aesopagency.com/

Bond, the UK network for organizations working in international development: www.bond.org.uk/news/2015/10/new-report-highlights-mental-trauma-caused-modern-slavery

Doc South: A digital publishing initiative sponsored by the University Library at the University of North Carolina, providing access to digitized primary materials that offer Southern perspectives on American history and culture: http://docsouth.unc.edu/

Hannah Rose Thomas: An artist working with former ISIS slaves on self-portraits: http://hannahrosethomas.com/art-with-former-isis-slaves/

The Gangmasters & Labour Abuse Authority: www.gla.gov.uk

The Global Alliance to Eradicate Forced Labour, Modern Slavery, Human Trafficking and Child Labour: www.alliance87.org/

The Global Slavery Index: www.globalslaveryindex.org

The Refugee Council. A UK Organization that works with refugees and people seeking asylum in the UK: www.refugeecouncil.org.uk

Trauma Recovery Center, University of California, San Francisco: http://traumarecoverycenter.org/

The UK Government website: www.gov.uk/

The UK Government Legislation website: www.legislation.gov.uk/

The UK National Audit Office website: www.nao.org.uk/

The UK National Crime Agency: www.nationalcrimeagency.gov.uk/

The US Congressional search engine: https://congressional.proquest.com/

The Works Progress Administration and the Slave Narrative Collection: www.loc.gov/collections/slave-narratives-from-the-federal-writers-project-1936-to-1938/articles-and-essays/introduction-to-the-wpa-slave-narratives/wpa-and-the-slave-narrative-collection/

UK Human Trafficking Blog: https://ukhumantraffickinglaw.wordpress.com

NGO websites accessed for narratives, reports and other data:
www.airecentre.org/
http://antislavery.ac.uk
www.antislavery.org/

www.artworksforfreedom.org
http://atleu.org.uk
www.barnardos.org.uk
www.bawso.org.uk
https://blackcountrywomensaid.co.uk/
https://city-hearts.co.uk
www.communitysafetyglasgow.org/what-we-do/supporting-victims-of-gender-based-violence/%EF%BF%BC%EF%BF%BCtara/
www.eavesforwomen.org.uk
https://freedomfund.org
www.freemovement.org.uk/
www.freetheslaves.net/
www.helenbamber.org
http://hopeforjustice.org
www.kalayaan.org.uk
www.medaille-trust.org.uk
www.midlandheart.org.uk/
www.migranthelpuk.org
www.mojatufoundation.org/
www.newpathways.org.uk
http://palmcovesociety.co.uk
www.p3charity.org
www.rahabuk.com/
www.refworld.org/
www.salvationarmy.org.uk
https://snowdropproject.co.uk/
www.sun-gate.org/
https://survivoralliance.org/
www.survivorsink.org
https://survivorsofslavery.org/
www.unseenuk.org
www.walkfreefoundation.org

# Index

abolition (antislavery) movement
  banned groups, 164
  contemporary slave narratives, use of, 4–5, 10, 13, 29–30, 37, 175
  'fourth wave', 2–3
  historic slave narratives, use of, 3–4, 19–20, 22–24, 26
  *see also* activism; survivor participation
abortions, 98
accommodation, post-liberation, 28, 133–34, 143, 164
activism
  education as, 92, 150, 158–65
  identity, 92–94, 155, 159
  narratives, 22, 42, 43, 46
  survivor guilt, 123, 124, 158
  trauma of, 156, 177–78
  *see also* survivor participation
addictions, 58, 59, 97–99, 134
Africa, 9, 20, 27
agency of survivors
  education, 150–51
  expressions of, 101, 110
  iconic victim, 169
  self-responsibility linked to, 128–29, 137
  telling, 44, 46, 92
  terminology, 152–55
  *see also* survivor participation
Aida, 106, 127
Ajok, 78, 96
Akallo, Grace, 32
alcohol addiction, 58, 59, 98

alienation
  definition of slavery, 50, 75–77
  narrative evidence of, 21, 97, 114, 121
  telling leads to recovery from, 45
  visualisations, 110–13
Alina, 87–88
Allan, Rev. William T., 52
amanuenses, 6, 7, 13, 14, 31–32, 37
Amasya, 140–41
Angel Coalition (NGO), 152
anger, 101–2, 117, 158
animals, people treated like, 50, 75–77, 96, 113, 175–76
Anita, 83–84
Annan, James Kofi, 95
anorexia, 64, 97, 99
antislavery movement. *see* abolition (antislavery) movement
anti-trafficking activities, 169–73, 175–77
anxiety, 28, 39, 117, 120
ashrams, 129, 134–35
ASSODIP (NGO), 28
asylum status. *see* immigration and asylum status
audience, narratives influenced by, 20–22, 28–31, 37
authentication, of narratives, 22–24, 31–34
Azad, 121

Bales, Kevin, xvii, 11, 50, 53
Beah, Ishmael, 32–34, 64, 148–49, 172
bearing witness. *see* telling (bearing witness)

Beatrice, 59, 103, 163–64
Beautiful Women (Minh Dang), 181–82
Blank, Art, 150
Blassingame, John W., 25
body
  gender, 85–86, 104
  graphic descriptions, 9–10, 36, 168
  *see also* death; genital mutilation
Bond, Scott, 122
Bradbury, Adrian, 32
Bruner, Peter, 21

Cadet, Jean-Robert, 1–2, 113–14
cannabis farming, 85, 105, 118
caring roles, post-liberation, 90–91, 121, 123, 147, 151, 160–61
Carla, 142
caste, 62, 84
Charlotte, 163
chattel slavery, xiv–xv, 1–2, 9, 75
Child, Lydia Maria, 23
child slavery
  Dwain, 67, 74–75
  recovery from, 147
  research recommendations, 180
  restavecs (Haiti), 1–2, 113–14
child soldiers, 32–34, 50, 64, 159
China, 108
Choti, 53, 101
citizenship, 67–69, 145–46
cognitive interviewing techniques, 13–14, 38–47
community relationships
  post-liberation, with non-survivors, 67, 93, 94, 108, 146–50, 156
  survivor communities, 47, 87, 94, 149–50, 163
  toleration of slavery, 26, 83
  *see also* ostracism
complex post traumatic stress disorder (C-PTSD), 96–97, 108, 121
Congo, Democratic Republic of (DRC), 28, 57
constructivist grounded theory coding techniques, xv, 13–18
contemporary (modern) slavery
  definition of, 6–7, 26–27, 75, 119
  statistics, 2
contemporary slave narratives
  abolitionist/antislavery uses of, 4–5, 10, 13, 29–30, 37, 175
  academic analyses of, 9, 10

cognitive interviewing techniques, 13–14, 38–47
comparison with historic narratives, 5, 26–27, 49, 56
culture of disbelief, 31–34, 140
length of, 27, 29–31, 36–38, 109
NGO case studies, 27–30
policy and legislation, 44, 177
research recommendations, 178–80
sponsors' influence on, 10, 14, 28–31, 35, 178
themes, summary of, 9, 174–75, 177–78
types, 5–6
control
  box metaphor, 112
  definition of slavery, 49–50, 60, 63, 66
  drugs, given by slaveholder, 83, 97, 139
  narratives, 31, 37, 42, 43, 88
  psychological, by slaveholder, 49–51, 53, 62, 77
corpus linguistics, 180
criminality
  arrest of survivors, 104, 116–19, 137–38, 141–42
  defence under Modern Slavery Act (2015), 141
  forced during enslavement, 51, 104, 116–18, 142–43, 146
  immigration status destabilised by, 119, 169
cultural identity, 78–84, 88, 102
cultural norms, 81–83, 99
culture of disbelief, 22–25, 31–34, 105, 106, 140
  *see also* willing victim myth

Dang, Minh
  Beautiful Women (poem), 181–82
  open letter to anti-trafficking movement, 175–77
  post-liberation experiences, 71
  researcher's standpoint, xvi, 36
  Survivor Alliance, 162–63, 172
  survivor participation, 169–72
Dara, 165
Davidson, Julia O'Connell, 50
death, 54, 57–61, 70
  *see also* suicidal ideation
debt bondage, 56–57, 85, 98, 118, 142

## Index

dehumanisation, 3, 45, 46, 50, 77
   objectification/owned status, 21, 48, 63, 74–77, 102, 113
   people treated like animals, 50, 75–77, 96, 113, 175–76
   see also alienation; spectralisation
Democratic Republic of Congo (DRC), 28, 57
deportation and repatriation, 116, 117, 119, 140–41, 143–44
depression, 64, 99, 143
detention. see prison and detention
Devi, Munni, 62
Dia, 147
Dina, 51, 62, 89, 113
disassociation, 58, 102–3, 151
disbelief, culture of, 22–25, 31, 32–34, 105, 106, 140
discovery events, 116–17, 129, 136–38, 164
diseases, 98, 99
dissociation, 60, 107–8, 110–13
domestic slavery, 67, 78, 85, 104–5
Dorothy, 165
Douglass, Frederick, 21–23, 178
drawings, 40–41, 110–12, 116, 119–20, 160–62, 179–80
drugs
   addiction to, 58, 59, 98, 99
   cannabis farming, 85, 105, 118
   to capture/control victims, 83, 97, 139
   smuggling, 83
Dwain (cognitive interviewee)
   drawings, 40, 110–12
   enslavement experiences, 74–75, 107
   post-liberation experiences, 67–69, 133, 145–46, 151
   telling, impact of, 43

editing/redaction of narratives, 24, 25, 29–30, 41
education
   activism through, 92, 150, 158–65
   for agency, 150–51
   language of host country, 28
   occupational skills, 28, 91, 151
   rights, 91–92, 150–51, 163–65
   survivor participation skills, 168, 169, 171–73
Egypt, 67
emotions
   freer post-liberation, 66
   memory, 40, 96, 109–10
   regulation difficulties, 63, 65, 97, 99
   repression, 58, 63, 106–9
   visualisations, 119
employment. see income and employment
enslavement. see slavery
Equiano, Olaudah, 19

FAIR Girls (NGO), 164
family relationships
   forced marriages, 60–61, 81–83, 162
   identity in, 54, 78, 102
   longing for, 58, 101–2
   micro freedoms, 55–56
   post-liberation difficulties, 62, 64–65, 84, 108, 120–21, 147–49
fear
   in discovery event, 129
   of freedom, 55, 61–63, 65, 136
   freedom from, 67
   post-liberation continuation of, 64, 65, 99, 122, 129, 130
   witchcraft, 79–80
female genital mutilation (FGM), 160, 162
Fisher, Ronald P., 38
Flores, Theresa, 37, 151
forced marriages, 60–61, 81–83, 162
Foster, Frances Smith, 20–21
Free the Slaves (NGO), 28
freedom
   absolute concept (binary with non-freedom), 57, 59
   abstract concept, 48, 52, 55, 56, 69
   barriers post-liberation, 51, 61–65, 69, 86–89, 99–100, 121
   from fear, 67, 122
   fear of, 55, 61–63, 65, 136
   immigration status and limits to, 116, 119, 120, 143–46
   innate desirability of, 52–55, 57–58
   micro freedoms, 48, 49, 55–57, 70
   relative concept (not binary with non-freedom), 48–49, 55–56, 69–70, 94
   resistance behaviours, 56–61, 70, 78–79, 174
   seeming impossibility of, 50, 51, 57, 61–62, 121
   slaveholder controls perceptions of, 49–51, 53, 62
   spinning top metaphor, 112
   survivor definitions of, 66–69
   telling as, 42–44, 46
Furaha, Benita, 28

Geiselman, R. Edward, 38
GEMS (NGO), 167
gender, 54, 62, 85–86, 103–5, 104, 162
genital mutilation, 85, 97, 98, 118
  female genital mutilation (FGM), 160, 162
Germany, 142, 143, 152
Ghana, 79–80
Global Slavery Index, 105
Grace, 27–28
Graves, Asia, 164
grounded theory coding techniques, xv, 13–18
Gupta, Rahila, 11

Haiti, 1–2, 113–14
Hall, Shyima, 32, 66, 67
Hart, Catie, 171
Harvard Bellagio Guidelines, 50
hereditary slavery (born slaves)
  Christine Stark, 50, 63, 89
  freedom as unknown concept, 52–55, 75
  Niger, 130
  post-liberation difficulties, 57, 63
Hestia (NGO), 105
hierarchy of needs, 147
historic slave narratives
  abolitionist use of, 3–4, 19–20, 22–24, 26
  academic analyses of, 9
  comparison with contemporary narratives, 5, 26–27, 49, 56
  culture of disbelief, 22–25
  length of, 20–22
  sponsors' influence on, 9, 20, 22–23
historic slavery, xiv–xv, 1–2, 9, 26–27, 56–57, 75
homelessness, 64, 144, 145
human rights, 9, 33, 50, 67, 91–92, 161
human trafficking. *see* trafficking

iconic victim, concept of, 168–69
identity (selfhood)
  activism, 92–94, 155, 159
  cultural identity, 78–84, 88, 102
  definition of, 71–72
  definition of slavery, 54
  narrative analysis focuses on, 74
  objectification/owned status, 21, 48, 63, 74–77, 102, 113
  post-liberation, 59, 64, 86–94
  pre-enslavement, 53–54, 75
  renaming, 48, 75, 76, 78–79, 107, 113
  shame, 83–89, 94
  telling, 20, 43–47, 72–74, 86–89, 92, 94
  identity documents, 68, 77–78, 145–46
  *see also* passports
imagery and symbolism
  beaded necklace, 60, 61
  bells, 107
  box metaphor, 40, 112
  citizenship, 67
  cutting hair, 83–84
  narrative length to allow for, 30
  river metaphor, 40, 120
  safe metaphor, 40, 112–13
  spinning top metaphor, 112
  travel and passports, 68, 112, 145–46
immigration and asylum status
  agency destabilised by, 137
  criminal charges have impact on, 141, 169
  education access limited by, 151
  freedom destabilised by, 116, 119, 120, 143–46
  research access limited by, 41
immigration law, 117, 137–38, 140–41, 143–46
income and employment
  during enslavement, 55–57
  immigration insecurity prevents, 145
  independence, 99, 100, 130
  less secure than enslavement, 62, 91, 133
  occupational skills, education for, 28, 91, 151
  prostitution, 84–85, 87–88, 89, 131
India, 83, 84, 139, 172
infertility, 97–99
injustice, sense of, 117, 119, 140, 143, 146, 176
International Criminal Court, 164
interpretative phenomenological analysis (IPA), xv, 13–18
interpreters, 41, 42, 137, 141
interview methods
  cognitive interviewing techniques, 13–14, 38–42, 42–47
  narratives influenced by, xv, 24–25, 30–31, 36–37, 109, 178
  structured and semi-structured, 30–31, 177
Iraq, 164
Irina, 117, 142–43
Islamic state (ISIL), 158, 164

Jacobs, Harriet, 23
Japan, 98, 99
Jennifer, 108
Jill, 63–64, 89, 99–100, 136
Joy, 80
Juan, 105
justice, sense of, 117, 119, 140, 143, 146, 176

Katya, 144
Kavita, 76, 90, 121, 129
Keitetsi, China, 32–33
Keith (cognitive interviewee)
  emotional detachment, 105, 126
  enslavement experiences, 56, 176
  post-liberation experiences, 58–59, 66
  visualisations, 40, 112–13
Kidder, Louise, xv–xvi

labour exploitation, 28, 104, 108, 116
Labov, William, 31
Lajeunesse, Helia, 50, 76, 91
Lane, Lunsford, 52
language ability, post-liberation, 28, 62, 129, 137, 141
language of narratives
  amended in transcriptions, 21, 22, 25, 30
  interpreters/translation, use of, 32, 41, 42
  verbal and visual, 40–41, 44, 160–62, 179–80
  verbatim transcriptions, 16, 27, 36, 43
law enforcement authorities, 167, 170
  see also police
leadership roles, survivors, 75, 159–63, 167–68, 171–73, 178–79
legal representation, 28, 119, 137, 141, 143
legal rights
  citizenship, 67–69, 145–46
  denied in enslavement, 51, 78
  denied post-liberation, 63, 64, 141, 143
  telling as assertion of, 45
legal slavery (historic), 23
legislation and policy, 2–3, 44, 163–65, 169–70, 177
Lewis, Damien, 32, 38
liberation events, 116–17, 129, 136–38, 164
listeners/listening, 35, 47, 73–74, 95–96, 177
literacy, 21, 24, 28, 46, 91, 150

Lithuania, 115
Lloyd, Rachel
  post-liberation experiences, 131
  recovery needs, 130, 149
  survivor participation, 153, 154, 159, 167–68
Lutnick, Alexandra, 172

Maiti Nepal (NGO), 139
Mann Act, 118
Maria, 50, 58, 80–81
Mariana, 151
marriages, forced, 60–61, 81–83, 162
Marsha, 152
Maslow, Abraham, 147
Mauritania, 55, 164
McKenzie, Shamere
  bearing witness, 46, 92, 124, 152, 172
  criminality, forced, 117–18
  legacy, importance of, 115, 159
  liberator role, 154
  Sun Gate Foundation, 163
memory
  cognitive interviewing techniques, 39, 40, 43, 44
  continuous trauma, 102–3, 123
  emotion, 40, 96, 109–10
  inaccuracies, 21, 25, 33–35, 73, 96
  post-liberation desire to forget, 34, 79, 91, 106–8
  repression, 102–3
  researchers' engagement with, 30, 37
Mexico, 115
micro freedoms, 48, 49, 55–57, 70
Miguel, 147
modern slavery. see contemporary (modern) slavery
Modern Slavery Act (2015), 141
Mojatu Foundation (NGO), 159–60
Muhsen, Zana, 32, 136, 152
Murad, Nadia, 158, 164
Murphy, Laura, 9–11, 109

narratives
  analytical approaches to, xv, 13–18, 74, 180
  authentication of, 22–24, 31–34
  definition/purpose, xiii, 13
  editing/redaction of, 24, 25, 29–30
  interview methods influence on, xv, 24–25, 30–31, 36–37, 109, 178
  narrative truth, 34–35, 73–74, 96

narratives (cont.)
  selection of, xiv–xv, 6–7, 11
  see also contemporary slave narratives; historic slave narratives
National Human Trafficking Training and Technical Assistance Center, 171
National Institute of Justice, 170
National Referral Mechanism (NRM), 119
National Survivor Network, 172
natural rights, 54, 91
Nazer, Mende
  family relationships, 101–2
  identity during enslavement, 48, 76–79, 114–15
  micro freedoms, 56
  narrative authentication, 32
  post-liberation experiences, 64–65, 121, 136
Nepal, 83, 84, 139–40
Netherlands, 117, 142–43
Niger, 130
non-governmental organisations (NGOs)
  banned groups, 164
  hereditary slavery projects, 52–53
  research location provided by, 38–39, 41
  statistics, 105
  survivor leadership/participation, 42, 159–60, 162–63, 171–72
  website case studies, 27–30
non-survivors
  epistemologies of, xvi–xvii, 15, 163, 165, 180–81
  participation/activism, 166, 172
  power imbalance with survivors, 165–66, 173
  trauma mishandled by, 166–68
normalisation, 83, 131–32
Nu, 98–99
Nur, Farhia, 67

objectification, 21, 75–77, 102, 113
occupational skills, education for, 28, 91, 151
Olney, James, 34–35
Osborn, Mike, 14
ostracism
  enslavement perpetuated by, 62, 130–31
  examples of, 84, 89, 99, 115, 118
  rights overridden by, 63, 88
otherness, 46, 50, 55, 76, 113–15
Oumoulkhér, 51
outsider status, 108, 118, 165, 166

ownership by others
  definition of slavery, 7, 48–50, 63, 75, 174
  and identity, 48, 63, 74–75, 102
  Niger, 130
  women's bodies, 104

passports
  confiscated by slaveholders, 77–78, 142
  false passports, 117, 142–43
  symbolic of acceptance, 68, 145–46
Patience, 79–80, 109, 115
Patterson, Orlando, 50
permanent residency, 145–46
perpetrators. see prosecution of perpetrators; slaveholders/traffickers
Phillips, Ulrich B., 24
poetry, 176, 181–82
police
  arrest of survivors, 104, 116–17, 117–19, 137–38, 141–42
  deportation of survivors, 140–41
  dismissal of survivors, 136, 144
  questioning survivors, 117, 119, 139–40, 142–43
  re-trafficking survivors, 138–39
  support for survivors, 116, 144
policy and legislation, 2–3, 44, 163–65, 169–70, 177
Post, Amy, 23
post traumatic stress disorder (PTSD), 28, 40
  complex post traumatic stress disorder (C-PTSD), 96–97, 108, 121
power balances
  gender, 103–4
  non-survivors and survivors, 165–66, 173
  researchers and survivors, xv–xvi, 25, 35
  sponsors and survivors, 30–31, 35
Pranus (cognitive interviewee), 41, 42, 66, 115–16
pregnancy, 98
prison and detention, 116, 117, 133, 141
  Carla, 142
  Irina, 117, 143
  Shamere McKenzie, 118
  Tung, 105, 119
prosecution of perpetrators
  narratives influenced by, 30, 41, 44
  support for survivors linked to, 133, 137–38, 169
  unsatisfactory outcomes, 119, 143
  use of 'victim' term, xiv

# Index

prostitution
 criminal charges for, 117–18
 decriminalisation, 163
 Nu, 98–99
 post-liberation, 84–85, 87–88, 89, 131

Ramphal, 146
Ravi, 134–35
recovery, key elements of, 130, 146–47
redaction/editing of narratives, 24, 25, 29–30, 41
re-exploitation, risk of
 deportation and repatriation, 119, 144
 education to prevent, 150
 fear and, 129, 130–32, 141
 sexual slavery, 130–34, 138–39, 151
relationships. *see* community relationships; family relationships
religion, 62, 67, 79–80, 122
renaming
 alternative name, 78–79, 113
 as 'animal', 75, 76
 bell instead of name, 107
 as 'slave', 48, 75, 76
repatriation and deportation, 116, 117, 119, 140–41, 143–44
repression
 emotions, 58, 63, 106–9
 memories, 102–3
researchers, responsibilities of, xv–xvi, 15, 35–38, 41
resilience, in survival, 122, 135, 160, 180
resistance behaviours
 during enslavement, 56–61, 70, 78–79, 153, 174
 post-liberation, 92, 150, 174
restavecs (Haiti), 1–2, 113–14
Richard, Anywar Ricky, 159
rights
 citizenship, 67–69, 145–46
 denied in enslavement, 51, 78, 101, 114, 117
 denied post-liberation, 63, 64, 141, 143
 education, 91–92, 150–51, 163–65
 freedom of speech, 19, 43, 46
 human rights, 9, 33, 50, 67, 91–92, 161
 natural rights, 54, 91
 telling as assertion of, 45
Rita, 138–40
Rosa, 115
Russia, 117, 142, 143, 152
Ruth, 155

Salma, 52, 55, 61–62, 63, 91
San Francisco Mayor's Task Force on Anti-Human Trafficking, 170, 172
Sankalp (NGO), 53, 135
Scott, Dred, 1
Seba, 10
Seeyawati, 123
Selek'ha, 51
self-blame, 100–101, 104, 149
self-destructive behaviour, 59, 64, 69, 99–100, 126, 174
selfhood. *see* identity (selfhood)
self-ownership, 31, 45, 50, 60, 152, 155
self-responsibility, 121–23, 130, 136–37, 156, 174–75
 agency linked to, 128–29, 137
sexual slavery
 addictions, 97–99
 definition of, 26
 gender, 103–5
 prostitution, post-liberation, 84–85, 87–89, 131
 re-exploitation, risk of, 130–34, 138–39, 151
 shame, post-liberation, 62–63, 84–86, 94, 99, 115, 119
 spectralisation, 88–89, 115
 willing victim myth, 104, 131, 139–40, 169
shame
 de-shaming through telling, 45, 47, 87, 119, 164
 and identity, 83–89, 94
 post-liberation treatment by others, 117–18, 139, 168
 sexual slavery, 62–63, 84–86, 94, 99, 115, 119
 survivor guilt, 123
 underreporting of male sexual slavery, 105
Shared Hope (NGO), 172
shelters, 28, 133–34, 143, 164
Sierra Leone, 33–34
slaveholders/traffickers
 drugs as method of control, 83, 97, 139
 passports, confiscation of, 77–78, 142
 prosecutions fail, 119, 143
 psychological methods of control, 49–51, 53, 62, 77
slavery
 conceptual boundaries, xiv–xv, 5, 20, 87
 control as defining aspect, 49–50, 60, 63, 66

slavery (cont.)
    legal definition, 7
    ownership as defining aspect, 7, 48–50, 63, 75, 174
    types, 18, 29, 96, 104–5
Slavery Convention (1926), 7
Smith, Jonathan A., 14
social acceptance and belonging, 145–47
    see also community relationships
SOS slaves (SOS Esclaves) (NGO), 164
spectralisation, 87, 88–89, 97, 113–15, 124
spiritual beliefs, 80–81
sponsors
    contemporary narratives influenced by, 10, 14, 28–31, 35, 178
    guidelines for, 37
    historic narratives influenced by, 9, 20, 22–23
    types of, 6
Spry, Tami, 154
St Petersburg Crisis Centre (NGO), 152
Stark, Christine
    bearing witness, 108, 155, 159
    enslavement experiences, 10, 50, 54–55, 76, 124–26
    legacy, importance of, 115
    post-liberation experiences, 63, 88–89, 92–94, 124–26
Stockholm syndrome, 131
structured and semi-structured interviews, 30–31, 177
substance abuse, 57–59, 97–99, 134
Sudan
    Ajok, 78
    Mende Nazer, 32, 64, 76–77, 79, 102, 114
suicidal ideation, 100, 115, 118, 121, 143
suicide attempts, 57–59
Sumara, 135
Sun Gate Foundation (NGO), 163
Survivor Alliance (NGO), 42, 162–63, 171, 172
survivor communities, 47, 87, 94, 149–50, 163
survivor guilt, 47, 90, 123, 124, 158
survivor participation
    barriers to, 165–71
    caring roles, 90–91, 121, 123, 147, 151, 160–61
    definition of, 157
    hereditary slavery, 53, 75
    leadership roles, 75, 159–63, 167–68, 171–73, 178–79
    recommendations for, 171–73, 176–77
    telling as, 37, 43, 44, 47
survivor voice, definition, 157
survivors
    epistemologies of, xv–xvii, 15, 87, 178–81
    use of term, xiv, 152–55
    warrior myth, 122–24
Sustainable Development Goal 8.7, 2
symbolism. see imagery and symbolism

Tamada, 108, 147
telling (bearing witness)
    activism, 156, 163
    education to enable, 151
    identity through, 20, 43–47, 72–74, 86–89, 92, 94
    trauma, 95, 104–10, 112, 119, 123
terminology
    'survivor', xiv, 36, 152–55
    'victim', xiv, 45, 81, 152–55
Thailand, 98
therapeutic effects of telling, 37, 43, 44, 46, 92
Togo, 79
trafficking
    anti-trafficking activities, 169–73, 175–77
    contemporary slavery, 2, 26, 36, 62
    police re-trafficking survivors, 138–39
    see also slaveholders/traffickers
trauma
    activism as potential cause of, 156, 177–78
    continuous, 102–3, 123
    definition of, 95
    dissociation, 60, 107–8, 110–13
    gendered exposure/responses to, 103–5
    identity impacted by, 72–74, 85, 88
    non-survivors mishandle details of, 166–68
    search for understanding of, 100–101, 114
    telling, 95, 104–10, 112, 119, 123
    see also post traumatic stress disorder (PTSD)
travel, post-liberation, 68, 112, 145–46
Trodd, Zoe, 11
*trokosi*, 79–80
Tung (cognitive interviewee)
    drawings, 40, 118–20

enslavement experiences, 56–57, 85–86, 118–20, 141–42
freedom, definition of, 67
post-liberation experiences, 141
telling, issues related to, 42, 43

Uganda, 32–33
Ukraine, 144
United Kingdom (UK)
  Dwain, 68, 85
  Farhia Nur, 67
  Grace, 27
  Mende Nazer, 64, 65, 101, 102, 114
  Pranus, 116
  shelters, 134
  Tung, 118, 119, 141
  Vera, 144–45
United States of America (USA)
  Jean-Robert Cadet, 1
  Katya, 144
  Rosa, 115
  Shyima Hall, 67
  survivor participation, 153, 163, 170, 172
Unseen (NGO), 27–28
U.S. Advisory Council on Human Trafficking, 170
U.S. Bureau of Justice Administration, 170
U.S. Office for Victims of Crime, 170
Utthan (survivor leadership program), 172

Val (cognitive interviewee), 40, 60–61, 81–83, 92, 106, 159–62
Vann, Sina, 85, 90–91, 109
Vera, 144–45
victims
  iconic victim, 168–69
  identification by authorities (or lack of), 119, 132–33, 137, 139–43
  training in identification for authorities, 164
  use of term, xiv, 45, 81, 152–55
  willing victim myth, 104, 114, 131, 139–40, 169
Vietnam, 56, 85, 118, 119, 141, 150
visualisations, 40–41, 110–13, 116, 119–20, 160–62, 179–80
voyeurism, 36, 37

warrior myth, 122–24
Whitman, Albery Allson, 52
William, 121
willing victim myth, 104, 114, 131, 139–40, 169
witchcraft, 80–81
Withelma, 164–65
Works Progress Administration (WPA), 21, 24–25, 31

Yazidi people, 164

Zamira, 107

For EU product safety concerns, contact us at Calle de José Abascal, 56–1°,
28003 Madrid, Spain or eugpsr@cambridge.org.

www.ingramcontent.com/pod-product-compliance
Ingram Content Group UK Ltd.
Pitfield, Milton Keynes, MK11 3LW, UK
UKHW032354120525
458466UK00002B/64